THE COMPLETE IDIOT'S GUIDE® TO

Trees and Shrubs

by Joshua Plunkett and Jeanne K. Hanson

ALPHA

A member of Penguin Group (USA) Inc.

ALPHA BOOKS

Published by the Penguin Group

Penguin Group (USA) Inc., 375 Hudson Street, New York, New York 10014, USA

Penguin Group (Canada), 90 Eglinton Avenue East, Suite 700, Toronto, Ontario M4P 2Y3, Canada (a division of Pearson Penguin Canada Inc.)

Penguin Books Ltd., 80 Strand, London WC2R 0RL, England

Penguin Ireland, 25 St. Stephen's Green, Dublin 2, Ireland (a division of Penguin Books Ltd.)

Penguin Group (Australia), 250 Camberwell Road, Camberwell, Victoria 3124, Australia (a division of Pearson Australia Group Pty. Ltd.)

Penguin Books India Pvt. Ltd., 11 Community Centre, Panchsheel Park, New Delhi—110 017, India

Penguin Group (NZ), 67 Apollo Drive, Rosedale, North Shore, Auckland 1311, New Zealand (a division of Pearson New Zealand Ltd.)

Penguin Books (South Africa) (Pty.) Ltd., 24 Sturdee Avenue, Rosebank, Johannesburg 2196, South Africa

Penguin Books Ltd., Registered Offices: 80 Strand, London WC2R 0RL, England

International Standard Book Number: 978-1-59257-698-2
Library of Congress Catalog Card Number: 2007937240

10 09 08   8 7 6 5 4 3 2 1

Interpretation of the printing code: The rightmost number of the first series of numbers is the year of the book's printing; the rightmost number of the second series of numbers is the number of the book's printing. For example, a printing code of 08-1 shows that the first printing occurred in 2008.

Printed in the United States of America

Note: This publication contains the opinions and ideas of its authors. It is intended to provide helpful and informative material on the subject matter covered. It is sold with the understanding that the authors and publisher are not engaged in rendering professional services in the book. If the reader requires personal assistance or advice, a competent professional should be consulted.

The authors and publisher specifically disclaim any responsibility for any liability, loss, or risk, personal or otherwise, which is incurred as a consequence, directly or indirectly, of the use and application of any of the contents of this book.

Most Alpha books are available at special quantity discounts for bulk purchases for sales promotions, premiums, fundraising, or educational use. Special books, or book excerpts, can also be created to fit specific needs.

For details, write: Special Markets, Alpha Books, 375 Hudson Street, New York, NY 10014.

Publisher: *Marie Butler-Knight*
Editorial Director: *Mike Sanders*
Senior Managing Editor: *Billy Fields*
Senior Acquisitions Editor: *Paul Dinas*
Senior Development Editor: *Christy Wagner*
Production Editor: *Kayla Dugger*
Copy Editor: *Tricia Liebig*

Cartoonist: *Richard King*
Cover Designer: *Becky Harmon*
Book Designer: *Trina Wurst*
Indexer: *Angie Bess*
Layout: *Chad Dressler*
Proofreader: *Aaron Black*

Contents at a Glance

Appendixes

Contents

Introduction

Our planet is richly green with trees and shrubs. Scientists estimate that just more than 60,000 different tree species populate the earth—about 630 of them conifers (evergreens) and the rest deciduous trees (which drop their leaves)—as well as thousands more species of shrubs still unnumbered.

Trees and shrubs twine their way through human history. We've used their fibers for cloth; their bark, roots, nuts, flowers, and leaves for medicines, dyes, poisons, and foods; and their wood for hearth fires, houses, furniture, tools, ships, utensils, weapons, and paper. They have been woven into our religions, too: think of the Buddhists and the bo tree, the Christians and the Christmas tree, the pagan Druids and their worship of the holly bush. Even Native Americans value too many trees to number.

In many ways, we've changed trees, too. Beginning with the ones found native to a given area, or ones imported to it, scientists and arborists have developed *cultivars*, or varieties of an original tree or shrub. Hundreds and hundreds of variants have been bred for their different characteristics, which means you can find plenty of trees and shrubs perfect for you and your yard.

These are our valued and ancient plants, well-established "citizens" of our yards, parks, and forests. So let's take a moment for time travel here, to look at when they first appeared. The first land plants that contained lignin—the raw material for wood—appeared as long ago as 420 million years before our time. Then came the first tree-size ferns and horsetail grasses; these began thriving about 400 million years ago. After that, came the first true trees, simple versions compared to today's versions, but hugely tall. (No one knows exactly how tall.) They grew in vast forests from 360 to 270 million years ago. Also thriving on the planet by about 360 million years ago were the first seed plants. Finally, by about 300 million years ago, conifers were spreading across the earth. Flowering plants, including all the deciduous trees that followed, began to thrive by about 145 million years ago. This advanced stage, the ability to flower, is the most recent—and perhaps the most elaborately beautiful—stage of plant development. It's amazing all that we have to enjoy.

We could go on and on, telling you about record-holding trees, curious facts about trees and shrubs, etc., but we'll save that for the following pages.

This book is not a field guide, teaching you how to identify various species of trees and shrubs. Instead, it's a how-to guide, giving you ideas about what to choose at your local nursery, gardening department of a large store, or online catalog; and how to make those trees and shrubs thrive in your yard—on an everyday basis, not after a major disaster such as a flood, forest fire, or avalanche. We help you make your new *and* existing trees and shrubs become and stay truly wonderful. Accompanying it all is a CD that contains photos of hundreds of trees and shrubs—to help you imagine them in your yard.

Keep in mind, too, that trees and shrubs are not identical and so aren't treated "in lock step" in the book. For example, you probably want to select the trees first in your yard "remodel" (whether with one new plant or many), and you probably want to consider flowering and other aesthetic issues even more in connection with your selection of shrubs. So some chapters have more information about trees, others have more about shrubs, and others have a balance of both in our discussion.

How to Use This Book

The book is divided into four parts to make your ventures with trees and shrubs as successful as possible:

In **Part 1, "The Seeds of Tree and Shrub Success,"** you learn that the best path to success is planting a tree or shrub in a good place.

In **Part 2, "The Growth and Life Cycle of Trees and Shrubs,"** we show you how trees and shrubs are like kids that never stop growing.

In **Part 3, "Tree and Shrub Maintenance,"** we cover maintenance from watering to pruning, and so on. We offer advice on taking good care of your trees and shrubs.

In **Part 4, "Tree and Shrub Diseases and Damages,"** we cover problems that can plague your trees and shrubs. Yes, lightning can strike (though not usually twice!)—and insects can be battled.

At the back of the book, the appendixes offer much more information.

How to Use the CD

Included with this book is an easily searchable CD featuring profiles of 101 of the most desirable trees and shrubs. In addition to full-color photos, each tree and shrub profile contains detailed information about the plant's mature height and width, nutrient requirements, foliage color and texture, flower descriptions, and more, to help you select the best trees and shrubs for your yard.

The trees and shrubs are organized by optimal growing zone. To find trees and shrubs in your zone, simply click on the appropriate zone link. If you're not sure what zone you're in, click on the Zone Maps link and locate your area on the map.

For your convenience, we've also included a complete alphabetized listing of all the trees and shrubs included on the CD. If you know which tree or shrub you'd like to see, you can go directly to it.

To use this CD, you need the following:

> *Equipment:* PC or Mac with a minimum 128 MB RAM
>
> *Operating system:* Windows 2000, Windows XP, Windows Vista, or Mac OSX
>
> *Browser:* Internet Explorer 6 or 7, Firefox 2, Netscape 7, or Safari 2

Extras

Throughout this book, you'll see boxed asides to the text. Be sure to check these out! Here's what to look for:

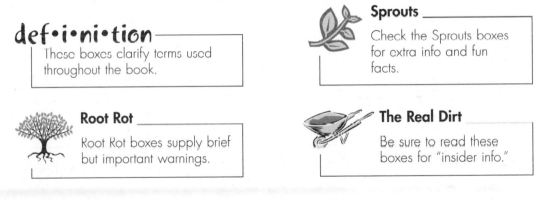

def•i•ni•tion
These boxes clarify terms used throughout the book.

Sprouts
Check the Sprouts boxes for extra info and fun facts.

Root Rot
Root Rot boxes supply brief but important warnings.

The Real Dirt
Be sure to read these boxes for "insider info."

Acknowledgments

We're grateful for Paul Dinas, our esteemed and intelligent editor at Alpha Books in New York—and he even has a great Boston accent.

Of course, we also want to thank our families and friends for loaning us the time to write this book. Josh was able to help quiet his toddler son with tree stories (sometimes), although his wife, Maureen, did it better (almost always). He would also like to thank Dr. Gary Johnson of the University of Minnesota, for special and expert mentoring.

Jeannie wishes to single out her children Jennifer and Erik; Jamie and his Pacific Northwest forester father, Ron; and her friends for thanks. And let's not forget her dog, Alice, for curbing her barking during times of greatest concentration.

Trademarks

All terms mentioned in this book that are known to be or are suspected of being trademarks or service marks have been appropriately capitalized. Alpha Books and Penguin Group (USA) Inc. cannot attest to the accuracy of this information. Use of a term in this book should not be regarded as affecting the validity of any trademark or service mark.

Special Thanks to the Technical Reviewer

The Complete Idiot's Guide to Trees and Shrubs was reviewed by an expert who double-checked the accuracy of what you'll learn here, to help us ensure that this book gives you everything you need to know about trees and shrubs. Special thanks are extended to Manuel Jordan.

Part 1

The Seeds of Tree and Shrub Success

Your yard needs something … maybe a tree here and a shrub or two there. But how do you know what to choose? What will work best in your yard, given your climate, soil conditions, light conditions, wind conditions, the temperature, etc. Welcome to Part 1. Here we take you through all you need to know to choose new trees and shrubs that match your yard conditions—and help you give your new plants the best chance to survive and thrive.

In the following pages, we also tell you about the basic "body parts" of trees and shrubs as well as the lifestyle issues that govern their successful growth. Along the way, we highlight plenty of specific trees and shrubs likely to work for you and your yard.

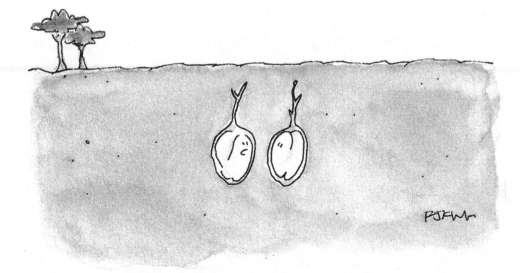

"I hear the sun up there is awesome."

The Basics of Trees and Shrubs

In This Chapter

- ◆ The nature of trees and shrubs and how they differ
- ◆ All about pollination
- ◆ Tree and shrub anatomy
- ◆ What you see ... and what you don't

Trees and shrubs are vital living things, although they lead unusual lives. Half their bodies are stuck underground where they encounter everything from tiny organisms such as fungi and bacteria (which may help or may attack), to furry burrowing animals, to large rocks that may be in the way of their roots as they try to grow. And they can't move after they've been planted, which means they encounter a range of forces above ground, too—plumes of fungi, hordes of insects, fierce winds, droughts, blizzards, and herds of deer—with no means to get out of the way. But trees and shrubs are put together and function well enough to thrive even through all this.

In this chapter, we cover the basics of trees and shrubs, including their anatomy and how they "work."

Introducing Trees and Shrubs

Since the days of the first woody plants about 420 million years ago, trees and shrubs have been evolving into the immense green bouquet we see today. No one actually knows how many species exist, and many surely remain to be discovered, but the number is surely many hundreds of thousands worldwide. Trees and shrubs are divided into two basic groups, *conifers* and *deciduous.*

def•i•ni•tion

Coniferous trees, the conifers or evergreens, are known as gymnosperms and set their seeds in cones. Deciduous trees, which drop their leaves, are known as angiosperms where flowers give rise to their seeds.

The difference between a tree and a shrub might at first seem pretty clear: both are woody plants; one you stand *under* and the other you stand *next* to! Well, that's part of it, but efforts have been made to make the distinction more precise. Trees can be defined as woody plants with one main trunk and a mature height of at least 15 feet (some sources say 13 feet). Some definitions go on to specify that to be a tree, the plant needs to have both a crown (the leafy part) and a vertical trunk of at least $4\frac{1}{2}$ feet when fully grown. Shrubs, on the other hand, have more than one thick branch in a clump, beginning at or near the ground level and reaching a mature height of fewer than 15 feet.

But these criteria don't always clearly define a tree versus a shrub. Young trees, trees that have multiple trunks, and trees growing under conditions such as pronounced cold or drought that don't allow for their maximum possible size are often called shrubs when they would otherwise grow to be trees under better conditions. And some plants that look similar to shrubs can end up growing as tall as 30 feet or more, making us wonder if they shouldn't be called trees. This flexibility—shape shifting, really—depends on how well the planting site and other conditions suit the tree or shrub; better conditions mean more growth. The geographic zone they're planted in makes a difference, too; farther south usually means bigger growth. (Geographic zones are the subject of Chapter 3.)

The Real Dirt

Not to really confuse you, but some vines can be trained to grow into shrubs. And some trees, in the process called bonsai, can be forced to remain as small as a house plant! And finally, a very few conifers actually drop their "leaves" (needles), so they aren't all *evergreen.* One example is the tamarack, a tree of northern wetland terrains. On its thin, graceful branches, the needles turn golden in fall before falling to the ground.

Trees and shrubs have basically the same body parts and the same "lifestyle"—they add wood where they need to keep their crowns stable as they grow, they adjust to wind, they cope with changing growth around them, and they repair damage from insect infestations or lightning. They also bend well, almost elastically.

The way we see it, it doesn't much matter if you call that green thing in your yard a tree or a shrub because usually we can all pretty much tell them apart. You care for them in many (although not all) of the same ways, so we discuss trees and shrubs together in most of the following chapters. The main exceptions are in the chapters on pruning, watering, and fertilizing and mulching, although even there, the differences in care are not extreme. And because trees are more particular to where they're planted than shrubs are, we focus more on trees in Part 1 and a bit more on shrubs in Part 2 in Chapters 10 and 11 on flowering, fruits, and foliage—areas where shrubs shine even more than trees.

Seeds, Flowers, and Cones

Every tree and shrub, from the giant "General Sherman" sequoia to the most modest barrel cactus, comes from a seed. This seed is housed either naked in a cone (as in the conifers) or in a flower (as in the deciduous plants, the ones that drop leaves). We can see the seeds in some conifers—pinecones, for example. But tree flowers? We think mostly about shrubs flowering rather than trees.

But many trees have flowers so small that you never see them, and sometimes you couldn't even see them if you looked hard (scientists call these "cryptic" flowers). At the other extreme you have the showy tulip poplar, with its large tulip-y flowers, and the Japanese lilac tree, with its lovely white blooms similar to fistfuls of snow. Large-scale blooms on trees are the exception. And of course, many shrubs don't have magnificent flowers either.

A Closer Look at Flowers

Flowers evolved to house seeds (as did the fruits that follow the seeds), and the flowers attract creatures for pollination. (This is how they get from flowers to seeds, as we'll see in upcoming sections.)

The flowers of the deciduous trees and shrubs, the angiosperms, typically have four major parts:

◆ Petals (all of them together make up the *corolla*)

◆ Stamen (the stalky part inside the flower, the male part)

◆ Pistil (the rounded, gourdlike part inside the flower, the female part)

◆ Sepal (the splayed-out inside part that once enclosed the flower before it bloomed)

Perhaps surprisingly, some flowers have both a stamen and a pistil—in other words, they're both male and female on the same tree, although each flower is either male or female. These are called the *monoecious trees*; for example, oak and birch trees are both monoecious. And some are *dioecious*, or have flowers that are both male and female at once. And almost as gender-bending, other trees such as the poplar and willow trees and the holly shrub are either all male or all female and need to grow near a fellow tree of the opposite sex. All this makes flowering trees less uniform than trees with cones because, in conifers, no cone contains both sexes at once. (More on cones coming up.)

Tree and shrub flowers don't just pop up suddenly the way garden flowers do. The ones that bloom in spring usually began in buds summer or fall before. However, the summer-bloomers usually start their buds during the spring. These flowers, if pollinated, develop a fruit—it's like their baby. Although the fruits of some trees and shrubs are edible—love those plums and cranberries!—most are not. The fruits—which are usually quite small, as with most tree and shrub flowers—contain the seeds that will form the next generation of the tree.

The Real Dirt

It's not your imagination that oak trees drop many more acorns some years than others. This phenomenon, called *masting*, has evolved to overwhelm the squirrels, in this case, as well as to focus the trees' energy on these years and to conserve it during other years for other functions. It also confuses the furry little predators, as one local area will be deluged with acorns while another experiences a lean year. The squirrels can't eat that many nuts at once, so some nuts are able to grow into new oaks.

A Closer Look at Cones

Cones—the "flowers" of the conifers—usually look even less like flowers than those of the deciduous trees. On most conifers, some of the cones are *pollen cones* and some are *seed cones;* other conifers have both sexes on the same tree. In a given species of conifer, the pollen cones are much smaller than the seed cones and tend to be the ones growing lower on the tree. Wherever they are, these "girls" and "boys" usually take 1 to 3 years to develop.

Cones form toward the top of the tree.

— pinecones

The seed cones of some conifers, especially pines, need high heat before they will release their seeds at all. By "high heat," we don't mean hot summer days—it takes a forest fire to create enough heat for conifers to release seeds. In this way, they have evolved to take advantage of natural forest fires caused by lightning strikes, rather than to be completely exterminated by them. The adult trees might burn, but their seeds launch a new generation. The jack pine is an example of this "phoenix" function.

The Birds and the Bees

Lacking Match.com, or even the mobility to get together physically, trees and shrubs still manage to reproduce, thanks to *pollination*. You and I wouldn't like to rely on wind or on insects in these matters, but this is only the beginning of the array of techniques used in your own backyard.

Wind pollination is the most common pollination method among temperate zone trees. (The continental United States is all temperate zone.) In fact, almost all conifers are wind pollinated. The seed cones are located

def•i•ni•tion

Pollination is the process in which pollen is transferred between the male and female parts.

higher on the tree and the pollen cones lower to facilitate this mixing by the wind. Gravity helps pull the sturdier seed cones down.

Worldwide, insect pollination is probably the most common method of pollination, and it enables plenty of American trees and shrubs to reproduce. And it's not just bees doing the work; so many species of insects help out! Bees, of course, stay busy, but almost everything from ants to beetles, to flies, to wasps have been known to move pollen to where it needs to go.

Even bats and birds pollinate some species. Similar to insects, they are attracted to flowers and tend to move pollen around within and among plants as they seek more flowers. They also eliminate seeds when they defecate after eating them, of course.

After a tree or shrub seed is fertilized, it needs to find a place in the soil. The narrowest part of a large seed needs to maneuver so that it faces up, and the whole seed needs to be tamped into the ground, at least slightly. Rain, snow, and even animals help with this process. Most of the trees that establish themselves the fastest after a forest fire, avalanche, other such natural event, or after logging are the ones with the lightest-weight seeds because the wind carries them from nearby. Trees with heavy seeds, such as acorns, usually rely on animals to plant them. Some even need scarification (a bite or scratch marks) to get them going. Shrubs establish more quickly because they require less space and fewer resources of all kinds.

The Foundation: Trunks and Roots

In Part 2, we describe more about the life cycle of trees and shrubs, from fertilized seed to a real tree or shrub with enough heft for the rest of its body parts to be obvious—and how you can help this growth to happen in the best ways, with plenty of examples. For now, let's examine these body parts as though the tree were already grown.

Sturdy Trunks

The *trunks* (or *stems*) of trees and the multiple "trunks" of shrubs are constructed with a key substance called *lignin* that toughens the plant's cell walls—which are made of the much more flexible *cellulose*. Think of lignin as the hardest area at the center of a carrot and cellulose as the stringy material in the outer layers of a stalk of celery.

Lignin enables a tree or shrub to withstand wind and also drought. (Plants without much lignin, such as your garden flowers, rely on water pressure to hold them up—so they wilt when they don't receive enough water.) This woody substance acts a bit like your skeleton, but it also transports water and nutrients through the tree's cells, as though it were not only the skeleton but the bloodstream, too. The most primitive version of this amazing substance dates back about 420 million years.

The trunk's *heartwood* and *xylem* are the woodiest parts of a tree or shrub. The heartwood, the very core of the tree, has the more limited role of the two. It primarily helps the tree stand up straight and acts to a certain extent against infections.

def•i•ni•tion

Lignin is one tough molecule, almost like cement between the areas of cellulose. It is the main thickener that enables trees and shrubs to stand without toppling over in the first breeze. **Cellulose** is the fibrous or "stringy" part of the wood.

Heartwood is the inner heart column of the plant. **Xylem** is the tissue inside the trunk that moves water and whatever is dissolved in it. **Dendrochronology** is the study of tree rings.

The xylem is a very active part of the plant. We see it as the "rings" when a tree trunk is sliced across; they mark the tree's growth because the xylem is always adding layers. (This pattern exists in plants, too, although it's a bit hard to see.) Unless you live in a place where the climate is truly constant (same temperatures and rainfall year round), your trees have a distinct ring for each year of their lives. These rings are thicker and farther apart in years according to when the growing season was favorable, and thinner when it was not. Even within a year, the xylem is different: springtime xylem is a bit lighter, wider, and thin-walled; summer xylem is narrower, darker, and sturdier. Generally, these merge into one ring for every year. The study of these tree rings is called *dendrochronology*. As the xylem gradually ages, it turns into heartwood. (Note it's possible to drill into the tree to gather this information, but it's dangerous to the tree. Scientists generally conduct this analysis on trees after they've fallen.)

The xylem is not only hard and surrounds the tree's even harder heartwood, it also performs several key roles for the tree or shrub. It provides great sturdiness, holding the tree or shrub up in a mechanical sense. It defends the tree's integrity by growing extra tissue to enclose and cut off fungal and bacterial infections, to block off insect invasions, and to seal off an injury by a force such as lightning by compartmentalizing it. (You can sometimes see these repair jobs as galls, or blobs, on the trunk.) It features channels, almost like blood vessels, that move the nutrient-rich water from the root system throughout the rest of the tree. (These channels are shaped differently in different species.) It even conducts long-term storage, holding food such as starches and sugars for the plant.

The trunk has other key areas: *phloem*, *cambium*, and *bark*. The phloem is the area between the xylem and the bark. The corklike cambium layer is where the main growth of the tree or shrub occurs. And the bark is the outermost layer.

> **The Real Dirt**
>
> Studying tree rings can tell about human history. One example: a group of people leaves a desert area entirely. Why? Was it because of a multi-year drought? Check a tree in the area to find out.

Shape-Shifting Trunks

Trees and shrubs react to conditions around them much more than most people think, changing their overall shape as necessary. The tapering of the trunk, the movement of the trunk, the effect of uneven shade, and the reaction of the branches to changes are only a few of these reasons for a tree to adapt to your yard. How we treat trees and shrubs is important, significantly affecting some aspects of the trunk's shape. (More on this in Chapters 15 and 16.) Here are some ways trunks transform themselves:

- ◆ Tapering
- ◆ Movement
- ◆ Shading
- ◆ Tilting
- ◆ Compartmentalization

> **The Real Dirt**
>
> Proper pruning is actually good for a tree (not just pleasing to the homeowner)!

Tree trunks add wood as they grow and when under stress. Typically, they become broader in areas closer to the ground and taper at greater heights. (Palm trees are an exception.)

For a tree to grow properly and be nicely tapered, its trunk needs to be able to move. Trees' natural movement can be hindered if they're part of a too-dense grouping (whether in your yard or wild in the woods) or if they're tied to stakes (in your yard). Staking even for a few months affects the tree, and the young tree will try to compensate by growing up instead of both growing taller and thicker at the same time. That's not what you want. It makes for a weaker trunk, and the next major windstorm could knock down your tree completely. It's similar to when you wear a cast after an injury; that part of your body weakens.

Proper trunk tapering flares out above the ground and narrows nearer the top of the tree.

Trunk shading is when a tree shaded on one side, within a grouping of trees, for example, grows fewer branches on the darker side. Even a small solid wood stake—the kind used near the trunk to buttress a young tree—can cause an area of shade on the slender trunk, which might make a real difference. If you must stake to keep your tree from toppling over immediately, use a single transparent stake only until the roots grow enough to stabilize (a few weeks), allowing the tree to compensate.

A tree with a trunk tilted away from the vertical or with bent branches will try to strengthen its branches and trunk to straighten the tilt. This sometimes works, although the new wood is always weaker and the tree tends not to grow as tall. This kind of wood is called *reaction wood* or *tension wood*.

Root Rot _____

Avoid tying trees to solid wood stakes, especially when your tree is young and growing vigorously. When unstaked, a tree tilts away from the stake and continues to do so—you'll end up with a crooked tree if you're not careful.

Trunk compartmentalization changes the visible shape of the tree's trunk by creating what looks like a large knob of wood on the trunk. This callus-type area shows that the tree was trying to enclose, and thereby cut off, a damaged area, which may be from an insect infestation, lightning strike, mechanical damage, or even poor pruning. (For more on pruning, please see Chapter 16.)

The Business End: The Roots

Just as important as the trunk of a tree or shrub are the roots. When the root system and the aboveground parts are mature, they weigh about equal. Unlike the branch system, the root system is hairy (yes, hairs stick out from it underground). It doesn't branch in the same way, either, and it also works even harder. (For more on how roots grow, turn to Chapter 8.)

Roots spread out from the trunk, not down.

(Illustration by Tamara Martin)

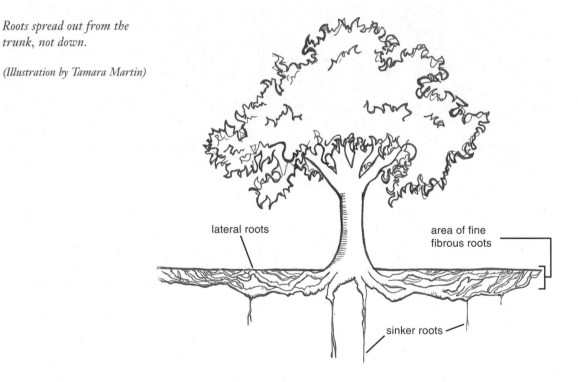

Roots work in four main ways. They ...

◆ Anchor trees.

◆ Pull in water and nutrients, mainly nitrogen and minerals.

◆ Store energy for growing and life processes.

◆ Synthesize materials for the needs of trees—such as fixing nitrogen and other organic products.

The anchoring makes sense. If you poked a stick in the ground and weighted it down with a lot of branches on top, the whole thing would fall over pretty easily. Roots prevent this. And in the case of a shrub, the whole plant helps because the plant is spread out and closer to the ground.

Drawing in nutrients along with water via the roots is the only way trees and shrubs can get the minerals they need. A root tip looks similar to a shaggy arrow, its solid part fringed with some slender lateral roots, then a long zone of root hairs, followed by an elongation zone (where its growing mechanism is), and a cap area at the tip. The water is pulled in mostly by the hairs and along the elongation zone. Nutrients such as nitrogen are taken in, thanks to soil fungi and bacteria working symbiotically with the tree's roots. Unlike in the case of parasitical relationships, these working relationships benefit both parties. (More on the nonbeneficial fungi and bacteria—and how they increase the all-important surface areas of the roots to help them absorb more—in Chapter 22.)

To do all this root work, trees have a *taproot*. This is a single root going straight down—maybe even 40 inches—when the tree is so young that it may still be just 3 inches tall above ground. This vertical root is usually either lost or vastly diminished after the tree is mature. Trees also have *heart roots*, which grow at an angle from the trunk, more spread out and continuing to splay out as the tree matures. Trees also have *sinker roots*, which grow out vertically from the horizontal ones, reaching down deeper for water.

All these roots follow the "line of least resistance," gradually growing around rocks (or through cracks in them) and other obstacles. A professional can dig small underground trenches to direct roots away from a major obstruction such as the foundation of your house.

Up Top: Leaves and Crown

These elements of a tree or shrub are the ones that take up and process energy from the sun. Without light to "eat," these plants couldn't grow.

All-Important Leaves

Tree and shrub leaves have a skin (*epidermis*), a waxy covering to hold in moisture (*cuticle*), and a mouth (*stomata*) to control water loss and transport carbon dioxide and oxygen. Leaves also have xylem and phloem in their veins, as does the trunk and *chloroplasts*—the "green machine" which handles the conversion of sun to energy, and other specialized tissues.

Under a microscope, leaves look like lace. But they're hardly delicate; they're actually more like little engines that turn solar energy into chemical/biological energy. The leaves nourish even more than the tree or shrub itself—insects, birds, and other creatures can use leaves in various ways, too.

> **The Real Dirt**
>
> Even an evergreen has "leaves"—its needles. It usually drops them over a 3- to 9-year period, not all at once, and not necessarily in the fall. The leaves of evergreens and deciduous trees and shrubs have similar parts and perform the same functions as coniferous trees and shrubs.

Leaves have a lot of work to do. Picture a sunny day after a nice rain—the best kind of day in the life of a tree or shrub. The roots have been drinking the soaked-in rain, and the nutrient-laden moisture from the soil has reached the leaf system. To keep from drying out in the first hour or two, the plant partly closes its stomata, allowing the leaf's waxy cuticle to block too much *transpiration*, or water release (read more about transpiration in Chapter 2). The stomata must stay open enough, however, for it to breathe out oxygen and breathe in carbon dioxide.

Leaves on the outer edges of the plant receive about 15 times more light, which enhances their growth. The loss of light makes a deciduous plant begin to transform and drop its leaves in the fall, when the days are shorter. (Leaf color changes are discussed in Chapter 10.)

The Crown Jewels

The *crown* of a tree or shrub is the size and shape of its canopy of leaves, from the lowest branches to the sky-scraping, arching top. This shape develops through buds and shoots growing larger and the underlying genetics of the tree species.

From a tip smaller than the size of the period at the end of this sentence, new shoots of a tree or shrub grow out, extending the structure until it gradually becomes a branch. On some trees, small shoots that won't develop into full branches are called *spurs.*

Buds grow out from the same tiny tip as well as from elsewhere on the shoots and branches. A bud can develop into a leaf or a flower or both, and it can become dormant from fall until the next spring. The arrangement and the shape of the buds vary depending on the species. Those trees and shrubs that have more spurs tend to bear more flowers and fruits. And trees like palm trees often have no budding from the sides of their trunks at all, giving them a long trunk topped by an explosion of leaves.

In a process called *shoot elongation*, shoots grow from tips every year. Some trees and shrubs elongate only for a few weeks in spring, others do so in one or more faster bursts, and others do so steadily throughout the entire growing season.

Watch out for sprouts that grow out—but not from the branches. These oddly named off-shoots are called *waterspouts* and *suckers* and can make a tree look cluttered and crowded, although they're usually only weakly attached. Both of these growing features look like mini-trees, complete with branches and leaves, but they grow upright out of the main trunk (waterspouts) or from the roots out of the ground very nearby (suckers). These sprouts can indicate either growth into a new clump of trees nearby or a last effort at vigor by a tree in trouble. Shrubs, because of their shape, don't have this issue.

> **Sprouts**
>
> Trees and shrubs can be most successfully planted and transplanted when buds are dormant, in the fall. The plant is better able to withstand the stress then.

Tree species genetics plays a role, too. The globe-shape crown of a tree such as an ash is formed because its side (or lateral branches) grows almost as fast as—or even faster than—the trunk. Conifers, in contrast, develop a conical shape as the tree grows along with the shoots and branches. Differences like these cannot really be overcome by human intervention—except sometimes through the chemistry of plant growth regulators (to be discussed in Chapter 14). The amount of sunlight the tree receives, however, can change its shape.

We talk more about tree shapes and sizes (and that includes crowns) in Chapter 12 because a balance of crown types in your yard is often desirable. This can be a bit tricky to achieve because tree species don't all grow at the same rate, but we do give you some pointers.

> **Root Rot**
>
> Trees that will grow tall and conically should not be planted under utility lines. They'll have to be pruned throughout their lives—maybe even removed—and they'll never reach their potential as a wonderful part of your yard.

The Least You Need to Know

- Trees and shrubs can have male and female parts on the same or neighboring trees or can contain two sexes in one.

- Every tree and shrub has seeds and pollen—the conifers in cones and the deciduous trees in flowers.

- The trunk contains the circulatory system and the plant's energy storage system.

- The root system, at least as extensive as the aboveground part of the tree or shrub, pulls in water and processes soil nutrition.

How Trees and Shrubs Work

In This Chapter

- ◆ How the tree or shrub gets its energy
- ◆ How plants breathe
- ◆ The life cycle of trees and shrubs
- ◆ Helping your tree or shrub live a long life

Trees and shrubs are pretty amazing when you think about it. All they need to live and grow are sunlight, carbon dioxide, and nutrients from the soil—and most of the time they get that on their own. In a natural forest, no one waters or fertilizes these plants, but they usually grow just fine there. And some homeowners don't do these things either, especially if their trees and shrubs are well established.

Trees can live a long time—some hundreds of years longer than others and shrubs up to several decades—but eventually they age and die like all other living things. This chapter helps you understand the life cycle of trees and shrubs, which, fortunately, is usually quite long.

The Magic of Photosynthesis

Although your yard's plantings appear to be inactive, just standing around looking pretty, that's not actually the case. Trees and shrubs are quietly very active, constantly engaged in *photosynthesis*, respiration, and transpiration.

Photosynthesis happens mostly in the leaves (although the trunks of young trees and even budding fruits can accomplish some of it), where the stomata—the leaf "pores" they use to breathe—draw in carbon dioxide, a pigment called *chlorophyll* makes a simple carbohydrate, and oxygen is released as a byproduct. The result: food for the plant.

def•i•ni•tion

Photosynthesis is the process by which trees and shrubs use light to turn carbon dioxide and water into the food they need to grow. The light comes from the sun (or a special indoor plant light). The carbon dioxide comes mostly from the air, with additions from the soil. The water comes mostly from the soil, with additions from the air. **Chlorophyll** is a pigment that makes trees and shrubs green.

Healthy photosynthesis requires the right amounts of water, nutrients, carbon dioxide, and temperature. The need for water is understandable. But nutrients, especially nitrogen and iron, are also important for photosynthesis. (These and other "fertilizers" are discussed further in Chapter 18.)

Carbon dioxide, the gas a tree or shrub needs to breathe, comes in through the stomata. In times of drought, trees must close these openings partway to preserve moisture—and that means they breathe less, too. Too much carbon from vehicle exhaust and factory effluents (especially coal-fired power plants) can strangle trees and shrubs. (Some trees and shrubs can tolerate more air pollution than others, and we mention those throughout the book.)

The temperature outside also has an immense effect on photosynthesis. Although trees can conduct this process in temperatures from as low as freezing up to a bit more than 100°F, these extremes are not ideal. Too much heat actually makes a tree pant, or breathe more quickly, and too little (as in winter) slows growth down to nothing or almost nothing. Photosynthesis takes a rest during this season.

Sprouts _____

Especially in the case of young trees and shrubs, which are growing most vigorously, the right amount of water is absolutely essential for photosynthesis. The process won't work without it. In droughts, you should set up a waterdrip (a hose that simply drips water out, from the mouth or more than one opening, at the rate of about 1 or 2 cups per hour; more on this in Chapter 15) for young plantings. Mature trees and shrubs can store water quite well and often don't need extra watering.

Understanding Respiration

After photosynthesis, next up is *respiration*, which happens in the leaves, shoots, growing parts of the roots, active parts of the trunk, and even in the young fruit of the tree. The younger the plant, the more it respires.

The Care and Handling of Roots

Because respiration happens in the roots, be sure to watch for soil compaction. Soils can get too low on oxygen if they become tightly compacted (by home construction equipment or heavy lawn mowers, for example). The tiny spaces between the soil particles that hold the air just collapse, and without enough oxygen for the roots, trees and shrubs can't conduct efficient respiration.

def•i•ni•tion

Respiration is the process by which trees and shrubs take the "food" energy they've made and use it for their life processes. The carbohydrates, in the presence of oxygen, become energy, along with some water and carbon dioxide.

Construction activities can destroy tree roots.

It's not wise to dig anywhere near a tree or to drive a large truck or lawnmower under a tree. A mature tree's root system covers even more area underground than the visible part of the tree does, and much of it is very close to the surface—often the top 3 feet of soil under and near the tree. That makes it easy to damage roots by accident. Remember that the roots are part of the tree's circulatory system, similar to blood vessels. (Shrubs are usually bushy enough to protect themselves because equipment can't get in as close.)

Plant "Hormones"

To help with respiration and conduct their bodily functions, trees and shrubs contain substances that behave much the same way hormones do in humans. For example, tomatoes and apples release the chemical *ethylene*, which helps them ripen when placed in a paper bag (the ethylene gets trapped in the bag and concentrates to ripen the produce). Ethylene also conveys messages to a tree's trunk to grow enough to adapt to the prevailing direction and strength of the wind. This chemical tends to be produced by the plant when it's under stress in general; in conditions other than wind, it can instruct the tree not to grow and/or to begin aging.

Another of these plant growth regulators, *auxins*, stimulates the tree or shrub to elongate its cells, push out more roots, and deal with its carbohydrate food supply. A synthetic form is the garden store chemical *2, 4-D*—the high doses included in it act as an herbicide. Another form of auxin can prevent the tree from sprouting around areas where it has been pruned.

Three other groups of tree and plant hormones have been identified—and, yes, younger trees have more of them!

Earning Their Keep

During respiration, trees and shrubs also freshen the air for us. They also absorb chemicals from the atmosphere that are unhealthy for us, such as smog.

The Real Dirt

Just for sheer oxygen production, a tree earns its keep: 1 acre of trees in a neighborhood park yields enough oxygen for 18 people to breathe. Take a deep breath!

Researchers have even put dollar signs on the benefits of trees and shrubs on air quality. In Atlanta, city trees removed so many tons of air pollutants that, based on an estimated cost of removing the pollutant load through industrial processes, each tree provided about 13 cents' worth of air cleaning service. In New York City, each tree turned out to be worth $1.82 in clean-up services. Trees and shrubs can become damaged if forced to absorb too much, so it may be necessary to replace big-city trees more often.

Transpiration

A tree standing in the middle of your yard, one crowned with an average canopy—say, 36 feet across—can release as much as 535 gallons of water per summer day—about 95 percent of what it took in. That's *transpiration*. Typically, more transpiration occurs when a day is light, warm, slightly breezy, moist at ground level, and low in humidity.

A tree's "plumbing system" is well adapted to manage water. Unlike garden plants that droop when they're low on moisture, trees' cell walls are toughened with lignin (you learned about lignin in Chapter 1), which creates pressure to hold in water until it's needed. Some species help manage their water by dropping leaves to avoid having to use water to maintain them.

Trees and shrubs filter dirty water as they move water throughout their bodies. The rainwater, sprinkler water, and snow that runs off all the roads, parking lots, driveways, and sidewalks is polluted with gasoline, oils, street salts, and tire rubber particles, among other things. A line of trees and shrubs along this pavement can help. Their roots are built to absorb water and the pollutants. This reduces the stuff that would otherwise make its way to our streams, rivers, ponds, and lakes via the storm sewer drains. They also absorb—and then gradually release—floodwater for us.

def•i•ni•tion

Transpiration is the process by which trees and shrubs shed water. Most of it "sweats" out of the leaves' stomata, although a little is also released through tiny openings in the bark.

Sprouts

Trees with a lot of leaves, those with thinner and with darker green leaves, and deciduous trees that keep their leaves longer into the fall, process more water. They need more water to begin with, and they transpire more, too. Keep this in mind when choosing the trees for your yard.

Trees and shrubs also prevent erosion; their roots hold the soil in place. Without this service, we'd be losing land and collapsing hills every time it rained. That soil would eventually clog up our waterways.

Tree and Shrub Aging

At 4,600 years old, the oldest tree found to date is a bristlecone pine in California. That's old for a tree. Trees that bear fruit—apple trees, cherry trees, members of the rose family, for example—tend to be among the most short-lived, possibly because of the effort it takes to produce the fruit. Shrubs tend to have shorter lives than trees, too, though there are some exceptions to this rule.

 The Real Dirt _____

Some trees move toward immortality by cloning themselves, so each new version starts off as a just-born organism. As the cloning continues, more and more young organisms grow up near the genetically identical parent. Any tree or shrub that makes a grove or "patch" by itself is probably a cloner—think sumac, aspen, or pawpaw. Self-cloning can have amazing results. Scientists have found huckleberry bushes that are about 13,000 years old, a creosote bush at about 11,700 years of age, and quite a few grasses and mushrooms that could date to the time right after the glaciers melted in the northern sections of the lower 48 states about 10,000 years ago.

You might not notice the aging of a tree or shrub for decades, and that's a good thing for the beauty and greenness of your yard. An easy way to influence this *senescence* is by buying longer-lived trees as opposed to trees that grow faster. It also helps a lot to carefully choose the best locations and conditions for any plant you buy. You can even buy *dwarf trees*. These trees are grafted and/or genetically engineered to have a dwarf root system—and they move through their life stages very slowly—more slowly than most shrubs.

def•i•ni•tion

Senescence is the process of pulling back nutrients and shedding leaves or more branches through the production of the plant hormone ethylene.

A Tale of Two Trees

Elderly trees, as with people, can be quite vigorous. Author Jeannie has two nice instances of this, one involving an oak tree and the other an apple tree.

When we bought our house, a 200+-year-old oak tree was growing out of the middle of the deck, which itself was probably 20 years old. The tree was not only surrounded by decking 8-feet out in all directions, but it was well established with an extensive root system. The tree gets its rainwater just fine and is still growing. In fact, we've had to enlarge the hole in the deck around its trunk every 2 to 3 years—the trunk is still adding that much girth.

The apple, a much shorter-lived tree, looks gnarled and twisted although it's probably only a twentysomething. But it drops tons of apples every fall—so many that they rot there after we've made all the applesauce we can stand from the apples.

It can seem pretty amazing that trees live as long as they do. Throughout their lives, they need to change their entire shape to gradually adjust to their own increasing weight as well as the sometimes severe stresses of wind, rain, snow, and ice. They do this by adding more wood to buttress themselves and by constantly redistributing the strain across their whole mass.

And different tree species have different life spans. Most birch live about 50 years, sugar maples and many oaks grow to be 200 to 400 years old, and sequoias and other temperate rain forest trees age to thousands of years old. Balance these numbers with another factor, though—usually the trees and shrubs that have the *shortest* life spans also grow the fastest. And of course, better care—and luck—means that any plant can be a bit above average.

Sprouts

We give you more information on choosing the best trees and shrubs for your yard in later chapters, but for now, a couple of examples. If you want fast-growing (but short-lived) trees, opt for a willow, aspen, poplar, or birch. For a long-lived tree, try a Douglas fir, white oak, sugar maple, or giant sequoia or California redwood. If you know that oak wilt is plaguing your community but you still want to plant an oak for your yard, choose a white oak instead of a red oak (the former is more resistant to this life-shortening disease). And remember that shrubs generally grow *very* fast.

Signs of Trouble

In nature—nature wilder than our yards and city parks, we mean—the main causes of tree and shrub death are disease (aboveground or underground), insects, fire, drought, and structural failure from causes as various as root rot and windstorms.

In your yard, the same causes figure in, but so does environmental degradation, ranging from air pollution to poor pruning, from too much watering to not allowing enough room for the tree's roots to spread or its leaves to stretch out to the sun. And quite a few trees and shrubs, as we'll see in Chapter 24, are susceptible to insects and fungi. After such pests become established, a tree's or shrub's death is usually inevitable, although it may be slow, even almost undetectable by us.

Most of the rest of the book advises you on what to do to allow your trees and shrubs to thrive, to live as long as possible in as good a shape as possible. But for now, walk around your yard: do any of your trees or shrubs look as though they're quietly asking for help? Leaves falling off in summer or large dead branches? Fungus up against the trunk at ground level in a disturbing, large blob? Leaning to one side, straining for sunlight? An "extra" root like an odd necklace around the base of the trunk? If you see any of these signs in your yard, you might want to read this book fast—or maybe even call a tree service company or arborist to see about extending that tree's or shrub's life. (More on the senescence of trees and shrubs, including the best ways to dispose of them after death, is found in Chapter 19.)

A Word on Temperature

We soon get you started in the right direction for choosing trees or shrubs that can conduct their lifestyles long and well in your yard. But first, a word on temperature, which is a key issue.

The Real Dirt

Different species also have limits on how *much* cold they can endure. These parameters are the basis for the geographic success zones discussed in Chapter 3.

It's important that a tree or shrub not be exposed to colder temperatures than it's suited for. In each temperature zone, trees need cold during the winter so their buds can break dormancy in the spring. You won't get any fruit from your apple tree in the northern states, for example, if it doesn't have a week or so of temperatures below 45°F; in the far southern states, those cultivars require only a couple days of this.

Slowing Aging

What seems to slow down your tree's or shrub's aging the most, in general, is to prune dead branches, fertilize if necessary, and keep the tree's or shrub's environment as stable as possible above and below ground.

It's best not to introduce new trees or shrubs near an elderly tree, nor compact the soil around it with machinery, nor radically change the amount of water you give it. Aging trees don't like change very much—it's even bad for them.

The Stages of Death

The first sign that a tree or shrub is becoming elderly is that it doesn't grow as much. This happens for various reasons in various species, and the balance of factors even in one species isn't well understood.

As your tree or shrub continues to age, you'll notice less fruit (if it's a fruit tree) and a general slight shrinkage of the tree. Underground, the roots are slowly degrading, and the tree is deliberately shrinking its crown to remain as stable as possible, given the mass of its root system. This happens with shrubs, too, although it's less noticeable.

As living tissue continues to be lost, both above and below ground, the tree loses stability. It becomes especially vulnerable to additional invasions by insects, fungus, bacteria, viruses, even woodpeckers. Eventually, your tree falls down dead or you have it taken down before it has a chance to fall on your house or another tree.

Consider keeping your dead tree pulled to the edge of your yard as a home for chipmunks or other creatures. Or saw it up, let the wood dry, and use it in your fireplace. (See Chapter 19 for more on disposing of the dead tree.)

Sprouts

When you plant a new tree to replace a large mature tree that's dying or dead, don't place it in the exact same location. The roots of the dead tree are still there, in the way, and will be for years, even if you paid to have the stump removed. Your best bet is to plant the new one off to the side.

The Least You Need to Know

- Trees and shrubs use sunlight as the energy for photosynthesis, turning it into food primarily through chlorophyll.

- Trees and shrubs inhale and exhale air, a respiration process.

- Trees and shrubs also "sweat," losing water in a process called respiration.

- Trees that grow faster tend to live shorter lives. It's a trade-off: do you want a tree that will grow fast or stick around for a while?

3

What Zone Are You?

In This Chapter

- ◆ A look at the temperature zones
- ◆ Finding your zone
- ◆ Tips for choosing the right trees and shrubs for your zone

If you've ever browsed through plant catalogs, you might have noticed the little box labeled "Zone" and a corresponding number. In this chapter, we talk about these zones and offer suggestions of the best trees to plant in your particular zone.

Zoning is much less of an issue with shrubs, most of which have varieties that have been bred to be appropriate for a broader zonal range. For that reason, and because a shrub can be tucked pretty easily into a sheltered area, *and* because trees are a much larger financial investment, we advise you to begin your yard enhancement with trees suitable for your zone. Later chapters focus more on shrubs, while others cover both trees and shrubs simultaneously.

On the Map: Finding Your Zone

Get ready for a small adventure! On the following zone maps, find your location. Write down the corresponding number in the front of this book or someplace handy so you'll remember it throughout the rest of the book and especially when you're shopping for new green companions. Of course, the nursery in town won't be selling Eastern white pines if you live in the Everglades or palm trees if your home is Wyoming—but they usually offer more than one or two zones.

This map shows the cold hardiness zones across the continental United States.

(©2006, National Arbor Day Foundation)

Here, cold hardiness zones are featured for Alaska and Hawaii.

(©2006, National Arbor Day Foundation)

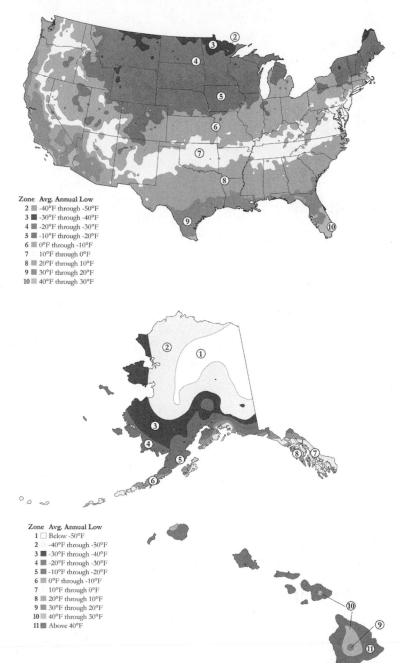

Zone	Avg. Annual Low
2	-40°F through -50°F
3	-30°F through -40°F
4	-20°F through -30°F
5	-10°F through -20°F
6	0°F through -10°F
7	10°F through 0°F
8	20°F through 10°F
9	30°F through 20°F
10	40°F through 30°F

Zone	Avg. Annual Low
1	Below -50°F
2	-40°F through -50°F
3	-30°F through -40°F
4	-20°F through -30°F
5	-10°F through -20°F
6	0°F through -10°F
7	10°F through 0°F
8	20°F through 10°F
9	30°F through 20°F
10	40°F through 30°F
11	Above 40°F

Next take a look at the temperature numbers shown on the map. If you live in zone 5, for example, you might be able to buy a tree from an adjacent zone (some of the store tags will even say "zones 4/5"). Ask the nursery if you're unsure how a tree will do in your yard, or consult Appendix F for plantings that do well across more than one zone.

Root Rot _____

Some homeowners push the zone envelope, choosing trees labeled one or more zones higher (a larger number) than their own zone. But be careful. You might dream of a saguaro cactus in your Indiana yard, or a lovely loblolly on your Portland, Maine, or Portland, Oregon, front lawn, but it isn't likely to survive. Unless you've got an incredibly warm corner of your northern yard or a truly cool spot in your southern yard, don't push your plantings more than one zone. Stick to the map.

The following sections offer some sample tree choices specific to each zone. These trees are considered common in and characteristic of their zone. (They are also found on the CD that accompanies this book if you want to check out what they look like.) We focus as much as possible on native trees, ones that have been growing in a given area for thousands of years and are especially well adapted to local conditions. Nurseries and universities typically begin with the native tree to create *cultivars*. You can also plant the native tree. But don't worry about getting the wrong cultivar of a

tree or shrub if you shop at a reputable plant seller. Just ask what kind of success they've had with it and for how long. This could be a concern, though, if you order from a catalog or online. Just check out our advice in Chapter 13 and also the list of top native trees in Appendix C.

def•i•ni•tion _____

A **cultivar** is a variant of a tree species, developed by scientists or arborists to more perfectly suit a given location. Some are tried and true by now; others are newer and still a bit experimental.

Zone 1

We're not including zone 1 in our discussion here because its extent within the United States is very minimal.

Zones 2 and 3

Very little of our country's territory lies within zone 2 (parts of interior Alaska, a stretch in northeastern Minnesota, and some high elevations within the Rocky Mountains), so we're combining it with zone 3.

White pine and paper birch do well in both zones, as premier trees of the North. Zones 2 and 3 were once highly glaciated, almost completely buried under 2 miles—or more—of solid ice. The soils tend to be thin.

The trees of this combined zone all established themselves after the glaciers began to melt about 10,000 years ago. Only a handful of tree species are native here, although they're present in incredibly vast numbers: balsam fir (*Abies balsamea*), tamarack (*Larix laricina*), lodgepole pine (*Pinus contorta*), black spruce (*Picea mariana*), white spruce (*Picea glauca*), jack pine (*Pinus banksiana*), all conifers, quaking aspen, balsam poplar (*Populus balsamifera*), paper birch (*Betula papyrifera*), and white pine (*Pinus strobus*).

Sprouts

It's helpful to know a tree or shrub's Latin name when you're ready to buy plantings. *Latin?!* Don't worry. You don't have to talk to Caesar or anything. But it is important to know a plant's Latin name because you'll probably find many varieties of the same tree, and the common English names for trees and shrubs can vary in different parts of the United States. And some plants have *only* a Latin name. Your local store will have these—and often a third name—to label the cultivars. Note we provide the Latin only the first time a tree or shrub is featured in the book as well as in Appendix F.

White Pine

At up to 150 feet tall and as broad as 5 feet in diameter, the white pine is a beautiful choice. It is also very long-lived, often able to thrive for hundreds of years. The trunks are so straight and its wood so desirable that in the heyday of massive clear-cut logging in this country in the nineteenth century, most were cut down. Residents who plant white pines are regardening the northern world.

What it likes: A white pine grows best in rich soil but also accepts the dry conditions of sand dunes and even a silty soil. It enjoys full sun but accepts a bit more shade than other pine trees. Easy to transplant, it is quite resistant to drought and certainly to cold.

What it doesn't like: Air pollution and road salt, being crowded, and too much heat.

Paper Birch

Paper birch trees—also called white birch and even canoe birch (grey birch is slightly different)—are just as iconic in zones 2/3. However, they are vastly less long-lived, with a natural life span of only about 50 years. This tree does grow fast, though, and its tiny seeds, blown in by wind, catch on well. Slender and beautiful, it puts on a bright yellow fall "dress." It's often clumped, which happens when dormant buds around the main trunk are allowed to grow instead of being cut back or naturally pruned by hungry wildlife. But even trees with a single trunk grow in immense stands in natural areas.

What it likes: Birch love disturbed habitats. After a forest fire, for example, it is often the first tree to become established. (In fact, when you see a large stand of birch, you can tell that something must have happened there before—you might be standing at the site of old logging, an avalanche, an insect invasion, or a fire.) Birch prefer full sun and slightly acidic, cool soil.

What it doesn't like: Too much heat. If July's heat averages more than 70°F, birch won't thrive, falling prey to insects. Too much moisture around its roots is a problem, too.

Root Rot _____

If your birch tree is developing dead branches, the condition is probably due to the bronze birch borer. Prune off the affected branches (after reading the pruning chapters), and if any other birch are nearby, consider administering one round of a nonspray insecticide in liquid, powder, or granular form.

Zone 4

This zone is still quite northerly, except where it dips down into mid-latitudes in Colorado, Nebraska, Iowa, and a small section of Utah. Bur oak and sugar maple are both classic trees for zone 4, although they grow in other zones as well. Bur oak is one of the 300 to 600 species of oak trees that thrive worldwide. Oaks grow in probably more different kinds of forests around the world than any other tree, from Europe, to the subtropics of Central America, to northern Africa. North America, though, has the most oak species of any continent.

Bur Oak

The bur oak (*Quercus macrocarpa*) is impressive, a shade tree par excellence. It grows 60 to 90 feet high and 50 to 90 feet across. It's an immense, craggy tree whose crown is a rough semi-circle. Its leaves turn a deep yellow-brown to russet in the fall. Even its acorns are large, measuring sometimes 2 inches across. And snow transforms a bur oak into a castle. Plant one now and others will enjoy it for the next 200 to 400 years.

The Real Dirt _____

Jeannie lives in a suburb that was, before humans arrived, an oak savanna with wetlands and ponds in between. There are still park areas where you can see groups of bur oak, widely spaced and immense, near small lakes.

Only in the farthest northwestern part of its range is the bur oak smaller. There it can even be the size of a shrub.

What it likes: Plenty of space and sun—and squirrels and other rodents that plant its seeds. The bur oak can tolerate extremes of precipitation and soil types from acid to alkaline, even forest fires. It can clone itself, after a fire, if necessary. This is one tough tree!

What it doesn't like: Being transplanted when it's mature; having its roots compacted by construction machines; the fungal invasion called oak wilt (although it's a bit more resistant to this than most other oaks); and having its soil drainage patterns altered by lawn projects.

Sugar Maple

Sugar maple (*Acer saccharum*) got its name for a reason you can probably guess (think pancakes). This is the premium sap-is-running-in-the-spring tree. (The process of harvesting and then boiling the sap is not as daunting a project as you might imagine if you ever want to try it.)

The sugar maple shows benefits year-round. In springtime, after sugaring season, its pale-yellow flowers create a glow before the leaves form. Summer finds them leafed out in either a dense, full-crown shape (if there's plenty of room) or as more of an elegant green candle effect. Autumn transforms them into the first blaze of any tree; gold, orange, and crimson are its palette. If you're careful, and perhaps select one of its equally spectacular close relatives, you can enjoy this tree as far north as zone 3 and certainly down in zones 5 and 6. Check Appendix F for details.

Sprouts

Jeannie has heard a tree make a loud cracking sound on an extremely cold (way, way below zero) day. This happens when ice, which expands as water freezes, penetrates some of its cells. Almost always, don't worry—the tree repairs itself inside.

What it likes: Moist, organically rich, well-drained soil to allow it to grow to its 60 to 80 feet optimal height. Air pollution and road salt are tolerated.

What it doesn't like: Lawn chemicals; even thick grass (because the grass roots disturb its roots) and lawnmowers (they also compact the soil and hurt the roots). Being planted with its roots a bit too deep in the ground. When the tree is planted too deep, it can develop *girdling* roots, which look a bit like a choker-style necklace around the trunk at ground level. (See Chapter 8 for more on girdling roots.)

Zone 5

This zone stretches like a smile across the middle of the U.S. map. For trees, think of the nickname for President Andrew Jackson of Tennessee—Old Hickory. And although they're hardly widespread, another nice feature of this zone is the cranberry bush (*Vaccinium macrocarpon*), the bog bush whose fruit we love to eat.

Shagbark Hickory

Shagbark hickory (*Carya ovata*) is probably the most classic of the hickory family, and it's excellent to plant in this zone. (Others are good, too, such as the bitternut hickory [*Carya cordiformis*], pecan hickory [*Carya illinoinensis*], and mockernut hickory [*Carya tomentosa*].) Its shaggy bark can look like the latest hairstyle. Although it grows slowly, this tree can live for a couple hundred years and stretch to as many feet tall. In the spring, its budding leaves look like tulips. By fall, it blazes pure gold. The nuts taste great to local rodents—and to us—although they have very tough shells. This is a pretty adaptable tree, and its wood is also particularly hard.

What it likes: Mostly dry and upland areas, the edges of a yard (not any manicured, "glossy" areas your yard might have).

What it doesn't like: Being transplanted; the heat of forest fires; construction equipment over the root area.

Flowering Dogwood

Flowering dogwood (*Cornus florida L.*) is one of the most beautiful flowering trees. Both George Washington and Thomas Jefferson planted them, and you can, too. The shrubbier dogwoods, more densely branched, have the most spectacular flowering, coming usually in white (which tend to be the sturdiest), pink, and red cultivars. In the fall, its cascading red leaves enrich the soil where they fall. The fruits are bitter to us, but birds enjoy them.

What it likes: Having its leaves in the sun and its roots in the shade—in other words, edge locations—as well as a bit of a breeze. It doesn't mind the gypsy moth or air pollution as much as many other trees do.

 The Real Dirt

In our own Minnesota, the dogwoods in bloom after a long winter have actually made us gasp! They join with the redbuds in a magnificent display. A spring rain or wind so quickly causes petals to fall, but even that forms an elegant arc of color against the still-bare ground.

What it doesn't like: Being transplanted within your yard, especially too deep and in alkaline soils.

Zones 6 Through 8

This zone begins its arc high in interior Washington State and some of Oregon and Nevada, slides into the lower part of its smile shape, and goes back up north into limited areas of Massachusetts, where it touches the ocean. (It's not generally a coastal zone, however.) This mid-zone area has myriad choices; elm and holly provide plenty of accents of green.

Zone 7, home to classic southern trees, stretches from southern New Mexico on far to the east, and going as far north as Delaware. You'll find loblolly pine and sycamore happy here.

Zone 8 is largely but not entirely the Deep South. It covers parts of Nevada and Arizona, dips down through Mexico, and reappears in southern Louisiana and through Georgia. The black tupelo and southern magnolia are classics for readers here.

American Elm (Zone 6)

American elm (*Ulmus americana*), the classic elm, although drastically affected by Dutch elm disease, still grows widely in North America. It's a great bet across zone 6. More should be planted to replace those trees killed, especially its new, healthy cultivars. This lovely tree is shaped like an upended broom—and a tall broom at that because it regularly grows to 100 feet. Springtime finds them one of the first trees to flower, turning branches to a pale red blur. They are golden in the fall.

What it likes: Moist soil, such as found in valleys and on flood plains, although it also grows on prairies and even rocky bluffs. It's a tough tree, easy to transplant and grow, and very long-lived, able to survive even in zone 2 when planted there. Sun or shade? No problem.

What it doesn't like: At sapling size, rabbits. And of course, the Dutch elm fungus.

The Real Dirt _____

One of the things we love about forests, in the United States and elsewhere, is the variety of wonderful, though not-so-useful names they have. *Cloud forests* live at and above cloud level on mountains. *Riverine forests* march along both sides of rivers. *Boreal forests* are in the high north, with only a strip along the North Shore of Lake Superior in the United States and high up in the Rockies. And these are only a few!

American Holly (Zone 6)

American holly (*Ilex opaca*) is a lovely tree or shrub associated with winter holidays, especially Christmas, and even the Druid religion, which uses it at the winter solstice. In the United States, 14 native holly trees and 2 native shrubs grow dressed in shiny green leaves and bright red berries, and if you count the cultivars, that number sprouts into the hundreds.

Some cultivars have black, orange, or yellow berries, the fruit of the plant—which birds just love! The holly's flowers are few and not as showy as its berries, coming in a whitish-green or a greenish-white.

In natural forests, holly grows in the shady understory, but in a yard with plenty of sun, it becomes more attractively dense and symmetrical. An evergreen, its new leaves push off the old ones in the spring.

Each holly is of only one sex, so be sure there's an opposite sex one somewhere reasonably near—and the opinion that matters is the bee's. Otherwise, you won't get the lovely red fruit, which forms only on the female bush or tree. (A few cultivars have been created that have both sexes together on one plant.)

What it likes: Moist, humid soils and temperatures. It's happy to grow under other trees.

What it doesn't like: Cold.

> **Sprouts**
>
> For a shrub very similar to holly, try winterberry or possum haw if you live in the southeastern United States or even as far north as southern Indiana. Its berries can be even more impressive than the holly's, because they stand out against yellow leaves in the fall or even the bare branches in winter.

Loblolly Pine (Zone 7)

Loblolly pine (*Pinus taeda*) has an odd but mellifluous name, bestowed upon the tree by early British settlers, who drew it from the word for a thick stew. This tree doesn't look "stewy" (whatever that would be)—but it grows in marshy lands such as wet places in woods.

Loblollies are a classic tree in South Carolina, Alabama, Mississippi, Arkansas, Louisiana, and Texas, where a natural woodland stand may cover 70 square miles. This tree grows fast, not minding poor soil, fierce wind, or salt spray, and can live 200 to 300 years.

What it likes: Marshy soil.

What it doesn't like: Beetles.

American Sycamore (Zone 7)

The sycamore (*Platanus occidentalis*) is huge, up to 100 to 150 feet tall and 6 to 10 feet across at the trunk. In fact, it is the most massive tree in the eastern United States, where it grows from Iowa east. Its flaking outer bark exposes the smooth, white bark underneath, making it dramatically white in winter. As it becomes very old, a sycamore opens a "cave" inside its trunk at the ground level where kids (and, in some larger trees, even adults) can crawl in for fun. These trees can live for 400 years.

What it likes: Bottomlands, where they are often found growing with oak, hickory, pecan, and cottonwood trees, and some upland sites that have been disturbed by human construction, where many wind-blown seeds can colonize.

What it doesn't like: A disease called anthracnose (see Chapter 21), and too much undercutting of its roots by stream water.

Stream water can undercut and erode the root system and foundation of a tree such as a sycamore.

Black Tupelo (Zone 8)

Black tupelo (*Nyssa sylavatica*), also called black gum, is common on the coastal plain/ low country of the zone 8 Gulf and Atlantic states, often with sycamores. Probably its best-known terrain is the tupelo-cypress swamp, where it can grow draped in both grape vines and poison ivy vines, its roots in the black water. But your yard, if low and moist, can be ideal, too.

What it likes: Wet roots.

What it doesn't like: Dry places, being transplanted.

Magnolia (Zone 8)

Magnolia (*Magnolia*), which can grow either to the size of a shrub or a tree up to 80 feet tall, can be planted from zone 6 down to zone 10. Its spectacular white and fragrant flowers against dark-green, glossy evergreen leaves make it one of the most beautiful trees in the United States. As an understory tree, it tolerates shade under other trees and also prefers the moister area of the southern coastal plains, such as the Georgia coast. Understory trees and shrubs don't grow as tall as other species growing around them and are content with less sun. Magnolias grow in both bottomland and upland areas, as long as rainfall or watering is sufficiently ample.

Sprouts

The magnolia is probably the oldest flowering tree on the planet—dinosaurs probably ate its fruit. To get help from your children when planting a magnolia tree, mention that it was dinosaur food! (Then be sure to allay any fears.)

What it likes: Good drainage, acidic soil, low elevations.

What it doesn't like: Your yard's grass too near to its trunk, flooding, and soil compaction because of construction equipment.

Zones 9 Through 10/11

This zone covers much of the Florida peninsula, dips down into Mexico, and comes back up in southern Arizona and parts of California. Because zones are defined by temperature, perhaps it won't seem surprising that the trees we feature in this varied zone are the mangrove and the saguaro cactus. Two trees could hardly be any more different in their approach to water: mangroves keep their roots in it all the time—you could call it wallowing—while saguaro have to struggle for moisture and save every drop. They're as dry as bones.

As with zones 2/3 in the high northern United States, zones 10 and 11 in the far south are combined because neither pair covers much territory in America. Only Hawaii and the southern tip of Florida, mostly the Keys, are in zones 10/11.

American Mangrove (Zone 9)

Mangrove (*Avicennia germinans*), with its prop roots, or legs, splaying out into the water to anchor the tree in the mud, is a tree for all seasons in Florida and across the world's tropics. This state has the most extensive mangrove swamps in the world.

Mangroves actually build brand-new islands by trapping bits of detritus and nutrients and forming new soil. Any reader in the position to a start a new island for a community park or a "yard" should plant mangroves! Even a small such barrier island can protect your area from storm damage inland.

The Real Dirt

Jeannie has a favorite bit of knowledge about bamboo, a southern plant that looks like a tree but is actually a grass. This speedy green creature can grow as fast as 4 feet in 24 hours, faster even than mangrove!

Mangroves become home to dozens of wood storks, egrets, and other birds nesting high; plenty of sea life (who take advantage not only of root hiding places but nutrition from the trees' leaves); and mammals such as raccoons who climb their trunks.

What it likes: Silts and muds to anchor themselves in water that's not too deep.

What it doesn't like: Solitude—they prefer to grow in vast swampy stretches.

Saguaro (Zone 9)

You might not think of the saguaro (*Carnegiea giganteus*), the giant cactus with "arms" that wave, as a tree—it has spines instead of leaves! If you've ever seen a dead saguaro, it becomes obvious that there's a "skeleton" or framework of woody ribs. And in spring, it features white flowers, with edible red fruit later as the season progresses.

The typical height for these cacti are 20 to 35 feet. In the United States, you'll only find them in Arizona.

What it likes: Desert, south-facing slope.

What it doesn't like: Too many of the gila woodpeckers and gilded flickers digging holes in it for their nests.

Eucalyptus (Zones 10/11)

The eucalyptus tree (*Eucalyptus camaldulensis*), common in the uplands of Hawaii and growing in more than 300 species worldwide, rises very tall dressed in thick, hard bark. It can grow up to 50 feet high and a couple feet across. Eucalyptus can live well on dry hillsides because its roots plunge very deep for water. Although we usually recommend native trees most enthusiastically, this ancient species original to Australia is well worth planting in Hawaii. Its sprigs can be woven into spicy-smelling wreaths (although wear gloves because they're very sticky), and the scent keeps some insects away.

What it likes: Its seeds won't germinate unless it experiences fire, or comparable heat. Buds under the bark also pop out when the bark is burned.

What it doesn't like: Lots of moisture and other plants nearby.

> **The Real Dirt**
>
> The crowns of the eucalyptus are a bit unusual—they actually can explode in a fire, when the fragrant oils that characterize this tree transform into a gas.

Live Oak (Zones 10/11)

The live oak (*Quercus virginiana*) just says the Deep South, spreading shade under its long gracious, bending branches. The crowns can be twice as broad as the tree is high, and when old, the branches brush the ground, creating a green kingdom underneath.

Live oaks grow as far north as Virginia and as far west as Texas but only in areas very close to the ocean. In its zone, a live oak is exceptionally drought-resistant, shade-tolerant, and long-lived. A draping of Spanish moss doesn't harm it at all—in fact, the combination seems perfectly in character.

What it likes: Growing in groupings called motts; sandy soils; salt spray is tolerated.

What it doesn't like: Fire and oak wilt.

That should give you a good idea of what you can expect to find in your zone. You can even start a "top choices" list now, to be filled in later with plenty of trees and shrubs perfect for your area. For more ideas, turn the page!

The Least You Need to Know

- ◆ The United States is divided into climate zones based on the lowest temperature point of the year.

- ◆ You can push your zone a bit when you plant trees and shrubs (one number higher or lower), if you have a particularly warm, or cool, place in your yard.

- ◆ Native trees that have grown in your zone for thousands of years are particularly sturdy and well adapted for your yard.

- ◆ Tree and shrub species have key features as well as likes and dislikes. Learning their preferences helps ensure success in your yard.

Chapter 4

Conditions for Success

In This Chapter

- Assessing your local conditions
- Too hot? Too cold?
- *Wiiiiiind!* and how it affects trees and shrubs
- Suitable trees and shrubs for your zone

In Chapter 3, we looked at the zones and offered a few suggestions of trees and shrubs to plant in each zone. That's a great place to start, but knowing your zone is only part of the tree- and shrub-planting success story.

Seasonal extremes and sudden temperature changes make a real difference and may be rather common in your city or county. An odd cold spell in spring or in a summer that's otherwise unremittingly hot, especially when these aren't unusual happenings, are important to keep in mind. Wind is a curious variable, too. Too little can be as difficult for your trees and shrubs as too much. Wind is the trees' exercise and also dating service, bringing male and female parts together in wind-pollinated plantings.

In this chapter, we take a closer look at your local area to help you determine what you should plant so your trees and shrubs will not just survive, but thrive!

Extreme Seasonal Temperatures

What we consider "extreme" in our area might be typical for your area. Remember those TV images of orange growers panicked over 30°F temperatures in Florida? That would be a winter heat wave in other areas of the country! Obviously you wouldn't choose a tree or shrub for your yard based on the chance occurrence of non-stop major hurricanes or tornados, freak ice storms, or the heat wave of the century. But do consider more normal extremes, or temperatures too low or high for a given season. Some plantings handle such swings better than others.

> **The Real Dirt**
>
> We focus more on trees than on shrubs in this chapter because your decisions about trees usually need to come first—they take up more space and cost more. As the book proceeds, we add in shrubs more and more, and we mention everywhere when a tree has a form or size that's more like a shrub. We also always note where what we say applies to both trees and shrubs, which is often the case.

def•i•ni•tion

Mesoclimate describes these factors for your neighborhood, city, or county. **Microclimate** is the pattern of temperature, light, topography, wind, and other such factors at the level of your yard. Both are important for the success of your trees and shrubs.

You might want to take a moment here to review the zones in Chapter 3 and note your geographical success zone number. In this chapter, we focus on trees for your zone that are especially tough when encountering seasonal temperatures. (The tree and shrub grid in Appendix F pulls this together for you, too.)

Although there are steps you can take to affect some of the other factors in this chapter, there are some realities here, too. After all, there's little you can do to change your city and county-wide temperatures (the *mesoclimate*) or the temperatures in your yard (the *microclimate*).

Too Cold/Too Hot

Many trees and shrubs have a set of preferred temperatures throughout the year—perhaps higher or lower when they're forming flower buds or creating fruit, for example. The temperature at night can be more important than in the daytime for them, too, especially when a plant is in bloom. Even within each zone, extreme, unusual, and sudden temperature changes are serious issues for your trees and shrubs to deal with.

The Effects of Cold

Seasonal temperature extremes are difficult for your trees and shrubs all year round, not just winter. In winter, in fact, the tree or shrub has completed this year's growing season and is much better able to tolerate a blast of cold.

Too much cold in spring or fall is hard on your plantings. Frost, especially when humidity is low and skies are clear, is stressful. A sudden drop in temperature, when winds sweep in with a new, colder weather system, is also challenging. The very coldest days of winter and cold days in winter that follow immediately after a winter warm period are difficult, too.

The Real Dirt

The process of winter adjusting, which trees and shrubs do at any age—and every year—is called *hardening.* Your plantings become *winter hardy.*

Seasonal extremes can lead to ...

♦ Death by frost damage to new shoots, flowers, or fruit (although the tree or shrub may well live to try again).

♦ Frost splitting or cracks in a tree's trunk or branches.

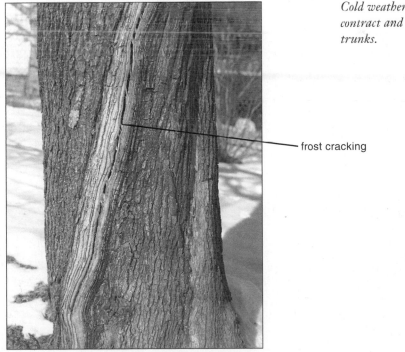

Cold weather makes cells contract and can crack tree trunks.

——— frost cracking

◆ Soil-heaving damage to roots, as freezing and thawing cycles shove them up a bit higher toward the surface than they should be.

◆ Sunscald of trunks and especially of exposed branches of trees from a sudden drop to below freezing temperatures or even the reflection of the sun off new snow.

The late winter sun is strong while temperatures are still low, and sudden changes can scald the tree.

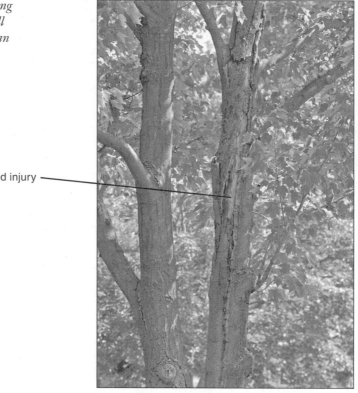

sunscald injury

◆ Winterburn or desiccation of conifers when they can't pull enough water up out of the frozen ground—they lose too much water through their needles.

◆ Death to the dormant buds of trees and shrubs (in winter), meaning they won't be there in the spring.

◆ Death to the entire tree or shrub, when even the roots die. This can happen from excessive cold (without a blanket of snow cover) or from the drying effects of excessive heat.

Note that temperature stresses more often "wound" trees and shrubs than actually kill them. But cracks in the trunks, death to buds, and other effects similar to these make the plant more vulnerable to everything later from insects to deer.

Here's what you can do to help, in addition to choosing sturdy trees and shrubs:

◆ Plant your more vulnerable planting choices on the south side of your house, garden wall, garage, etc. Or the side that gets less wind.

◆ Plant near to your house, while allowing room for roots, because a house sheds heat, no matter how energy-efficient it is.

◆ Plant in well-drained locations, which will lead to less ground frost from water within the soil.

◆ Don't leave a plant in a container outside in cold winter climates; its roots are not sufficiently protected in it.

Looking on the good side of cold weather, the trees and shrubs of the temperate zones (virtually all of America) actually need *some* cold. Buds chill out gradually, beginning in fall. Then in winter they actually require an average of 4 to 8 weeks of temperatures between 24°F and 50°F, depending on the tree. Without it, buds don't open in springtime. Lower temps for a shorter period doesn't work—plants require a winter to some degree because they react so much to the length of the day, the *photoperiod*, also. (See Chapter 5 for more on the photoperiod.)

Sprouts

Watch out for cold snaps! If you know one is coming, you could string an electrical cord outside, hang a 100-watt bulb amid a group of shrubs, and plug it in. Even a little bit of heat such as this can help!

This need for winter is a way to see evolution at work. The native trees and shrubs we have today are the ones that survived winters over the years—and even came to count on them. Fruit trees and shrubs are especially picky. Without a period at 45°F or less, for 1,000 to 1,400 hours, apple trees won't produce apples. Neither will pear or apricot trees. Peach and almond trees need less chilling time than apple trees do. Chilly fogs blowing in from the ocean help boost this winter chilling necessity in some areas. Cultivars have been developed to push these envelopes somewhat, but the trees and shrubs native to your area have had thousands of years to adapt to it, as opposed to perhaps 5 to 10 years for a cultivar.

The Effects of Heat

Seasonal temperatures that have ratcheted up well above normal for your area can be as dangerous for your trees and shrubs as extreme cold temperatures. Heat dries out leaves, which means they don't absorb as much moisture as trees or shrubs need to use for transpiration. When the balance is off for awhile, trees and shrubs can cope—but not forever.

Sprouts

Although we'd love to, we can't sit with you in your yard and detail what you should plant or where. More information, especially on issues of mesoclimate, is often available from your local university's extension service, local weather service office, or from a major local nursery.

Sudden changes in temperatures that have been unchanging even for weeks—from a generally cool spring, for example, to a hot, dry, breezy period—can also be a problem. Because of a chilly spring, young trees may have developed leaves that are too tender to handle a quick sweltry period.

Temperatures that remain higher at night than usual can make your trees and shrubs breathe so fast that they can't move their carbohydrates beyond the leaves where they formed. They're just huffing and puffing.

Of all the parts of the plant, the roots are the most vulnerable to the heat. This is why slow-drip watering can save leaves, roots, and even the tree itself. (See Chapter 15 for more on watering.)

Planting for Success in Your Zone

It makes sense to buy plantings with the best chances of success. Here are some good-bet ideas for each zone.

Note we have offered only partial information about each plant—the features that we feel are more salient in a first introduction of them—but of course each tree or shrub mentioned can also be found in Appendix F.

Quaking Aspen (Zones 2/3)

The quaking aspen (*Populus tremuloides*), with its rough, whitish-gray or whitish-green bark and its paddle- or heart-shaped leaves, is the tree with the broadest range within North America. Most of that is Canada—so this is a tough tree for winter temperatures in zones 2/3. It grows tall and slender in huge stands and in many kinds of soils across the main breadth of these zones in the United States. (It also dips down to mountainous elevations in northern Virginia, Arizona, and New Mexico.)

Although the quaking aspen grows fast—and can spread quickly throughout your yard on its underground *rhizomes*—it's not long-lived. If you don't want more than one, mow or pull the tiny sprouts as they come up. But if you have the space and want free trees, just sit back and let it spread into a small grove. If you're looking to buy a quaking aspen, note that it is a poplar variety.

def•i•ni•tion

Rhizomes are the underground propagation engines that some species, such as the quaking aspen, use for reproduction. Each tree is like a stem off the same root. The record number of new trees from one root system is 47,000 trees! These trees are essentially clones, and they can keep cloning, too. One aspen grove has kept it up for 8,000 years.

Green Ash (Zones 2/3)

Green ash (*Fraxinus pennsylvanica*), also widespread, is a good bet for the seasonal "theatre" of zones 2/3. A native tree, it grows from the bottomland woods to the prairies, provided the soils are somewhat damp. But it really isn't picky, tolerating flooding, street salts, soils that would raise your hair on end (toxic gravels, etc.), and even gypsy moths. If it gets a nicer row to how, however, the green ash will grow much taller and fuller.

In fall, the green ash is an elegant yellow. To minimize the middle-age spread of its crown, pruning works well. (See Chapter 16 for more on pruning.)

River Birch (Zone 4)

The river birch (*Betula nigra*) is known for its attractive cinnamon-colored, peeling bark that stands out in winter; its resistance to the bronze birch borer insect (compared to other birches); and its tendency to grow as a tree with several trunks. This tree also comes in a dwarf form whose mature size is about the size of a large shrub. It does *not* need to be planted near a river, as the name might suggest, although it can tolerate flooding and will shed leaves in droughts. The river birch can also tolerate higher temperatures than some other zone 4 trees. Its only demands are for full sun and no ice storms (which can bring its branches down). Along with white pines "flowering" with snow, this birch may be the most beautiful winter tree.

Spirea (Zone 4)

Spirea (*Spiraea*) is a shrub that cascades with boughs of white flowers in late springtime. It grows to about 4 to 6 feet high, depending on the cultivar and conditions. One cultivar is nicknamed bridal wreath, and an armful of its boughs would grace any bride. (Of course, it's best to keep most of the branches on the bush!)

Although these shrubs love the sun, spirea can be planted under deciduous trees because trees leaf out later than the spiraea does. Give it plenty of space, though, so its profusion of branches can grow uncrowded. Spirea grows well as far south as Missouri and Ohio and in North Carolina's mountains, as well as north from these latitudes well into Canada.

Douglas Fir (Zone 5)

The Douglas fir (*Pseudotsuga menziesii*) can grow as high as a skyscraper—literally. Along with other giants such as the western red cedar, western hemlock, and lodgepole pine, you can find them in upland or mountainous Pacific Northwest forests. With its thick bark and straight trunks, these trees have been around for probably 40 million years. If you live around the Northern Rockies or the Cascades, this tree is a great choice.

Ohio Buckeye (Zone 5)

The Ohio buckeye (*Aesculus glabra*), a relative of the horse chestnut, is a sturdy, medium-size tree that sometimes grows only to the height of a shrub. It does well under larger trees because it leafs out earlier than probably any tree you have or might plant in your yard. It's also an early announcer of fall, providing pleasant orange, yellow, or tan foliage.

The Ohio buckeye has large flowers that bloom after the leaves and are popular with hummingbirds. Squirrels love its large, smooth brown nuts (toxic to humans and deer); the tree's name comes from the lighter spot on these nuts.

This buckeye does nicely all across the center of the country and even up to zone 3, preferring moist soil. If your tree gets too dry, it will shed its leaves (but grow more the next spring). It's not especially vulnerable to insects.

Sweet Gum (Zone 6)

The sweet gum (*Liquidambar styraciflua*) has sweet-smelling leaves and large green flowers, stretches high (60 to 100 feet), and is shaped as a conifer when young. Its fruit is prickly brown balls about 1 inch in diameter. The sweet gum is probably most common in the southeastern sections of zone 6, but it also does well up to southern Illinois and Connecticut and to Texas and California. Its "gum" is found on the inside of the bark and can indeed be chewed.

Although the sweet gum prefers the moist soils of bottomlands, it can grow in dry and upland ones, too, as long as the soil isn't a heavy clay. This tough tree is usually susceptible only to fire and animal browsing.

Red Maple (Zone 6)

The red maple (*Acer rubrum*) is spectacularly red, orange, or scarlet in fall and shows a hint of this blaze in the spring when its early buds, red flowers, and red seeds are nice to behold. This medium-size, resilient tree grows in large stands all throughout the Appalachians. In fact, it needs other trees of some kind around it to protect it from high winds.

Sun or shade, woods or swamp, uplands or bottomlands, poor soils? No problem. The red maple can tolerate those; it just doesn't like the dry heat of the prairie, being planted near the street, or a short list of insect predators. (For more on insect problems in trees, see Chapter 24.)

The Real Dirt

The red maple tree can change its dominant sex (every red maple has a balance of both sexes) in response to stress.

Pawpaw (Zone 7)

The pawpaw's (*Asimina triloba*) name even sounds southern and fun. A medium-size tree—most are less than 30 feet tall—it makes a nice ornamental understory planting; people often say it looks tropical. It has the largest berries of any tree native to the United States. It grows 6 inches long and sometimes in bunches similar to bananas. They're even edible, except for the seeds. Fall is the top season for the pawpaw because of its yellow foliage and fruit.

A sturdy tree, it thrives from zone 6 south, grows fast, and doesn't require fussing over. If you want a single trunk, prune accordingly—otherwise, you'll have a nice "pawpaw patch."

Baldcypress (Zone 7)

Baldcypress (*Taxodium distichum*) is a tree at home in the swamps of the South, although its range extends up to southern Indiana, Illinois, Delaware, and also through Tennessee and Kentucky. It likes to have its "feet wet"—so plant it in a very moist lowland area (if you don't live on a swamp, river, or shallow lake). These trees can live at least 1,000 years—one has been located that had 1,350 birthdays—and stretch 100 feet high. Herons love to nest in them, and tree frogs rest there, too.

Unusually, it is a deciduous conifer. The leaves turn a rich reddish-brown and drop for fall. The cones look like little soccer balls. The base of its trunk flares out into a solid circle, and it can be surrounded by "knees"—*pneumatophores*, or separate roots sticking out of the ground or water that help pull in oxygen.

Palmetto (Zone 8)

The palmetto (*Sabal minor*) is a sturdy understory plant, easily either a tree or a shrub, and one that naturally prefers growing under taller trees. It's found naturally in thickets with plants such as prickly pear cactus and gallberry shrub, all able to thrive in the sandy soils of the Atlantic coastal plain from North Carolina south and west through Florida to Texas' Gulf Coast. It can also grow in quite moist soils around ponds. When exposed to direct salt air, it remains dwarfed (as in North Carolina's Outer Banks) but lives out its life under these conditions.

Root Rot

If you like eating "hearts of palm," know that the palm tree had to be killed to retrieve it. The whole tree.

Its fronds emerge close to the ground and may be either somewhere between blunt and sharp, or actually sawlike. As a palm, its trunk doesn't thicken as it grows taller. These trees are virtually impossible for the wind to blow down.

Slash Pine (Zone 8)

You can find the slash pine (*Pinus elliottii*) towering over the palmettos and tupelos, or, in its drier terrains, presiding over deer, fox, and the occasional marsh rabbit, in many of zone 8's Atlantic and Gulf Coast locations. But it's not always tall—in fact, it makes a nice, medium-size garden tree. Its mottled bark is attractive, as are its long needles and slender trunk. Birds such as blue herons and eagles nest in its branches. These trees lose some "leaves" in winter to conserve moisture through the dry season.

Monterey Pine (Zone 9)

The Monterey pine (*Pinus radiata*), which shares a name with California's Monterey Bay, is now rather rare in the United States, although it has been planted successfully in places from New Zealand to South Africa to Chile. A native of the foggy area on the central California coast, it's a tall (50 to 100 feet) conifer with ornately furrowed bark and pointed cones. The cones open to release seeds in a forest fire; on very hot summer days, they also open up occasionally, with a distinct snap. These trees last a long time unless their main nemesis arrives—the five-spined engraver beetle. Pruning the Monterey pine during its spring growing season attracts insects in general, so don't do it.

California Redwood (Zone 9)

The California redwood (*Sequoia sempervirens*) is a beautiful tree if you have the right place to plant it. It can be tough and is certainly famous for being long-lived, surviving up to 1,000 to 2,000 years. Once growing prolifically across the planet, it now lives along the California coast from Big Sur up to Oregon's border, where it towers over everything!

The California redwood drinks fog, getting about a third of its water this way, as night and early morning transmute the fog to drips of water, which cover the whole tree and the ground underneath it. It's quite resistant to fire, although it doesn't like flood conditions. As the tree grows taller—up to more than 300 feet—and forest soils build up under it, the California redwood creates a new set of stabilizing roots closer to the surface than its older ones were. It is a member of the sequoia family.

Silk Oak (Zones 10/11)

The silk oak (*Grevillea robusta*) does beautifully in Hawaii, creating a show-stopping blast of flowers on branches with a very horizontal pattern. It grows to about 60 feet high.

Saw Palmetto (Zones 10/11)

The saw palmetto (*Serenoa repens*) is a shrub about 8 feet tall, often growing in thickets. With leaves about 3 feet across and featuring sharp spines, it grows prolifically in both Hawaii and Florida. (Another nice small palm is the European fan palm.)

For those of you in Florida, note that trees and shrubs that require dryer "feet" can be planted on the *hammocks*, even in low-lying wet areas; the rare mahogany tree is one of these.

def•i•ni•tion

Ecologically speaking, a **hammock** is a raised, moundlike area where drainage provides slightly dryer soils.

Blowing in the Wind

Tornadoes, hurricanes, and other drastically strong winds can tear apart, uproot, and smash trees. (Shrubs often hunker down and escape this trauma.) Even lesser winds than these can dry out trees and shrubs when temperatures are high and humidity is low. And it might seem odd, but even one medium-strong wind from the opposite direction of normal can blow down a tree. (Trees get used to things, strengthening their trunks to adapt to prevailing winds.) Conifers generally can suffer more damage from winds than deciduous trees do—the wind actually burns them when it's too fierce. Isolated in your yard, instead of grouped as in a natural forest, they can especially be at risk. Pruning for structure can be important to combat these problems (see Chapters 16 and 17).

Trees and shrubs have evolved in the presence of wind, and many have ways of coping with it—when it isn't ferocious, at least. They develop a strong root system to anchor themselves and also roll up their leaves from the tip in to reduce wind resistance. Many trees also grow their trunks thicker rather than growing taller.

The Real Dirt

Ordinary wind levels are not detrimental to trees. In fact, trees couldn't live without wind. Many trees, including virtually all conifers, are pollinated only by wind; it moves the pollen from the male flower to the female one.

Choosing the right trees and shrubs to cope with the typical winds in your area can be complex. City dwellers often experience wind tunnels created by buildings that funnel the wind, sometimes to fierce levels, as well as areas where other buildings may block the wind almost entirely. One suburb with lots of old trees might have plenty of wind breaks that slow the wind, while another newer suburb or exurb, with fewer trees and less building density, may be considerably windier. One side of your house is probably a lot windier than the others. And all this within a few miles!

Because wind is so intensely local to your yard and because most of the trees in your zone cope well with the wind, we aren't offering specific lists here. If you have special wind conditions, choose the area of your yard that experiences less ferocity, noting that prevailing winds in the northern hemisphere are out of the west but that the worst storms may come from the east.

Sprouts

Looking at it from the other direction, remember that trees and even shrubs block the wind *for us*. A couple trees or a cluster of shrubs on the side of the prevailing wind can shelter your house or garden from blowing rain or snow, or even just a dusty or chilly wind. If you live in places with pronounced winters, your benefits will be the greatest—and think thick evergreens.

To assemble the list of trees best for your yard, remember to continue jotting down what you like from your zone while reading these chapters. Consider adjacent zones, too, because some trees do well in more than one zone, as detailed in Appendix F.

The Least You Need to Know

- Beyond your geographic zone, seasonal extremes matter locally.

- Unusual or sudden periods of heat or cold in quick succession can damage trees.

- Although some wind is damaging, some is necessary for conifer reproduction, as well as for some deciduous trees.

You Light Up My Life

In This Chapter

- ◆ Trees and shrubs need sunlight
- ◆ Shade—plusses and minuses
- ◆ Morning light versus afternoon light
- ◆ Best-bet trees and shrubs for your light situation(s)

The sun is the elixir of life for trees and shrubs, as well as all plants, kicking off their life-sustaining photosynthesis process. But trees and shrubs differ quite a bit in how much light they need. Understory plants—the ones you see growing underneath other trees in a natural forest—are well adapted to a diet of minimal sunlight. Others grow tall simply to have their leaves experience the most intense light. (See Chapter 1 for how trees and shrubs gather and use sunlight to grow.)

How Much Sun Is Enough?

Garden flowers can be particular about the amount of light they need. Trees and shrubs can be, too, at least during the growing season. Every tree needs sun, although some need more than others.

Sun Versus Shade

But here's where it can get tricky. Your house might cast shade over the leaves of a small or medium tree all afternoon and over lower shrubs for sometimes a significant part of the day. Maybe your neighbors' houses and their trees, landscaping structures such as garden sheds, and even large vehicles if they're usually parked in certain places, cast shadows on your plantings, too.

Some trees and shrubs are fine with this—in fact, those that grow in the understory underneath other trees can actually have their chlorophyll-processing structures killed if they experience too much sun. A sun-loving tree or shrub, on the other hand, is only "out of the woods" when—and if—it grows tall enough to gather light from above. Otherwise, its trunk and branches can become spindly, its leaves thin and pale—and it may even die from lack of light. A generally cloudy summer as opposed to a sunnier summer can make a difference, too, in its level of growth.

> **The Real Dirt**
>
> Scientists are adapting the photosynthetic chemicals trees and shrubs use to turn the sun into energy to create better solar cells for home and industry energy use. It's part of a trend in scientific research called *biomimicry*—scientists try to mimic nature as they make technological products, on the theory that nature has been trying different approaches for many millions of years.

Have you ever seen a sunflower bend toward the sun? All plants do this to a certain extent, either growing or leaning more toward the sun (by elongating chemically), at least during growing season. This is less noticeable in shrubs, but you can often see this in trees when they get sun from mostly one direction—they can grow more horizontally than vertically.

The Growing Season

Trees and shrubs vary quite a bit in their response to the *photoperiod*. Some even have slightly different leaf shapes depending on where the tree is within its range of geographic zones because the length of day changes so much according to latitude. Trees typically grow taller and fuller in the parts of their territory that have more sunshine during the year.

> **def•i•ni•tion**
>
> The **photoperiod** is the response of a plant to the length of daylight hours versus darkness within a 24-hour period. This varies throughout the seasons and also changes more during the year at the higher latitudes; daylight hours change very little near the equator. Day length is the main reason trees and shrubs grow more in spring and summer, no matter where they are.

Planting for Success in Your Zone

Most trees and shrubs native to your area will also do fine in full sun (although they might need watering if temperatures rise high), so in the following sections, we focus on trees that tolerate shade or only partial sun. Again, we're focusing mostly on trees because shrubs are more flexible—and cheaper.

Red Oak (Zones 2/3)

The red oak (*Quercus rubra*) is the large oak most tolerant of shade (though, as with most large trees, it also loves full sun). These trees are also adaptable in other ways— a medium amount of moisture, average soil, being transplanted, all are acceptable to it. It is a common tree for this zone but also extends to eastern Oklahoma as well as to the coastal plain of the southeastern states and beyond. The red oak can grow to 120 feet, its trunk extending about halfway up to this height and its spreading canopy providing the rest. Smooth, striped bark; tiny red flowers in spring; and deep orange, crimson, or russet leaves in fall are its other pleasant features.

Balsam Fir (Zones 2/3)

Balsam firs (*Abies balsamea*), elegantly formed, medium-size trees, might be called the Christmas trees that could. This tree does just fine in the shade, smells fragrant, loves the cold, and even does well in wet soil. You can plant one and see it draped with snow from its pointed top down to its heavy, lower branches, from the border between Canada and the eastern half of the United States down to Iowa and Illinois and southeast to the highland parts of Virginia. This fir is even resistant to air pollution and gypsy moths, unless it's planted south of its natural range. Balsam firs are, however, quite sensitive to fire and the spruce budworm. Squirrels and birds love its seeds.

Northern Catalpa (Zone 4)

The northern catalpa (*Catalpa speciosa*) grows to full size—about 100 feet tall with a trunk up to 6 feet thick—in zone 4 where they can live for a couple hundred years. The very large leaves are shaped as hearts; the early summer's large, fancy white flowers are striped in yellow and spotted with purple inside. The long and thin seed-pods are unpopular with some homeowners, although they remain on the tree as an interesting winter visual feature. This tree isn't picky about anything, including some shade.

Black Locust (Zone 4)

The black locust (*Robinia pseudoacacia*) is a fast-growing, tough tree that reaches especially tall heights—up to 95 feet with a more than 7-foot trunk—in the full sun. But it does fine in the shade, too, creating fewer suckers and producing blue-green leaves in late spring and then white flowers that smell lovely and also attract hummingbirds. If you don't watch this tree, it could take over your entire yard!

White Spruce (Zone 5)

The white spruce (*Picea glauca*) is more common in the eastern and midwestern sections of zone 5 but is also found in the Rocky Mountain section. This is a hardy northern tree that does well up through zones 2/3 and is even more common in Canada. After the glaciers melted about 10,000 years ago, it was one of the most common trees in all North America.

Steeple-shaped, this is a classic Christmas tree. But whatever holidays you celebrate, you'll enjoy this fast-growing, tall (100 feet or so), dark-green-needled tree. It doesn't mind wind or cold, being transplanted, or poor soil. It doesn't like a sweltering summer, salt spray, air pollution, fire, and spruce budworms.

> ### The Real Dirt
> We love quirky stories about word origins—especially those of tree names—and here's one: *Spruce* was originally *Pruce*, which came from the word *Prussia*. Prussia was once part of Germany, where the custom of putting up a Christmas tree began.

Canada Hemlock (Zone 5)

The Canada hemlock (*Tsuga canadensis*) is in no way confined to Canada; its range extends from the Great Lake states to New England and down the Appalachians to Alabama and then up into the Smokey Mountains. It's the state tree of Pennsylvania, too. These trees do like cool, however, and although they can chill the soil around them a bit by themselves, they prefer streambeds and other naturally cool areas—they don't do well much below the southern borders of zone 6.

This is a tough tree, long-lived (several centuries), impressive, a willow-y style of conifer with lacy branches. Canada hemlocks prefer a moister, well-drained soil and dislike fierce wind, salt spray, and air pollution, although they're pretty adaptable. Shade is fine, too.

> ### Root Rot
> When a Canada hemlock gets accustomed to its location, it doesn't do well when conditions change. Southerners, don't push its zone.

The Canada hemlock has many nice dwarf cultivars for use in areas such as rock gardens. And some shrub varieties exist between these two sizes.

Blackhaw (Zone 6)

Blackhaw (*Viburnum prunifolium*) is the name for a pleasant, sturdy shrub in the viburnum family that can also grow as tall as a small tree (10 to 20 feet high on average). Excellent in the understory, it remains a shrub if it leads a "shady" life in zone 6. It also does well in zone 5 and is even adequate in zone 4.

Its glossy, dark-green leaves set off sweet-smelling white flowers and then turn crimson for fall. The fruits, small and dark similar to raisins, are edible for humans and birds alike. If you've heard of nannyberry, note that this is the blackhaw's northern "cousin."

This adaptable viburnum can handle some drought conditions, isn't picky about soil, and has no major enemies in the insect world. Just don't plant it where salt spray from highway or ocean can reach it.

Red Buckeye (Zone 6)

Red buckeye (*Aesculus pavia*) is another shade-tolerant shrub that can grow to a tree if given the room. Common in the Southeast, its range extends west to east Texas and north to Illinois.

Its leaves emerge pleasantly early in the spring, but its fame lies in its spectacular red flowers, which crowd the tree with their beauty. Its nuts are similar to those of the Ohio buckeye but are a more golden brown. But beware the red buckeye leaves—they're toxic.

Plant the red buckeye up through zone 4, mulching it enough to keep its root system cool and moist no matter where you plant it. The red buckeye is sturdy and you can anticipate skipping the major insect traumas. Expect its leaves to drop off early in the fall.

Hornbeam (Zone 7)

Hornbeam (*Carpinus caroliniana*) sports the nicknames "blue beech" (thanks to its blue-gray bark) and "musclewood" (thanks to its strong wood and sinewlike stems). It is a sturdy, shade-tolerant choice. Usually the size of a shrub or small fruit tree, it stretches much taller in the parts of its zone outside the United States (to the south).

This tree boasts an elegant silhouette of many branches, well textured and with a nice spread; a fall color as dark as crimson, yellow, or orange; and plentiful stock of tiny nuts, perfect for attracting songbirds. If it's mulched to keep the roots moist, it won't cause you any problems.

The hornbeam is a southern cousin to the birch and has one of the broadest ranges of any American tree—cultivars do fine from zone 2 down to the Caribbean.

Cabbage Palm (Zone 7)

The cabbage palm (*Sabal palmetto*) is common and hardy, thriving through the eastern parts of its zone 7 home. Tall and slow-growing, it sheds it leaves *and* its stalks as new ones emerge. (This does not happen all at once or in any one season.) Its little fruit, the size of a pea, is edible for humans as well as for larger birds such as blue jays, gulls, and wild turkeys, who gobble them up off the ground.

Cabbage palms not only look different from other trees—they *are* different. They get the diameter that they'll live with for life before growing tall—and so have no tree rings like other trees. Its girth depends on the species. This palm is excellent at blocking the wind from major storms and hurricanes, generally bending but remaining upright through almost anything.

Root Rot

The cabbage palm shouldn't be climbed in golf shoe spikes or any other kind of spiked boots used by a pruner! The trunk will never recover.

Cabbage palms enjoy the sun as much as any inhabitants of Florida and the coastal plain of the southeast United States, but they tolerate partial shade and even salt spray well (unlike a lot of the tourists). Any soil with good drainage is acceptable to these palms unless the roots are in salt water.

Fringetree (Zone 8)

Fringetrees (*Chionanthus virginicus*) can be grown either as shrubs or trees. In the shade, they are large shrubs or small trees; they grow taller in full sun. From eastern Texas and southern Missouri through the Southeast and even up into zone 4, fringetrees are tough, sturdy trees for the shade (although they love full sun, too).

Wispy white flowers give it the nickname of "snowflower." Fringetrees are exceptionally free of problems as long as deer don't get to them or they aren't planted near walnut or hickory trees, which poison the soil for the fringetree's roots.

Mesquite (Zone 8)

Mesquite (*Prosopis*) is a very adaptable tree and one you are likely to admire in this zone unless you are a cattle rancher who wants to drive a pickup out on the range—its thorns hurt both hoofs and tires while the tree is young, and it crowds out good plants for your cattle to eat. Thorn-free cultivars have been developed.

A tough southwestern tree of modest size, it has fragrant yellow flowers. It can survive even desert conditions. It is a shade (and sun) tree that can grow nicely green in your zone 8 yard (as well as in zone 7 and sometimes zone 6). The "honey" in its name refers to the fact that bees love it and make its pollen into a nice honey. A close relative is the Palo Verde.

Northern Spice Bush (Zone 9)

The northern spice bush (*Lindera benzoin*), which also grows well up into Apppalachia, is a nice shade inhabitant. It's even good in the full shade of an elaborate woodland garden. This shrub produces very small yellow flowers, followed by red berries, followed by bright yellow leaves for fall. Its name comes from the fact that its twigs, leaves, and berries can be used to make teas or used sprinkled in sauces. The spice bush can thrive up through zone 5.

Sourwood (Zone 9)

Sourwood (*Oxydendrum arboreum*) is another impressive small shade tree, especially in fall when it blazes scarlet with sometimes tones of maroon or yellow. Summer is a good season to enjoy it, when it features creamy-white, ball-shape fragrant flowers.

The sourwood likes plenty of water and shelter from the wind. This good-bet plant grows up through zone 5.

Camellia (Zones 10/11)

Camellias (*Camellia japonica*) are showy shrubs that seem never to stop blooming (the flowers don't come out all at once). Cultivars are available that range far beyond the classic white, coming in yellow, pink, pinkish-white, crimson, even mauve and maroon. They can also be found in single or doubled form. Even when no blooms are present, the glossy-green leaves of this evergreen are beautiful. It is a lovely shade-happy plant for this zone.

Hibiscus (Zones 10/11)

Hibiscus (*Hibiscus lunariifilius*) blooms late and is an excellent choice to stretch out your garden's flowering season. Its trumpet-shape flowers can be yellow, pale pink, white with red veins, lilac-colored with darker red veins, or even purple. Some of these cultivars can be planted up to zone 8 or even zone 6. The white variant, though, is classic zones 10/11.

The Real Dirt

Whether your city swelters for months or blazes red for only a few days each year, shade is beneficial—and not just for trees and shrubs. In regions with the longest, hottest summers, planting on the east, west, and northwest sides is the most advantageous to cooling your home the natural way—with shade from trees. Some cities even offer free or low-cost trees to its residents because the energy savings have become so significant. One estimate found that California's 177 million trees save $573 million in energy costs each year.

The Least You Need to Know

- ◆ Most trees enjoy full sun. But not all do, so do some research before shopping.

- ◆ Some trees and shrubs won't thrive—or even live—in shade from your house, garage, other trees, cars, or trucks. Other trees and shrubs grow well in partial shade, even if they prefer full sun, although they may not grow as tall or as broad.

- ◆ In natural forests, it's easy to see that some trees and shrubs are adapted to understory life, spending their lives under other trees—they'll work in the shade for you.

Chapter 6

A Look at Elevation and Moisture

In This Chapter

- ◆ Evaluating elevation ecological zones
- ◆ Understanding forms of moisture
- ◆ Tree and shrub suggestions based on water needs
- ◆ Trees and shrubs that like it dry

In Chapter 3, we provided information on top choices of trees and shrubs for your basic geographic zone. In Chapters 4 and 5, we zeroed in on planting ideas based on seasonal patterns, sun versus shade, and wind in your city and county. Now we take the issues to your very own yard.

As you probably remember, the basic zone lines of the United States, based on coldest annual temperature, cross mountains, valleys, plains, deserts, lakes, and rivers. But elevation matters! Your yard may be high in the Rockies or in a mountain valley. You might live on the flat plains or up against an area of foothills. You could live near one of the Great Lakes. In each of these cases, you could well be in or very near zone 4. Similar differences in elevation can occur in other zones, too.

So in this chapter, we discuss your area's elevation related to what's very common in the Pacific Northwest, the Northeast and Middle West, the Southeast, and the Desert Southwest and Great Plains areas. Both your ecological region as well as your topography and drainage work together with the amount of water your trees and shrubs receive. Some live to get their feet wet and some don't. Only swamp trees want nonstop water, and only desert trees can tolerate very low levels of rainfall.

We include shrubs in our discussion, of course—we love them—but we do focus more on trees in this chapter. Shrubs are smaller, cheaper, and far more flexible. But still, choose your trees first. Fortunately, some of the plantings we recommend here come in varieties from smaller trees to larger shrubs.

U.S. Elevations

Elevation is important, and the United States boasts four general areas along this dimension:

- Pacific Northwest (including Alaska for our purposes)
- Northeast and Middle West
- Southeast
- Desert Southwest and Great Plains

If you live in the Pacific Northwest, your area is probably either mountainous or temperate rainforest near the coast. You're highly likely to be in conifer country, home to many kinds of evergreens.

If you live in the Northeast and Middle West, a broad sweep of the United States, your elevations generally aren't extreme. New England has mountains, of course, and the Middle West has some impressively flat lands, but neither compares to the high elevations of the Pacific Northwest or the low country of the Southeast and the Atlantic coastal plain. You have a lot of choices in this part of the United States, from conifers to deciduous trees. (The section of the Middle West that is about the Great Plains—the Dakotas and parts of Nebraska—is discussed along with the Desert Southwest because both are dry and enjoy full sun across large proportions of their terrains.)

The American Southeast, although it includes a long broken line of Appalachian Mountains, is generally low in elevation. This "low country" extends from the Carolinas south, all around Florida, up through the Gulf Coast all the way to the

Texas coasts. The higher areas in this area usually have similar trees and shrubs to the East and Middle West, so we focus here on the predominant lower Atlantic coastal plain, which extends quite far inland.

In the dry Desert Southwest and the Great Plains, trees and shrubs have had to adapt to infrequent but sudden and heavy rains. If you live in this area, you'll want to plant accordingly, instead of overusing the water supply by choosing plants from elsewhere and constantly having to water them. Plenty of good choices are available.

> **Sprouts**
>
> If you haven't checked it out yet, turn to the trees and shrubs grid in Appendix F, which, if we do say so ourselves, is a real mother lode of information presented in an easy-to-find format. It offers more details about all the trees and shrubs we describe in this book.

The Pacific Northwest

Alaska yellow cedar (*Cupressus nootkatensis*). Tall and slender with fragrant wood, this Pacific Northwest tree loves wetter mountain soils, but it can also grow in lower inland areas in the farther north part of this area.

Austrian pine (*Pinus nigra*). This hardy, common conifer is fast-growing, is dense, is medium-tall (about 60 feet), and sports yellow-brown cones. It grows throughout this area, except in the colder parts of Alaska. This tree doesn't like really hot or really dry weather.

Bristlecone pine (*Pinus aristata*). These extremely long-lived conifers (the oldest one known is pushing 5,000 years) can grip onto high rocky slopes. Although it naturally looks scrubby there, it grows fuller and taller (20 to 40 feet) in more fertile soil.

Lodgepole pine (*Pinus contorta*). This pine loves the mountains, preferring the well-drained soils there. From Alaska to southern California, its range also extends east to the Rockies in Colorado and even into the high Black Hills of South Dakota.

Pacific yew (*Taxus brevifolia*). A mid-size evergreen of about 50 feet tall, this yew grows fine in the *understory* of a conifer forest or under other yard trees, also in moist areas near streams or in canyons.

Sitka spruce (*Picea sitchensis*). This is the largest spruce worldwide (up to about 160 feet tall and 3 to 10 feet in diameter). It loves the coasts, especially foggy areas.

> **def•i•ni•tion**
>
> The **understory** is formed by the trees and shrubs that have adapted to grow *under* the taller trees and shrubs.

White fir (*Abies concolor*). Tall and conical, this conifer prefers moist, rocky soils in the mountains. Its range extends from southeastern Idaho down the spine of the Rockies to New Mexico, in addition to the Pacific Northwest (although not in Alaska). It's the fir that accepts the warmest weather.

The Northeast and Middle West

Black (or wild) cherry (*Prunus serotina*). This medium-tall tree or shrub grows well across the East and Middle West, blooming in beautiful white. Its wood is widely used in furniture, its ripe fruit is used in wine and jelly (along with plenty of sugar), and its bark is used in cough syrup. Give it full sun and good drainage.

> **The Real Dirt**
>
> In one year, the black cherry tree can feed more than 100 species of wildlife and house more than 200 species of butterflies and moths.

Black willow (*Salix nigra*). Even more characteristic here than the weeping willow, this tall, fast-growing multi-trunked tree has a similar grace. It likes bright sun and wet soils, akin to those other willows and the cottonwood prefer.

Boxelder (or Manitoba maple) (*Acer negundo*). This tree thrives far south of Manitoba, Canada, growing well from Vermont, west through New York, and south through this entire area. It's a small or medium-size tree—it could even fit where you're thinking of planting a shrub—with light green leaves. Fast-growing, it prefers moist valleys or wetter stream banks, although it isn't very picky.

Chinkapin oak (*Quercus muhlenbergii*) or chestnut oak (*Quercus prinus*). This plant, which can grow to be anywhere from a shrub (its popular dwarf form) to a tall tree, grows in the southern parts of New England and the broad mid-section of the United States centered on Missouri, Illinois, Indiana, Kentucky, Tennessee, and farther south. It likes dry and rocky soils. Unlike most oaks, the chinkapin has vivid yellow or pale orange leaves in fall. Its small acorns fit nicely into chipmunk cheeks, too!

American mountain ash (*Sorbus americana*). Both the most northerly and the highest altitude sections of this area are home to this large shrub or medium-size tree. In fall, its golden-orange leaves set off large clumps of brilliant reddish-orange fruits that last long after the leaves and attract birds all fall and into winter. The mountain ash prefers full sun or light shade. In late spring, these trees also shine, bearing large, fragrant, white flowers.

Scotch (or Scots) pine (*Pinus sylvestris*). This full-crowned tree is adaptable to a broad range of conditions, including city pollution, across this area. It's tall (about 70 feet) with distinctive reddish-brown bark. Think Christmas tree.

Wild plum (*Prunus americana*). This dense shrub or small tree is a delight across this area, growing widely except for in northern Michigan and northern Minnesota. Its large, white flower clusters in spring and scrumptious plum-red fruit in summer are prolific in moist, slightly lowland yards. (Unlike the fruit of the damson plum, these plums may require a bit of sweetener.) With enough sun and good drainage, wild plums are easy to grow.

The Real Dirt _____

Plum trees can make memories. Children can snack delightedly at a backyard plum tree, when the fruiting season seems to go on forever!

The Southeast

Barberry (*Berberis*). This attractive shrub has thorns. The darwinii cultivar sports yellow flowers for spring, glossy green leaves, and bluish berries for the birds. This shrub is not at all picky about soils or temperatures and might even take over your yard if you let it!

Boxwood (*Buxus*). This is the shrub you see planted in sculptured hedges, formal knot gardens, or even pruned into topiary, although you need not be so ambitious with it. Densely leaved and healthy through a range of soil and temperature conditions here, boxwoods grow slowly but live long. They even smell good.

Pecan (*Carya illinoinensis*). In the hickory family, this tree likes moist river bottom areas, although not high humidity. It can grow huge, even 6 feet in diameter with a canopy 100 feet across. Enjoy its nuts in fall not only in the Southeast but up the Mississippi and Ohio River in the Middle West. Some 500 cultivars have been developed of this tree.

Seville orange (*Citrus × aurantium*). Also called "sour orange," this small, elegant evergreen tree has spicy-smelling leaves and fragrant white flowers, followed by very attractive but very sour orange fruit too bitter to eat. It grows to about 30 feet tall, preferring moist soils and hot weather in the southeast region and even into Hawaii.

Tulip tree (*Liriodendron tulipifera*). This tree, sometimes also called the yellow poplar, can grow as tall as 200 feet. Its spectacular flowers are about the size of a garden tulip; very fragrant; and apricot-colored, lime-colored, or a two tone of orange and yellow. This tree is characteristic of the eastern part of the Southeast and throughout the East. Although not particular as to soil, tulip trees should be planted where high winds, air pollution, and ice cannot reach them; where the soil is well drained and moist; and where its roots won't be disturbed by lawn or construction equipment. It likes sun at the level of its leaves.

Peach (*Prunus persica*). This lovely small fruit tree has pink flowers before the luscious fruit appears. Originally planted in the Southeast by the first Spanish colonists and Indian tribes, the peach tree now grows as far north as Michigan, as far west as California, and through the eastern states, too.

> **Sprouts**
>
> When we discuss shrubs and small ornamental trees in this and other chapters, you'll notice that we mention specific cultivars more than we do when discussing trees. This is because so many shrub and ornamental cultivars have been developed, much more than for the average tree. Blooms and other features can be quite different among cultivars.

The Desert Southwest and Great Plains

Cottonwood (*Populus deltoides*). This tree signals that water is nearby, often growing along the entire length of a stream in an area that's otherwise completely dry in the Great Plains or Southwest. It requires full sun. It is a huge, impressive tree with a rugged look and is probably the fastest-growing large tree in the country. The older ones can become hollow, with a large enough cavity for many kids or several adults to fit inside. The Eastern cottonwood and Plains cottonwood thrive in this area; the Rocky Mountains are home to another species, as are the Pacific Northwest and the swamps of the Southeast. All are closely related, look similar, grow fast, and are brittle and fragile. And all throw out the fluff that gave them their name. If you don't like the cotton of the cottonwood tree, buy a male tree.

Foothill Paloverde (*Parkinsonia*). Called also yellow paloverde, this tree is small and spiny and doesn't have leaves for most of the year. (Leaf production and maintenance requires a lot of water.) Its branches and twigs are green, however. A southwestern tree, it is found in overlap with the saguaro cactus in the extreme Southwest.

Joshua tree (*Yucca bievifolia*). This unusual tree in the yucca family is a mid-size evergreen with large fistfuls of green daggerlike leaves; a twisted, cracked trunk; and a smell sort of similar to mushrooms. Love it or hate it, it's a wonderful desert choice for higher elevations, as on the Colorado Plateau of the Four Corners area, or in the California desert.

Juniper (*Juniperus osteosperma*). Growing along the south rim of the Grand Canyon as well as in many other southwest locations and up to Montana, this "Utah juniper" is the most common juniper in Arizona. A craggy, short tree (15 to 40 feet tall), it has yellow-green leaves and shredded bark. It likes rocky soils, growing slowly and more twisted as it goes. The "berries," more like seeds, are edible, although bitterly pungent.

Prairie crab (*Malus ioensis*). Before Johnny Appleseed ever came around, this was the *crabapple*/apple of the Great Plains (and the parts of the Middle West near to them). Small in scale and with fruit palatable to wildlife, it is a beautiful tree or a large shrub for springtime. The pale pink or white flowers can be up to 2 inches across and really perfume your yard. You can eat the fruit—just check for bugs and worms and grab the sugar! These trees prefer full sun and need good drainage. Some 500 wonderful cultivars exist, adapted to conditions throughout a large section of the United States.

Netleaf hackberry (*Celtis laevigara*). This shrub or small tree is native to the western states and is found all across the Southwest and up into the southern Great Plains, wherever it can grow near a stream or moist drainage area of a canyon or hill. Its height is 20 to 30 feet, and it bears berries that taste sweet to birds and small mammals. This hackberry is known for its "witches' brooms"—bushy growths off the branches. A larger hackberry (*Occidentalis*) is native to the Great Plains, grows well in full sun, and prefers bottomlands. There, with enough water, it can grow as tall as 100 feet. On slopes and in rocky soils, it tolerates drought and air pollution, although it won't grow as tall under those conditions. Hackberries look like elm trees and are related. The dwarf hackberry is also popular, staying smaller than 30 feet tall and turning a rich yellow color for fall. Here, it's found mostly in Nebraska and eastern Texas. If you want to find black walnut saplings in the wild, look for places where hackberries are growing.

> ## def•i•ni•tion
> A **crabapple** is any apple tree whose fruit is less than 2 inches in diameter.

Moisture and the Trees That Love It

A major determinant of your success with various trees and shrubs is how much moisture they get. (We say *moisture* and not *water* because your trees and shrubs benefit from more moisture sources than just rain and sprinklers—but more on that in a minute.) Not many trees like soggy or bone dry conditions, but within the middle range, some trees and shrubs need a lot more moisture around their roots than others do. Shrubs tend to be less picky because everything about their system is smaller in scale. That said, would a prickly pear cactus do well on the shores of the Great Lakes, even in summer? Not likely. Nor would a bald-cypress tree enjoy Tucson, even after a rain.

> **Root Rot**
> Dousing your trees and shrubs constantly wastes time, money, and the environment. So plant what's appropriate to your zone and moisture levels. (See Chapter 15 for more on watering.)

Let's take a look first at where your trees' and shrubs' moisture comes from:

- Fog
- Dew
- Snow and ice
- Rain

Fog can provide up to 30 percent of the moisture needed, at least for trees best adapted to fog such as the native trees of the "temperate rain forest" on the Pacific coast. But trees and shrubs anywhere can use fog because fog drips down, or precipitates out, becoming drops of water as the air chills. As an added benefit, fog also drapes the trees' branches and slows down evaporation of the water already present in the tree.

Dew typically affects the branches more than the roots. It condenses on the branches and slows evaporation of a tree's inner water supply.

The moisture content of snow and ice varies considerably. Powder snow is only 5 to 12 percent water, whereas the kind of heavy snow that bends your conifer's branches to the ground can be up to 50 percent water content. Ice isn't bad in moderation because it often melts. But heavy loads that encase each branch and twig can break branches and even kill trees.

Yearly rainfall varies, even in the same general area. But patterns do exist. In the "temperate rainforest" part of the United States (largely the Pacific coast), summer generally brings much less rain than other seasons, whereas inland areas tend to experience moisture that's pretty well balanced throughout the year.

 Sprouts

If you live away from the coasts, your mature trees and shrubs can tolerate as much as 3 weeks of drought. On the coasts, native trees can generally make it through the typical summer drought of 4 or 5 months. But in any location, some trees will simply drop their leaves for the season to help themselves if the water supply is too low. Trees can usually recover from this, although they don't always do so.

Although all trees and shrubs need water to survive, too much rain is not a good thing. It can cause the soil over a tree's roots to become severely eroded, rot roots, reduce underground oxygen levels, and even wash away plantings.

Riverbank erosion can quickly expose vulnerable roots.

Following is a grab bag of trees for each zone, ones that have a preference: first those that enjoy or can accept a lot of moisture for their roots, followed by zone listings for those that do well in dry conditions. Shrubs are more flexible because they have smaller "bodies" that drink, so they'll be mentioned only incidentally. Remember to check the tree and shrub grid in Appendix F for more about these plantings.

Balsam Fir and Tamarack (Zones 2/3)

Balsam fir, one of the best choices in zones 2/3, has also been discussed in earlier chapters, so we'd like to add the tamarack (*Larix laricina*), which likes wetland environments although it doesn't absolutely require them. A tall tree, its graceful branches "drip" with tiny cones. It also does well in an ordinary yard, provided it receives enough water.

Sugar Maple and Boxelder (Zone 4)

The sugar maple (*Acer saccharum*) and the boxelder (*Acer negundo*) notably tolerate high moisture at the root level so they work well in zone 4.

Black Willow and Willow (Zone 5)

Black willow (*Salix nigra*), or any good native willow or willow cultivar, does well in wetter areas.

Persimmon and Red Hawthorn (Zone 6)

Red maple (*Acer rubrum*), described earlier, can be joined by the persimmon and the red hawthorn (*Crataegus mollis*). With enough moisture and full sun, the persimmon grows especially tall (considerably more than 100 feet) and healthy. A long-lived member of the ebony family, it has dark heartwood so heavy it sinks in water! The orange fruit on the female trees tastes nice when completely ripe and can be cooked into various delicacies.

The red hawthorn, also called the red haw, tolerates moisture in zone 6. It usually grows 20 to 30 feet tall and sports clusters of white flowers and edible fruit called thorn apples. This sturdy, adaptable tree does well in either full sun or quite a bit of shade, along streets contaminated with road salt, and almost anywhere between soggy and drought-y.

Swamp White Oak, Overcup Oak, and Willow Oak (Zone 7)

Baldcypress and pecan, discussed earlier, can be joined here with three other choices for wetter soils: swamp white oak (*Quercus bicolor*), overcup oak (*Quercus lyrata*), and willow oak (*Quercus phellos*).

Swamp white oak is an attractive, broad-crowned cousin of the bur oak, with peeling or gnarly bark. Sometimes you can even eat its acorns raw, and the leaves' fall colors are elegant in orange and gold. Lots of moist soil is best, but this tough tree can grow without it, too. City conditions don't even faze it.

Overcup oak is even more tolerant of flooding.

The willow oak, not a willow but part of the red oak family (its name comes from its narrow leaves), likes warm and wet. In these conditions, it grows not only tall (up to 120 feet), but also broad across the canopy (again up to 120 feet). Although the willow oak likes full sun, it's very tough and can be planted along city or suburban streets.

Red Alder (Zone 8)

Red alder (*Alnus rubra*) works well in zone 8. (Virtually any alder anywhere likes quite moist soil.) Also called the western alder, this conifer grows up and down the Pacific coast from north of Los Angeles through Alaska. Its bark is reddish, and it is a tough tree for wet conditions. It easily takes the form of either a tree or a shrub.

Arizona Alder and White Alder (Zone 9)

Arizona alder (*Alnus oblongifolia*) and white alder (*Alnus rhombifolia*) are moisture-lovers in zone 9. As with the red alder, they're members of the birch family. The Arizona is tall and straight (up to about 80 feet tall), growing well in wet places whether by a mountain stream or in any kind of gully or rocky canyons. The white alder is similar.

Soapberry (Zones 10/11)

Soapberry (*Sapindus saponaria*) is our first choice for zones 10/11. Its name comes from the fact that its berries—poisonous to some livestock—have been used to wash clothes. It grows all across the Desert Southwest and up into the southern Great Plains. Soapberry is a large shrub or mid-size tree that likes moist conditions.

Root Rot

Soapberries can cause a rash in many people when touched. They're also inedible.

Dry Conditions and the Trees That Love Them

Especially dry conditions also fit with quite a few trees. Oaks, junipers, and pines tend to do quite well in these conditions, as do many of the hickories, elms, hackberries, and some of the stone-fruit trees and ash trees.

Red Pine and Jack Pine (Zones 2/3)

White pine and mountain ash, described earlier, can be joined by red pine (*Pinus resinosa*) and jack pine (*Pinus banksiana*) for this geographic zone.

The red pine has yellow-green, fluffy needles and reddish bark. Growing very large (more than 100 feet easily, with a trunk up to 3 feet in diameter), it enjoys sandy soils and full sun. It doesn't mind some air pollution.

The tough, winter-loving jack pine can manage with even less moisture in soil. It's smaller and not as long-lived.

Bur Oak and Hackberry (Zone 4)

Bur oak, covered earlier, goes well with the common hackberry (*Celtis occidentalis*), a tree that loves the dryness of the Great Plains from the Dakotas down to Texas but also grows well across the United States to the Atlantic coast. This medium-size tree can thrive even on rocky ridges and under the onslaught of salt spray and air pollution. It prefers full sun, however. An acid in its fallen leaves is bad for your grass—so rake the leaves up or use mulch under these trees instead of growing grass there.

White Oak and Staghorn Sumac (Zone 5)

White oak and a large sumac shrub called staghorn sumac (*Rhus hirta*) work well in zone 5.

White oaks are immense and long-lived trees whose canopies can stretch across 100 feet. Its "white" name comes from the color of its new leaves, although they can also be pinkish. In fall, it blazes crimson. This tree needs full sun and doesn't require watering.

The stag's horn sumac provides a beautiful red glow for autumn, especially if you allow the plant to clone itself to make a clump. Its velvety berry clusters, a bit like the antlers of a deer, are found on the female tree and last well into the winter. The sumac likes full sun and a dry corner of your yard, where it can become quite tall. Be sure not to confuse the stag's horn sumac with the poison sumac, which can give you a ferocious rash that looks—and itches—just like poison ivy! (And it's hard to tell them apart just by looking.)

Post Oak and Red Cedar (Zone 6)

Post oak (*Quercus stellata*) and red cedar (*Juniperus virginiana*) trees do well in a dry part of your yard.

Post oaks can grow in soils so dry that you'd be amazed—and they can do so for up to 400 years. Not quite as tall as most other oaks (about 80 feet or so), they grow slowly to form a gnarly shape. They do well throughout the Southeast, East, lower Middle West, and down to northern Texas. These trees like full sun and, as with most oaks, don't tolerate soil compaction from construction or lawn equipment.

The red cedar is a juniper, one of the families known for doing well in very dry conditions. It grows tall (up to 50 to 100 feet or so) where soil is richer but can also live out of almost bare rock, growing only about 1 inch a year there. This tree has a huge range, from the East to the Middle West and down South. For fall, it may remain green or become a purplish bronze. And in winter, the profusion of blue "berries" on the female trees (these are actually its cones) are colorful. Any extreme condition is accepted, except for dense shade or swampy areas.

Shortleaf Pine and Oneseed Juniper (Zone 7)

Shortleaf pine (*Pinus echinata*) and a juniper such as the oneseed (*Juniperus monosperma*) are good choices for zone 7.

The shortleaf pine is an eastern tree, characteristic of the more eastern part of this zone. These tough trees are tall (up to 110 feet or so) and thick (perhaps 5 feet in diameter at the trunk). If the tree experiences fire or lightning damage, it can resprout itself from dormant buds on older branches, but ice storms can bring it down. This pine likes full sun and is happy to have its dry soil be quite rocky or sandy.

The oneseed juniper is a bushy shrub or a small tree with a short trunk and lots of branches. It is one of the most common trees of its size in New Mexico and also grows in Arizona, Colorado, and southwestern Texas. The "berries" (really cones) are dark blue and softer and juicier than those of most junipers.

Mesquite and Mexican Pinyon (Zone 8)

Mesquite (*Prosopis*), described earlier, is joined by the Mexican pinyon (*Pinus cembroides*) as good choices here.

Also known as the "nut pine," the Mexican pinyon is a tree perfect for dry parts. Compact at about 16 to 20 feet tall, this tough evergreen has orange or reddish-brown cones called pinyon nuts edible for humans and area rodents alike. These trees grow well along with a juniper in your yard.

Foothill Paloverde Joshua Tree, and Prickly Pear (Zone 9)

The foothill paloverde and the Joshua tree, described earlier, are excellent here, as is the prickly pear shrub (*Opuntia*). The prickly pear cactus loves dry sandy soils and its ping-pong racket–shape leaves are graced with bright yellow flowers in springtime. An adaptable desert plant, it grows as far north as the dry lands of eastern Montana.

Slash Pine, Scrub Oak, and Sand Pine (Zones 10/11)

Cabbage palm and sumac shrub, described earlier, are joined by the slash pine (*Pinus elliottii*), scrub oak (*Quercus turbinella*), and sand pine (*Pinus clausa*) in this zone. Their names say it all, and you'll see them growing naturally in the dryer hammocks of the Everglades as well as even dryer areas outside of that national park. They'll do fine in your dry yard, too.

The Least You Need to Know

◆ At any elevation—Pacific Northwest, Northeast and Middle West, Southeast, and Desert Southwest and Great Plains—you have plenty of good-bet tree and shrub choices.

◆ Some trees prefer moister soils, some do fine with dryer ones, and some aren't at all picky.

◆ Your plantings can get moisture from fog, dew, snow, and ice, not just rain.

◆ Choose the right tree or shrub suitable to your yard's elevation and moisture levels—don't waste resources with constant watering!

Chapter 7

Analyzing Your Soil

In This Chapter

- Dirt defined
- A closer look at your soil's texture, depth, and chemical nature
- Analyze your yard's soil
- Match trees and shrubs to your soil

Just as the atmosphere surrounding the aboveground part of a tree or shrub matters, the soil surrounding the root system is important. It's much more than just a simple pile of dirt! The soil in your yard must allow your trees' and shrubs' trunks and canopies to remain stable, provide space for the roots to spread, hold some degree of moisture while the tree or shrub gradually uses it, supply underground air space, and offer the nutrition necessary for your tree or shrub to thrive. And it must be a deep enough layer for all this to happen.

Not every soil is right for every tree and shrub. Some plantings prefer sandy, silty, or clay, or (often) a loamy or peat-rich combination of all the above. Some prefer acidic as opposed to alkaline soil. Some do well in a salty soil near the ocean or even a crack in a rock high up a mountain. But not every type of soil is suitable for a growing plant; in a few areas, the soil would fail almost any tree or shrub: absolutely solid rock, a yard where construction and re-grading equipment have compacted the soil several feet down, an area that has very recently burned (the soil there can be as hot as 1,500°C), or a place that receives constant, drenching salt spray from the ocean. But unless that describes your yard, you're likely to find some good bets for your yard in the following pages.

It's All Just "Dirt," Right?

Not really. Soil is more than "dirt." It's a complex mix of mineral particles from rocks broken down long ago; organic matter from dead leaves, dead flowers and fruits, and dead creatures; water; air spaces; and a whole unseen world of living things from countless fungi and bacteria on up to maybe a few moles, prairie dogs, and chipmunks.

Think of it this way: soil is the grocery store for your trees and shrubs. If that's just a convenience store stocked with junk food, your plantings might grow, but they won't grow very well or for very long. Your trees and shrubs need more than that. We'll offer plenty of examples of how to match your trees and shrubs to an average soil in this chapter, especially if your yard has more than one kind.

You don't have to be a soil scientist to understand what kind of "store" your yard is, and you probably already know some things about your soil, such as whether your whole yard is sandy or not. In this chapter, we tell you how to conduct simple soil tests to determine what you're working with. (If that's more than you want to handle, you can send off the sample to be examined.) And it's easy to just look around at what your soil is already doing well. You could even try to improve your soil a bit (see Chapter 8)—good soil is that important for the roots of your trees and shrubs.

Sprouts

As you begin to think about which trees and shrubs would work best in your soil, don't forget to read or re-read the examples for high- and low-moisture yards in Chapter 6, because sogginess or dryness are important parts of your soil, too. And keep your geographic success zone in mind (see Chapter 3).

Soil is always changing. To begin with, trees change the soil around them—the roots of one 45-year-old pine were found to have chemically doubled its own soil's ability to feed the tree. And it can take more than 25 years to actually build up $1/2$ inch of soil under ordinary climate and latitude conditions—that's slow change, but it's still change. Soils are constantly evolving in the largest sense, too—the earth was once only a ball of hot volcanic rock, after all! And under all the layers of soil in your yard, deep down, it still is.

Getting to Know Your Soil

It's worthwhile just to spend a few minutes thinking about and examining the nature of your soil. Your trees and shrubs will thank you for it!

First, let's look at the most obvious part of your soil, the physical part. All soil has texture, structure, and depth.

Soil Texture

A soil's texture is determined by how much sand, silt, or clay it has and the size of the mineral particles; the particles that make up sand are the biggest, clay particles are the smallest, and silt's are in between.

Clay improves a soil's ability to retain water so the moisture is there a bit longer for roots to use. It holds nutrients in place, too, but it isn't very good at filtering the water or remaining aerated. Clay soils clump together in globs and occasionally seem almost solid, potentially interfering with the expansion of root systems. As you can guess, some plants like clay soils more than others, but many plants want at least some of it in their soil.

Sand allows water to filter through quickly and maintains good aeration. It can hardly hold water or nutrients, though, or even hold itself together. Few trees and shrubs can grow in pure sand, but many of them like some of it.

Silt holds water fairly well but doesn't filter it out at all well. It does a medium job at holding water and nutrients.

And there are combinations, of course. Loam, for example, has more than twice as much sand and silt as it does clay, making it an excellent combination for many trees and shrubs. Probably the best overall soil choice for the greatest percentage of trees and shrubs is a combination of sand, silt, and clay. No extremes!

Soil Structure

The physical structure of your soil matters, too. There are three basic kinds of structure: coarse, medium, and fine—easy, right? In the coarse texture category, you'll find sand or a sand/loam combination. Medium texture is a silt/loam combination or just loam. A fine-texture soil is a combination of everything except sand.

 Sprouts

Don't let your soil's rich top layers vanish because of your own activity. The roots of trees, shrubs, and even flowers and grasses hold down the soil, keeping it from eroding away.

When someone tells you that a tree or shrub likes well-drained soil, it's usually a coarsely structured one. It's a bit on the crumbly side. As you can guess, a medium structure is just right, holding moisture and air in the proper amounts for the right length of time.

Soil Depth

Depth is the simplest physical characteristic of soil. Your yard soil may be shallower or deeper. Shallow soil, for trees and shrubs, means less than 10 to 12 inches deep. This is a bit dicey for trees—and even for shrubs—to grow in. A deeper soil goes down 48 to 60 inches. The deeper soils have much more room before the tree hits rock, or any other highly compacted substance (clay included).

> **Sprouts**
>
> Your yard's soil varies in depth depending on elevations in your yard. The tops of hills, even small ones, tend to have shallower soils than the gullies because material gradually erodes downward. The steeper the hill, the bigger the difference.

If you think your top soil may be too shallow, simply dig a hole and measure it. If it's shallow, you could add some good soil on top and work it in well. While that works for spots here and there, if this is the situation in part of or all over your yard, you'll probably do better with shrubs than trees in that area.

Soil Chemistry

Good chemistry is important for happy, healthy trees and shrubs. Your soil has better chemistry if it's more fertile and in balance between acidic and alkaline.

A soil's fertility comes from both the organic material and the mineral particles. Organic material usually varies between 1 and 6 percent of the soil—so it's not much. (Adding mulches and composts can raise it a bit within these parameters.) The mineral aspect might sound strange as a part of fertility, but the mineral bits in your soil, all originally from rock, allow soil chemistry to take place as it interacts with the soil's moisture to make the nutrients available to the roots.

> **Root Rot**
>
> Soils that are near a concrete foundation or curb, or have experienced this kind of rocky past, tend to become alkaline as rock gradually breaks down, bit by bit. This is common in urban areas.

A lot is taking place down there under your grass, most notably what's called *soil reaction*. This is the balance of acidity and alkalinity in your soil—it's what you hear called the *pH*. The pH balance affects plant growth as it changes the nutrients in the soil. (More on this later in the chapter.)

Most trees like a soil pH of less than 7 up to 7.5, or acidic to slightly alkaline, but many do well in either acidic or alkaline soils. If your yard isn't in that range (we show you how to find your yard's pH number later in the chapter), you can try to improve your soil. Or even easier, you can just plant trees and shrubs that aren't too picky.

Sprouts

If you'd really like to "dig in" to the nature of soils, check out one of our favorite natural history books: *Gathering Moss* and *Dirt* (see Appendix B).

Testing Your Soil

The process of testing your soil might seem difficult, but it can actually be fun! What you want to figure out is your soil type/texture, its pH, and its nitrogen and phosphorous contents. Really, it's not as hard as it might sound.

Testing Soil Type

The first soil test determines your soil's type and texture, and the tools are easy to find—your fingers! Here's how to do it: when the ground is moist but not wet, rub some dirt between your fingers. How does it feel? If it's rough, even gritty, and comes apart easily, it's sandy. Clay soil feels more like play dough—more sticky and liable to form a blob. Silt feels a bit slippery when it's slightly wet.

Remember that soil can vary slightly from place to place, even in the same yard. For example, the top of even a small hill can differ from its "valley," having thinner soil above. Soils can receive a lot of moisture in one area but not in another. When in doubt, test in several places, or sample from many more places, and take the average.

Testing Soil Type 2

The second test is almost as easy:

1. Find a quart-size container with a tight-fitting lid, a spoon, and some Ivory liquid dish soap.

2. Without letting your hands touch the soil, push away any sticks and stones.

3. Use the spoon to crumble up some soil. Shovel some in the quart container to about halfway up the side.

4. Add water and 2 tablespoons of soap to reach the top, put on the lid, shake the container hard, and let it rest for 12 to 24 hours.

5. Measure the percentage of sand/silt after they have formed layers to determine the type of soil you have.

Testing Drainage

1. Choose a morning after a night without rainfall. Begin by digging a hole 24 inches deep.

2. Fill it with water. Let it drain completely, no matter how long it takes.

3. Fill the hole up again. This time, watch the clock every so often, to check whether the water has drained out.

If the drainage takes about 24 hours, congratulations—you have soil that's ideal for most of the trees and shrubs of your zone. If drainage takes longer, that's okay too, provided that the sogginess isn't typical within the growing season. If the water vanishes more quickly than 24 hours, you'll need to go with those choices for dry conditions.

Testing drainage is important. After all, you don't want to plant most trees in soggy soils (except for willows, baldcypress, and so on). Neither should you try to match every tree and shrub to arid soil conditions, unless you're planting something such as a saguaro cactus.

Testing pH

We won't go into all the pH-testing details here because garden stores sell various soil testing kits to help you determine how much nitrogen, potassium, and phosphorous are present in your soil. This is important to know because you don't want to add any of these elements if you don't need to.

Sprouts

Some kits come with lists of trees and shrubs appropriate to the various results, which you could use in addition to the good-bet ideas in this chapter and also in Appendix F.

If your pH is too high or too low, your tree or shrub cannot absorb the nutrients in your soil, and no matter how much fertilizer you offer it, the plant eventually starves to death. In the correct amounts, however, nitrogen encourages your tree or shrub to grow full, green, and healthy. Too little nitrogen might make the plant more susceptible to diseases and infestations. And too much encourages the plant to grow its greenery but not develop its flowers or seeds.

Phosphorous gives your plants a jump-start. It encourages faster root growth, height, blooming, and seed setting. It's like a steroid … which should tell you not to overdo it. In fact, you probably don't need any at all (see Chapter 18).

The Real Dirt

If all this testing sounds like more than you can or want to handle, you can always call a professional. An agricultural extension office at a nearby university can analyze your soil's pH and many, many other tests. Call them for their procedures, telling them that you are a homeowner, not a farmer. Once they receive your sample, results usually follow in 3 to 5 days. Costs should be in the $15 to $35 range.

Good Choices for Various Soils

These recommendations focus more on trees than on shrubs because the latter are much less picky about their soil. As always, be sure to check out Appendix F, too.

Planting for Success in Clay Soil

Clay soils tend to clump together, creating a bit of a problem for root systems to spread. If you have a problem corner of your yard like this, try one of the following trees or shrubs:

The Real Dirt

Most conifers, especially the large juniper family, are not soil-picky.

Trees   Silver maple, Ohio buckeye, hawthorn, most ash trees, honeylocust, Kentucky coffeetree, apples, crabapples, aspens, cottonwoods (although they like moistness, too), oaks (such as bur, eastern pine, and swamp white), willow, linden, and elm.

Shrubs/small trees   Honeysuckle, forsythia, lilac, arborvita, Russian olive, potentilla, snowberry, cranberry, and others in the viburnum family such as the nannyberry.

If they're in your local store or nursery, they'll probably work well for you. Just be sure to check the tag to see how much sun, moisture, and acidity or alkalinity each prefers.

Planting for Success in Alkaline Soil

Alkaline soils, around pH 7.5 but not completely rocky, can be challenging, too—many of us want a tree or shrub to grow fairly near our house's or garage's foundation where alkaline soils may well have developed. Here are some good, common choices; just be sure they match your site for sun versus shade and wet versus dry.

The Real Dirt

Jeannie has a Japanese tree lilac at the edge of her yard, where it's doing well, although the soils have got to be contaminated. It's a medium-size tree with very attractive, large, creamy-white flowers that bloom in clumps. The kids used to call it the "Kleenex tree" because the blooms look like handfuls of wadded up Kleenex.

Trees   Amur maple, hornbeam, golden chaintree, Japanese tree lilac, arborvitae, basswood, some lindens, hawthorn, honeylocust, Kentucky coffeetrees, black walnut, eastern red cedar, California palm, blue ash, golden raintree, and gingko.

Shrubs/small trees   Barberry, ninebark, butterfly bush, boxwood, hackberry, buttonbush, cotoneasters, and redbuds.

Trees that do well in high pH soils (somewhere between 5 and 7) include white and green ash, amur corktree, ginkgo, hackberry, and Russian olive.

Planting for Success in Any Soil

Nonpicky trees and shrubs, or those adaptable to any soil, are always good choices. Here are some best bets per zone:

Zones 2/3   In addition to the sumacs, green ash, northern catalpa, and hackberry mentioned in earlier chapters, try the silver maple or autumn blaze maple.

Silver maples (*Acer saccharinum*) grow very fast, stretching up to about 100 feet tall, spread into clumps, and sending out roots readily. The reddish flowers are a nice, first sign of spring. These trees prefer moist soils but grow almost anywhere. Note that black maples are also willing to grow in most soils. Your garden store probably has various maple cultivars.

Sprouts

Kids sometimes call the silver maple the "helicopter tree" because of the winged seeds that pirouette and whirligig down in a summer wind. Get your own kids interested in trees as part of nature. Encouraging them to think up nicknames is one way.

Zone 4   Besides the juniper, pine oak, and Ponderosa pine described earlier, you could plant the sassafras tree (*Sassafras*). As long as this tree has plenty of sun and no road salt, it grows well in soils across most of the East, South, and Midwest. Growth is quite fast, and it clones itself to form thickets (although you can pull up the small, new trees). The best things about it, though, may be its fragrance and its color. To experience its perfume, just crush a leaf. In early springtime, the sassafras' small yellow flowers come out in pleasing clumps. Summer means dark blue fruits, and fall brings a blaze of orange, red/gold, or even purple leaves, with the fruits turning to scarlet.

Zone 5   In addition to the buttonwood and tulip tree described earlier, we recommend the wahoo (*Euonymus atropurpurea*). This small tree, whose more attractive nickname is the strawberry tree, likes understory shade but also grows nicely in full sun. It can tolerate quite a bit of air pollution, although it needs enough soil moisture during the growing season. In springtime, its twigs are lime green; by summer the fruit has transformed from white to a rosy tone of pink; by fall and winter, the seeds are an attractive red to match its leaves. It's related to the burning bush, but it blazes in a less magenta tone. This tree thrives throughout the middle United States.

Zone 6   In addition to the red cedar and the Western larch, the Kentucky coffeetree (*Gymnocladus dioicus*) is a very wide-ranging tree that's not soil-picky. It is slow to leaf out in the spring, so shrubs planted under them have plenty of time to bloom and leaf. Even when in full leaf, the coffeetree's leaves are so fernlike and feathery that quite a bit of sun reaches the ground below to nourish smaller plantings.

 The Real Dirt

The Kentucky coffeetree isn't only a resident of that state but is, in fact, found through the country's mid-section, from the Finger Lakes of New York State to southern Minnesota and east through Tennessee and Virginia. In autumn, its gray bark, yellow leaves, and red leafstalks are an attractive package as the seed-housing pods form. By late fall and winter, the female trees are decorated with many of these pods. The seeds can be roasted as a coffee substitute, but they're toxic when raw.

Zone 7   For zone 7, try the cotoneaster and the gingko. Cotoneasters (*Cotoneaster*) are a large and popular family (tiny shrubs up to small trees), all which do fine here. Clumps of creamy-white flowers that yield to red berries is a common picture, but some cultivars sport pink flowers, purple leaves, or more orange-y berries. These are tough plants that accept fierce wind and shade in addition to almost any soil. They're so adaptable that they might try to take over your yard! It is also an easy tree to prune into a variety of shapes.

The gingko (*Gingko*) is an ancient and lovely middle-size tree with distinctive leaves shaped somewhere between a fan and a heart. It prefers moister soils but is quite adaptable, as befits a tree that's been around for hundreds of millions of years. If you don't want seed fall, buy a male tree.

Zone 8   For this zone, we feature the black hawthorn and the western hornbeam/hophorn. The black hawthorn (*Crataegus douglasii*) can grow as a thicket of shrubs or as a small tree of about 30 feet. It has attractive white flowers and shiny black berries. This hawthorn is found mostly in the western part of zone 8.

Root Rot

One crucial reason for understanding your soil is so you don't waste money on fertilizer you don't need or won't do much good. (Excess fertilizer run-off is a major waterway pollutant.) On the other hand, you don't want to condemn your new tree or shrub to death by starvation, either.

The western hornbeam/hophorn, also called the ironwood (*Ostrya virginiana*), is a shrub or a small tree with fruit said to taste like the hops used as an ingredient in some beers. This adaptable tree is found in the Southwest, including around the Grand Canyon.

Zone 9 Among the good choices for this zone are the honeysuckle (*Lonicera*) and mockorange (*Philadelphus*), as well as the soapberry (covered elsewhere in this book). We also recommend the incense cedar (*Calocedrus*) and the pepper tree (*Piper*).

The incense cedar, a western tree found mostly in California, gets its name from its especially fragrant wood used for cedar chests as well as for pencils. It grows 60 to 150 feet high and forms a columnlike shape for most of its life.

The pepper tree, a native of Peru, likes sun and sea, hot weather—and poor soils! Dry weather, even droughts, doesn't particularly bother it. In fact, it's quite the aggressive tree! The foliage pattern is light, airy, and drooping; the berries are the size of peppercorns, hence the name.

Zones 10/11 The silk oak (*Grevillea robusta*) is a nice choice here. Its silky leaves arranged in a fernlike shape are evergreen; the small flowers are yellow or orange; and its fruits are curved, black, and podlike. Not really an oak, it's an Australian immigrant that prefers sandier soils and grows well even along streets in zones 10/11.

The Least You Need to Know

◆ Soil provides nutrients to roots from its organic material, water, fungi, and even bits of rock.

◆ Soils are predominantly clay, sand, or silt with additional organic material, and, of course, combinations.

◆ You'll have healthier trees if you know about your soil's texture, pH, and nitrogen/phosphorus levels.

◆ Trees need topsoil at least a couple feet thick; shrubs tolerate a bit less.

Part 2

The Growth and Life Cycle of Trees and Shrubs

Now that you've gotten the picture on which trees and shrubs are likely to thrive in your yard, let's pause before you rush to the garden center to cover what you need to know before you actually buy and plant your new trees and shrubs.

In Part 2, we describe how young trees and shrubs settle in, flower, and produce fruits and foliage each year. Plenty of choices specific for your zone are offered, too. We also provide landscaping tips, buying tips, and the best planting methods for your new yard companions.

"Whatever! There's no way he got that big without artificial growth fertilizer."

Chapter 8

Roots Come First

In This Chapter

- The down and dirty inner life of roots
- The importance of roots
- Good dirt makes roots happy
- Dealing with root problems

They might not be the best subject for a *New York Times* bestseller, but your tree and shrub roots are worth reading about. Similar to the trunk, they might not look as though they're doing anything underground, but believe us: they're busy *all* the time. Without these growing "green engines," your new tree or shrub would topple over in the first stiff breeze. And roots aren't just the anchors for their own plant; they also help keep the soil in your yard in place.

For all their good work, roots can sometimes create problems, too, including interfering with pavement and underground pipes, disrupting building foundations, and girdling their tree. Roots can be stubborn!

The Life of Roots

Let's take a closer look at roots and all they do, including how they grow, where they grow, and other facts about roots we bet you didn't know—but should!

How Roots Grow

Roots grow outward not from the tree's or shrub's trunk but from their own tips, little probes shoving into the soil to seek out and pull in water, oxygen, and food. Roots have skin, many small hairs that stick out at close to right angles from the tips of new roots, a circulatory system, and nutrient storage chambers, among other parts.

Roots mastermind all their necessary activities through a cellular structure called the *cortex*—notice that's the same word used for the outer layer of the human brain. Their "brain" orchestrates the absorption of tiny pockets of oxygen, water, and food (in the form of mineral bits) through the tiny hairs on its skin and makes sure that most of the nutrients are stored as starch. As the root's cells fill up, the goodies are pushed closer to and then into either the trunk or cellular storage.

The Real Dirt

Autumn is roots' favorite season. They grow as fast in the fall as the shoots, branches, and leaves do in spring and summer. Roots continue working hard in all seasons, "shopping" for potential food in the soil and then chemically transforming it for use by the tree and storing it.

As a root system grows by both spreading and thickening, it shoves from the inside out through each root's skin from a point just behind a protective root "cap." Other parts of the root are similar to the trunk's woody structure (cambium, xylem, phloem, and so on—see Chapter 1).

If you break off a few root tips when planting your new tree or shrub, the root system recovers by growing not one but several new tips. These tips don't branch out but instead elongate—a process that makes the tips different from the hairs. The hairs don't grow up to become roots; they multiply into more hairs. A tree can add hundreds of millions of these tiny filaments every day. They typically last for only up to a few weeks, depending on the species.

Roots are adaptable. Although the fertility of the soil around them makes a difference to roots' vigor, they're genetically programmed to move and seek nutrients. Depending on the species, roots can move primarily horizontally, shoot up vertically, or form a structural I-beam shape to avoid a soggy area or maintain their compass direction after encountering and bypassing a large rock. Roots also tend to favor a certain depth of soil to live in, usually the top 3 feet or so.

Roots rarely grow down when the root system is mature. When young, though, the roots of some tree and shrub species are mostly taproot (one long, thick root pointing down), a fibrous mass, or somewhere in between in shape. A little acorn, for example, can grow a 40-inch taproot in 6 months, much longer than its aboveground parts at this stage. These taproots generally atrophy somewhat after the multi-directional roots have become established.

Roots become incredibly extensive. You might have heard that a tree's root system extends as far out from the trunk as its branches do, but really, the root system can extend much farther out, even two or three times farther. The weight of the root system and the weight of the branch system (minus the trunk) are approximately equal under normal conditions, so if you fertilize, irrigate, and aerate your trees too much, you'll get more branches, but at the expense of the root system. (This is why highly fertilized container plants bought from the store tend to have weaker roots.)

Underground Relationships

Roots develop relationships primarily with fungi and bacteria that live underground. These can be either good or bad relationships. One fungus might be a friend, helping the roots as its very existence multiplies their surface area. In turn, the fungus consumes some carbohydrates from the tree. Some bacteria enable the roots to capture nitrogen (a fertilizer) from the soil, again receiving some "carbs" in return. These are the good guys. (We cover the good and the not-so-good guys later, in Chapters 22 and 23.)

Sprouts

Roots act as miniature chemical factories, combining organic materials to synthesize new ones the above-ground tree or shrub can use.

Improving Your Soil

My yard is just fine, you might think. But is it really? Consider the following:

- Lawn chemicals blown or washed down into it can damage your soil.

- Salt, sand, and tars used to treat or repair your road can get pushed off onto the edge of your yard.

- Has any fill dirt resulting from street or neighborhood construction been dumped in your yard? Even if it's not happening today, your yard—way before even the neighborhood and its housing was developed—might have been a dump for fill. You would only know this now if you have an area where the grass is scrubbier than in other areas. That means that the "good" soil layer placed long ago on top of fill can be pretty thin.

Significantly changing your soil is difficult, expensive, and sometimes impossible. Smaller-scale changes are possible and often easier. Of course, the easiest way to amend the soil is through mulching, either before or after planting an individual tree or shrub. Composting, working into your soil a rich mix of decayed and decomposed organic material, helps, too. If you don't have a compost heap of your own, you can purchase bags of compost materials.

> ### The Real Dirt
>
> Clay soils are difficult for trees and shrubs to thrive in because the clay particles bind to water, locking it up away from the roots. The clay can even block the movement of oxygen in the soil. (This is why clay soils feel gummy when wet.) "Amending" the soil by adding a couple bags of manure or sandbox sand only makes things worse. To really improve clay soils, you need to treat an area at least 10 feet × 10 feet × 6 inches during relatively dry conditions. Work in coarse sand (also called builders' sand) and particularly coarse organic material (not peat or the packaged manures), a cubic yard each. Nature will do the chemistry—across several months or even a couple years.

Changing Your Soil's pH

The soil chemistry around your roots relates to its pH, or balance of acidity and alkalinity. Raising the pH, lowering the salinity (or salt content), and getting rid of herbicide residues can improve your tree's or shrub's chances of success.

Increasing or decreasing your soil pH is sometimes smart, although it's a major yard project that could take 10 to 20 years!

Boosting pH a bit can be done for the very short term, though, with various forms of lime: ground limestone, quicklime, and staked lime. For faster action, use the smallest particle size available. Spread the lime evenly across the area and work it in down through the top 2 to 4 inches of soil. As an alternative to lime, you could use a combination of wood ash (possibly from the fireplace) and leaf compost.

> ### Sprouts
>
> Of course, you can always plant trees and shrubs that aren't picky as to pH. To find some, check out Appendix F.

To decrease your pH, use agricultural sulfur, finely ground and wettable sulfur, iron, or aluminum sulfate. Spread it evenly and work it down 2 to 4 inches. Sulfuric acid reduces the pH but is too dangerous for your tree and shrub roots in the area.

Amending Salty Soils

Salty soils can develop even in one season, perhaps from excess street salt/de-icing chemicals administered during a snowy winter, windstorms that bring in salty dust even from far away, irrigation water that may be saline, or a high water table (where groundwater is heavy with dissolved rock leaching into your soil). Salty soil can also result from salt spray off the ocean, but you won't be able to fix that.

What to do? Soak the area with clean water, which forces the salts lower into the soil, below the tree's or shrub's root level.

Sprouts

If you plan to plant a tree or shrub near a street where de-icing chemicals are used, you might want to plant it in springtime so it has time to grow a bit before the winter onslaught.

Roots Behaving Badly

For all the good they do, roots do have some unfortunate tendencies! Roots girdle trees and cause problems with pipes, pavement, and even buildings!

Girdling Roots

Girdling roots often result from poor practices by the grower; the nursery probably cut into a main root when digging up the tree, and the girdling then is the tree's way to try to compensate. But they can also develop later. One preventable cause is allowing soil to build up too close to the tree's trunk when it's planted. Be sure to clear away the soil from the trunk—3 or 4 inches out when planting. After a girdled root is in place, you can cut it off without killing the tree, but this is best done when the tree is young.

def•i•ni•tion

Girdling roots form a thick "necklace" around the base of the trunk near or at ground level. These roots can cramp the growth of the trunk, making it hard for water and nutrients to reach the leaves and canopy.

A watchful eye can detect girdling before they become a problem for your tree.

girdling roots

Roots Versus Pipes

Roots interfering with underground pipes are quite common in metropolitan areas. Water, gas, electricity, and sewer lines are all hidden under your grass—primarily in your front yard, so they can connect to larger pipes buried along the street. If you have trees planted in the vicinity of these pipes, you might have root versus pipe problems sometime later—trees seem to be responsible for more than half of all sewer blockages nationwide. If you have large trees in your front yard, it's smart to have the sewer pipe "roto-ed" out once every 1 or 2 years to avoid problems.

The bigger and older the tree you have, the more likely you are to have problems. Tree species that grow naturally in damp or river bed environments, such as the silver maple, elm, and cottonwood, are especially likely offenders. When a tree root touches a pipe or even a root from another tree, its reaction is to expand, or what's called "pillowing out." If in the process, it feels a crack in an old pipe or a leaky joint between sections of the pipe, it moves right in. The pleasant warm and humid conditions inside the pipe make the roots grow more … and that expands the crack. Soon the tree can really clog up the pipe!

> **The Real Dirt**
>
> Regular roto-rooting out pipes is far better than deliberately plugging the line in sections temporarily and then filling the pipe with herbicides, foams, or copper sulfate. That's not good for the tree.

Roots Versus Pavement

Roots prefer to live in the top 3 to 5 feet of the soil, near to pavement level. Now think for a moment about the force of even a small wildflower shoving aside soil, mulch, perhaps even snow, to pop out of the ground in springtime. Then imagine the far, far greater force of a large shrub's or tree's root trying to get where it wants to go.

In addition to their brute force against pavement, trees can also pull out enough water from the soil under a sidewalk to make the soil subside and the sidewalk crack. (This is most common after severe droughts.) If the soil hasn't been drastically compacted by the equipment used to create the sidewalk pavement to begin with, the tree will be able to shove its roots out and through, at least to a certain extent. "Lifted" sidewalks and curbs are dangerous to bikers and walkers. And some trees can be repeat offenders after the sidewalk has been repaired.

What to do? Don't plant a new tree any nearer to a sidewalk, driveway, or street than 5 to 20 feet, depending on the size of the tree at maturity. Ask your city or suburban government to slightly reroute any new sidewalks so they bypass your existing mature trees by a safe distance or at least to limit the amount of digging required. It will save them repairs later (and make you happy now).

Arborists such as the one who works as your community forester have lists of tree species that tend to do a little versus a lot of damage to sidewalks, and city engineers can sometimes use improved sidewalk technology, but our best advice is to simply avoid planting close to any pavement. The sidewalk may end up intact, but it clearly isn't ideal for the health of your tree. If a buckled sidewalk is the handiwork of your tree and an accident occurs, you could even be party to a lawsuit.

Root Rot

All trees forced to encounter surface pavements will develop shallower—and so less secure—root systems. Pavement can also prevent the necessary water and air circulation from reaching areas of the roots, and road salts concentrated between sidewalk and street can also contaminate soils.

Roots Versus Foundations

Trees can also disturb building foundations—and that building might be your house!—especially if the initial grading wasn't done well enough so all the water drains *away* from your house. You don't want roots finding and enlarging cracks there because that would allow water in when the ground is saturated.

Arborists use the term *mining* in connection with trees, whose roots *mine* the soil for water. This is most likely to occur if a tree is within 20 to 30 feet of your house, if it's a large tree, if you have clay soil, or if your rainfall pattern often features sudden large rainfalls alternating with very dry periods. Oaks and poplars seem to be the worst offenders; shrubs or small fruit trees are much less apt to interfere, as are conifers because their root systems tend to be a bit more fine and fibrous than other trees.

What can you do if a large tree is already there near your house? You can water it, only slightly but regularly, to keep the soil from swelling and collapsing during major changes in the moisture level. You can also mulch it heavily to keep moisture more consistent. And if the problem becomes extreme enough that your foundation is leaking, you might have to pull away all the soil from around the house in that area, install a barrier such as thick plastic sheeting, and replace the soil. Expensive! You could also get rid of the tree and perhaps plant a pine, cypress, chinaberry, dawn redwood, or gingko there, depending on where you live and what you like.

Root Rot

If your house sits on a concrete slab as opposed to an excavated foundation, you're also more likely to have problems. There's just a lot more cement in the way.

The Least You Need to Know

◆ Roots, growing from tip out, anchor the tree and move water and nutrients in from the soil.

◆ Roots have skin, hairs, a cortex, and most of the same body parts as the trunk.

◆ A tree's or shrub's root system can extend 2 to 5 times farther out than the aboveground branches do.

◆ Although you might be tempted to improve the soil in your yard, be aware that it's difficult to do except in small areas.

◆ Tree roots can develop problems such as girdling and interfering with urban infrastructures such as pipes, pavement, and foundation structures.

Chapter 9

Aboveground Growth

In This Chapter

- ◆ The basics of tree and shrub growth
- ◆ What influences how trees and shrubs grow
- ◆ Which do you want, fast growth or long life?
- ◆ Fast-growing and long-lived trees and shrubs for your zone

As we saw in Chapter 8, the root system of your new tree or shrub grows first and does so even through the fall and winter, when everything else above ground seems to be dormant. After the plant has established itself, though, the twigs, branches, leaves, and trunks, having prepared for this the previous autumn, really get their day in the sun.

Trees destined for a long life, such as the live oak and saguaro, do not tend to grow fast. And the speedier growers—including most shrubs and trees such as the arborvitae, cabbage palm, and cottonwood—don't live long. It's a trade-off, and you can't get both features in the same plant. In this chapter, we give you plenty of examples of both long-lived and fast-growing trees and shrubs. You'll probably want to have both in your yard.

Helpful Hormones

Most trees and shrubs grow between 1 and 6 feet per year up and out from their branches and shoots—enough to be noticeable. Young plants need good soil nutrition, water, and light to grow up and bulk out this way. And they need hormones, or plant growth regulators, as we saw in Chapter 2.

One hormone, a form of auxin called *IAA*, directs the plant to grow toward light by bending, reorienting its leaves, even contorting its body to capture more sunlight. This hormone directs the cells near the tips of the shoots and roots to elongate. If one side of the tree or shrub is in the shade, the hormone builds up on that side until the cells there stretch out to grow as fast as they can. (There are limits, of course, to how much a tree can bend.) IAA also helps control which buds grow, when leaves drop, which branches grow more horizontally, and other key functions.

The Real Dirt

Unlike people, a given plant doesn't have a maximum height. (Each species does have genetics that provide a range of possible maximum heights, which is why some bushes can grow into trees.) But with plenty of room; ample food and water; and freedom from lightning strikes, insect infestation, fire, or a nasty microbe, your tree or shrub will keep on growing.

A second set of growth-related hormones called *gibberellins* are also involved in the plant's light sensitivity. These growth regulators direct cell division and elongation, work to create flowering and fruiting, and instruct the upper leaves to stretch and reorient themselves to receive more sunlight. Again, there's a limit to what growth a tree can accomplish, especially in very low-light conditions. Interestingly, understory trees that have evolved to live well in the shade don't react in this way. They seem happy to grow just the way they are under the shade of taller trees.

The third large group of hormonelike growth regulators are the *cytokinins*. Their job is to fight the aging of the plant, expand the leaf system to boost photosynthesis, and enlarge the cellular structure. More cytokinins are produced in a nitrogen-rich soil. This hormone also turns seeds around in the soil when they sprout so the right part is pointing up.

The chemistry that governs the movement of new shoots isn't completely understood, although it does involve other hormone activity. Time-lapse photography has shown that new shoots actually swing their tips in circles, almost as though they are checking for interference from another plant or your garden wall. The gibberellin hormones seem to have an additional role in controlling seed sprouting.

Tree and shrub aging—of the year's leaves, as well as of the whole plant—is also hormonally controlled. Ethylene directs the ripening both of the plant's fruit and its senescence (aging). It also thickens a plant's trunk. And *abscisic acid* actually inhibits growth but usually only in response to a stress such as a drought.

Sprouts _____

One year is not independent of the next in plant growth. The size of the bud you see now depends on its growth and development last year. And there are odd "delayed reactions" in groupings of trees or in natural forests. If the canopy trees are destroyed, the understory trees grow more vigorously, but not for several years, even though they have been given a new place of full sun.

Grow, Grow, Grow!

For a plant that stands in place, trees and shrubs are actually very active in their growth. Their shoots, twigs, branches, leaves, and even their trunks are constantly working, moving, and growing, even if you can't see it.

Shoots

Every shoot starts with what's called an *apical meristem* (to distinguish it from a flower bud). This is the name for the tip of the shoot and of the branch itself. Growth is orchestrated in just the top 1 millimeter of this bunch of cells, even out to the leaves and each one's placement to capture maximum sunlight. The angles at which the stems and branches do branch out—and, therefore, create the overall shape of the tree or shrub—is instructed from this area as well.

The Real Dirt _____

Have you ever seen new shoots coming out of a trunk that looks dead? This can happen if a trunk has been damaged or stressed or if a more favorable growth situation such as more light has reached the tree. These buds-in-the-bank can pop out to give the tree a new lease on life.

Twigs and Branches

Twigs and branches grow by elongation from the tip. They gradually add wood weight as sections move farther out from the trunk. In winter, take a look at a bare deciduous tree or shrub. You can see the branch's breathing pores (called *lenticels*), which look like small bumps scattered along the twig or branch; the leaf scars, where the tree sealed off the opening left by the leaves when they dropped off; and the *bud scales*, places where the buds of the new leaves will come out in the springtime.

Leaves

Leaves might be the most amazing feature a tree or shrub has to offer. Evolutionally, the annual renewal of leaves probably developed as the only way to adapt to winter—the tree or shrub couldn't survive if it maintained that array of moisture-laden, chlorophyll-rich appendages under the dry and low-light conditions of the cold season. The plants that could renew themselves were able to survive. But think how much energy it must take the tree or shrub to start so much all over again each year!

Leaves are light traps. They expose as much of their surface as possible to the sun and are just transparent enough to welcome the light in so it can nourish all their cells. The leaf veins also transport water and food throughout the leaf and from the branches and trunk. Some trees and shrubs attach the leaf directly to the stem, while others have a kind of ball-bearing structure called a *petiole*, which enables the leaf to turn and twist more with the wind. The plant has so many leaves, each conducting all these functions because, when damaged, a leaf doesn't repair itself.

def•i•ni•tion

A **petiole** is the leaf's stalk or base, where it connects to the branch.

We won't go into all the leaf types, leaf body parts, leaf edges, and leaf tip technologies here because we realize that most people don't choose or maintain their trees and shrubs on this basis. Especially appealing leaf colors and leaf change in the fall do, however, come up quite a bit in Chapter 11.

Trunks

The trunk grows, too, of course. A thin layer of cells, called the *cambium*, sheaths the plant under the bark, from its roots to its leaves. Within it, stem cells orchestrate the thickening of the trunk from the inside out. At the same time, they constantly form fresh tissues just inside to conduct the life processes of the tree's circulation without interruption. (A palm tree is the only one that does not do this, which is why its trunk is the same thickness all the way up.)

def•i•ni•tion

Cambium is the corklike layer where the main growth of the tree or shrub occurs.

Controlling Tree and Shrub Growth

Some homeowners may confront unwanted sprouting—*suckering* or waterspouting, discussed briefly in Chapters 1 and 5—in their trees and shrubs. These extra and awkward-looking branches don't appeal to most homeowners.

Suckers form from roots and pop up all around the base of the trunk, creating a bit of a nuisance. Waterspouts do the same, sticking out from the trunk (higher up) or in the canopy. Some trees do this a lot more than others, and some homeowners are more particular about it than others. If you're in the latter group, avoid littleleaf lindens, crab apples, olives, plums, crape myrtles, English oaks, and black walnuts because they do it a lot. You could paint or spray the area of the ground with products from the garden store containing NAA to avoid the annoying sprouts. Or you could just dig up these sprouts (and do it again, when they return)—but be very careful not to damage roots or trunk. Sprouting from the trunks of trees that have been cut down can be handled with herbicide. Or you could pay to have the stump completely removed.

def•i•ni•tion

A **sucker** is a smaller offshoot of the tree, coming up directly from its root and growing close to its trunk. And watersprouts are those emerging from the trunk elsewhere on the tree.

Root Rot

Electric power companies often use chemicals to reduce the number of times they have to trim trees under power lines. Don't try this yourself, though. Their application is best done by a professional.

Suckers can be removed by pruning.

Some homeowners might want to control the flowering or fruiting of their trees and shrubs. Here again, chemicals can be used; one such chemical, Florel, can be sprayed on, at least once, when the tree or shrub is in full bloom.

Most homeowners want their trees and shrubs to grow *more* and often put in lots of labor mulching, fertilizing, and pruning (see Chapters 16 through 18). No commercial chemicals will speed along that process really, just nature!

Sprouts

"Growing up" takes a while for a tree, often 10 years or more. It is considered juvenile until it can flower (provided the environmental conditions are within a favorable level), and until the time when it can no longer be rooted easily from cuttings. You can't really tell whether a tree is mature just by looking at it. The evidence is all in the tips.

Planting for Fast-Growing Success in Your Zone

If you want to fill a space vacated by a tree or shrub that died, or if you're just eager to have a new tree or shrub in a particular place, you might want a fast-growing addition to your yard. Maybe you even plan to sell your house soon and want to even out your landscape or block something that isn't particularly attractive. As mentioned earlier, fast-growing trees don't live as long—about 50 to 60 years is average—but do grow about 2 to 6 feet per year. Shrubs tend to grow faster than trees and also have shorter life spans. Everything is a trade-off!

The Real Dirt

Fast-growing trees tend to have weaker wood. Their shape and branch structure can compensate for this, but only to a certain extent.

So with that in mind, here are some "fast ideas" for your zone. We focus here a bit more on trees because fast or slow shrub growth still yields a smaller-scale plant that's easier to picture in your yard. As always, check out Appendix F, too.

Paper Birch, Yellow Birch, and Arborvitae (Zones 2/3)

We recommend birches and arborvitae for zones 2/3. The paper birch, also called white birch and canoe birch, described earlier in this book, is wonderful here.

The American arborvitae (*Thuja*) and its cultivars, especially the ones that easily form hedges without any pruning, grow even faster. These trees quickly shield your house, provide privacy, or block any view or wind that you want blocked—a few of them make a solid mass when planted close enough together. They're also fragrant and grow in any kind of soil.

Sprouts

The paper birch is also called the canoe birch. Native people in the north made canoes out of them (and still do sometimes).

Black Locust, Aspen, and Spirea (Zone 4)

The black locust and quaking aspen, both fast-growing, have been described earlier. (This aspen also does well in zones 2/3, quickly spreading by rhizomes to make a clump of trees for those who have the space.) The big-toothed aspen, closely related, joins them here. And the spirea bush is also a favorite for this purpose.

Sumac, American Smoketree, and Norway Maple (Zone 5)

The sumacs, such as the staghorn mentioned earlier in this book, are attractive shrubs if they're allowed to spread out to make a fast clump. They are known for their dramatic fall foliage in a range of scarlets and reds.

The American smoketree (*Cotinus obovatus*) is a popular fast-growing shrub or small tree in the eastern part of this zone. Its flower clusters look like smoke; the native tree might be preferable because many of its cultivars don't look as "smokey."

The Norway maple grows dense quickly and also does fine near a street. It can grow to about 80 feet tall.

Tulip Tree, Chokeberry, and Alder (Zone 6)

Besides the tulip tree, described earlier, we'd like to suggest the chokeberry and the alder for quick growth in zone 6.

Chokeberries (*Photinia*), native to the Appalachians but with cultivars widely available, have pleasant off-white flowers in spring and orange/red/scarlet foliage in fall. They're very flexible as to shade or sun, wet or dry—they'll grow fast almost anywhere.

All the alders (*Alnus*) are fast-growing and shrub-size and prefer damp soils. In this zone, the hazel or common alder is an excellent choice. It's native to the Southeast, forms thickets, and can grow to about 20 feet.

Loblolly Pine, Austrian Pine, and Elderberry (Zone 7)

The loblolly and the Austrian pine, both good choices here when you need speed, have already been featured.

The Austrian pine does well across most of the United States, disliking only extreme heat. It grows dark green and lush up to 60 feet tall.

We also recommend the elderberry (*Sambucus nigra*), especially the *aurea* cultivar. It grows quickly to become a large shrub in golden yellow and isn't picky about light conditions.

Hackberry, Pawpaw, and Cherry Laurel (Zone 8)

The netleaf or western hackberry, as mentioned earlier, ranges in size from a shrub up to a small tree with sweet fruit in autumn. It grows from the Southwest up into the prairie states and is a fast-growing native tree choice. We also like The Georgia (or dwarf) hackberry as it does well in the southeastern part of zone 8.

The pawpaw, already featured, has the nickname "false banana" because its 3- to 5-inch-long fruits, although brownish, resemble small bananas. This eastern tree's range can extend quite farther north through Indiana and Ohio.

Sprouts

Pawpaw fruits are pleasantly edible, for humans as well as possums, raccoons, squirrels, and birds.

The fast-growing cherry laurel (*Prunus laurocerasus*) makes a nice, small tree that's amazingly unpicky about conditions. It's an evergreen with fragrant white flowers.

Spice Bush, Sourwood, and Slash Pine (Zone 9)

Mentioned earlier, the spice shrub grows fast and looks decorative. They really shoot up in the South's warm climate.

Sourwood (*Oxydendrum arboreum*) is a small tree with brilliant scarlet leaves in autumn and lovely, creamy-white flowers in spring.

The slash pine (*Pinus elliottii*) is native to the Gulf Coast, mostly Georgia through Alabama, except for southern Florida. It is so fast-growing that it's used in tree plantations.

Buttonbush, Willow, and Black Mangrove (Zones 10/11)

The buttonbush (*Cephalanthus*), whose nicknames are "honey balls" and "globe flowers," sports white flowers and then fruits similar to little buttons. These shrubs or small trees can reach 20 feet high. They like wet soils and grow fast across the entire United States east of the Mississippi and somewhat west of it.

Also for fast growth, any willow (*Salix*) or cottonwood (*Populus*) for sale in your zone is a good choice if you have enough soil moisture. In the Gulf or Pacific regions, try an elm tree such as the Chinese elm.

Root Rot _____

If you own livestock, don't plant the buttonbush near where they graze. Its foliage is poisonous to them!

In addition to the American mangrove, mentioned earlier in the book, the black mangrove (*Avicennia*) is a nice choice, especially if you live a bit inland in this zone and near a creek or river. It yields an excellent honey, much paler than most bottled honey you find in the store. A very cold winter will kill it, however.

Planting for Long-Lived Success in Your Zone

We think it's so satisfying to plant a tree that will live long, into many future generations, adding its beauty to a yard, street, or park. Long-lived trees tend to be the ones you think of as very tall trees—it took them a long time to get that tall! Although no shrubs are terrifically long-lived, keep in mind that cultivars with purple or yellow leaves are a bit slower-growing and longer-lived than green-leafed ones.

The Real Dirt _____

Jeannie's grandfather often said, "To plant a tree is to love your grandchildren." The Russian olive he planted has looked wonderful for a long time!

Juniper, Bur Oak, and Red Pine (Zones 2/3)

Junipers and bur oaks, discussed earlier in this book, are both good bets for a long life in zones 2/3.

Sprouts

Junipers are fragrant even in winter. Crush a bit of the foliage, or even use the bluish berries in cooking. They're excellent with grilled salmon.

The red or Norway pine (*Pinus resinosa*) is common across eastern Canada, New England, upper New York State, northern Michigan, and parts of Minnesota. It grows 70 to 80 feet high, adding one row of branches every year. The "Norway" nickname, arborists say, is more likely to have come from the town of Norway, Maine, rather than the Norway in Europe. Both the white pine and red oak, discussed earlier, would be superb as long-lived trees here.

Northern Catalpa, Sugar Maple, and Pin Oak (Zone 4)

In addition to the catalpa and maple described earlier in this book, we'd like to suggest the pin oak (*Quercus palustris*) for a long-lived tree in this zone, working well in moist or dry conditions. When the stems are new, they are pleasingly reddish, as are the leaves throughout a long fall. It's native to the eastern United States and grows to about 70 feet tall.

Hickory, Red Cedar, and European Silver Fir (Zone 5)

We've already described the long-lived hickory and red cedar (a juniper). Another sturdy, long-lived tree, the silver fir (*Abies alba*) grows larger (up to 100 feet) if it has more space, but it is also a steady, moderate-size garden resident with a pleasing pyramid shape. Fine in the shade as long as the soil is moist, it is indeed silver-y. It will enjoy your yard for ages.

Persimmon, Boxwood, and Post Oak (Zone 6)

In addition to the persimmon and boxwood, both excellently slow-growing but long-lived, the post oak (*Quercus stellata*) is a winner in zone 6, too. Ranging from 30 to 70 feet when full grown, its prime area is the southeastern two thirds of the United States. The acorns are more elliptical than round and have deep cups. This oak likes soils from sandy and gravelly all the way to the moist loams of riverbanks. The pecan is another good choice here.

Sycamore, Baldcypress, and Monkey Puzzle (Zone 7)

In addition to the stately sycamore and the water-loving baldcypress, described earlier, the funny-named monkey puzzle (*Araucaria araucana*), so named because it looks like a monkey would have a hard time climbing it, also does well in zone 7. Also called the Chilean pine, this tree boasts dark green leaves like scales with sharp points and has a pleasing shape. This 50- to 80-foot tree isn't picky about its growing conditions.

Tupelo, Scarlet Oak, and Japanese White Pine (Zone 8)

In addition to the black tupelo, described earlier, the scarlet oak (*Quercus coccinea*) is a long-lived tree that's easily adaptable to urban conditions. It lives up to its name in the fall, when the exquisite leaves last for weeks.

The Japanese white pine (*Pinus parviflora*) is an interesting slow-but-long grower, so much so that it's used for bonsai gardens. Its needles are bluish-green, and if its growth isn't controlled by pruning, it eventually reaches 30 to 70 feet high.

Monterey Pine, Great Sequoia, and California Redwood (Zone 9)

The Monterey pine is a classic, dramatically large pine that lives a long time. It was mentioned earlier in the book.

The giant sequoia (*Sequoiadendron*) is the ultimate in a "take your time" tree because it plans to grow for 3,200 years! This huge tree, now rare, can be planted anywhere along the Pacific coast.

The California redwood (*Sequoia sempervirens*) lives so long that your grandchildren will have grandchildren and so on and so on while it still grows. Planting one of these two trees is a magnificent gift to the future.

Live Oak, Coconut Palm, and Silver Beech (Zones 10/11)

In addition to the huge live oak, discussed earlier in this book, the coconut palm (*Cocos nucifera*) is a nice tree for its longevity. Tall and slender and growing up to 80 feet high, its leaves were once used for thatch, its trunk for small canoes, and its nuts for food.

Also, don't forget the silver beech (*Fagus*) if you have a cooler spot. It's slower-growing, but it eventually reaches 50 feet tall and has a silvery trunk. In the meantime, watch its small leaves dance in the wind!

The Least You Need to Know

- ◆ Roots establish themselves in the fall and rest in winter, and then the trunk and canopy take over the growth for spring and summer.

- ◆ Hormones guide the development of the plant, keeping it alive and growing in the right pattern.

- ◆ Deciduous trees are unusual among living things because they discard and then replace much of their body mass each year.

- ◆ Homeowners can find both fast-growing or long-lived trees and shrubs, but not both features in the same plant.

Chapter 10

Stop and Smell the Flowers

In This Chapter

- Tree and shrub flower power
- Flower anatomy
- The timing of flowers
- Colorful flowering shrub choices

Among the most wonderful things about trees and shrubs—and especially shrubs—are their flowers. Many people buy plants based solely on their blooms. Maybe a palette of yellows, whites, pinks, violets, oranges, and reds is your goal. Or maybe you want a mass of all-yellow shrubs or a few shrub accents of any color among your trees. Whatever you're looking for flower-wise, you'll find it in this chapter.

And although every woody shrub flowers, not every one has showy flowers, or even visible ones unless you get up close (with some, you need a magnifying glass to see the tiny flowers!). Some shrubs even look almost pitiful in the flowering dimension, and some are actually unattractive! This chapter covers those shrubs with distinctly visible and very attractive flowers, and we focus on shrubs here since they're so much more dramatic than trees in this department.

Understanding Flowers

We've touched on flowers in an earlier chapter, but let's take a closer look. Flowers are part of the plant's life cycle, and they mostly evolved to attract bees, birds, and pollinators for reproduction—luckily for us humans who also appreciate the beauty of the blooms (although for sometimes different reasons). Botanists have developed cultivars—custom versions, in a way—of trees and shrubs to extend the appeal of plantings to us.

Flowering, fruiting, and foliage should be considered together because each phase lasts for only part of the year (be sure to read Chapter 11 along with this one). An individual native plant species typically flowers anywhere from 1 to 2 days up to a couple weeks, fruits are a feature until they are eaten or rot, and foliage fades—that's life, but if you choose your shrubs accordingly, your yard will be beautiful all summer long!

Flowering: It's All Timing

Most, although not all, flowers form in response to the photoperiod (remember that from Chapter 5?). A shrub species requires anywhere from 10 to 16 hours of light per day, during several days, to start its blooms. The shrub also needs to have grown enough in mass to not only support the extra weight of the flowers, but also to hold enough nutrition to develop the reproductive organs that the flowers become. Species differ, but it typically takes between 1 and 5 spring seasons for a shrub to be mature, or grown up enough to be fully beautiful.

In other words, your plantings are teenagers at their first flowering stage, *and* they can also tell time! Every year they measure the dark hours to contrast them to the light ones. Only in response to that difference do they start to create flowers, instead of leaves, from their buds. Scientists still haven't figured out all the sexual hormone chemistry of this amazing flowering system.

Outside in your yard, your plantings are careful to begin blooming late enough so they get enough light and, therefore, adequate food from the sun (through photosynthesis)—and early enough to be able to complete their entire reproductive cycle before the colder and darker period of the year shuts them down again. Every tree and shrub is trained to the sun the way we are to our alarm clocks and calendars.

> **The Real Dirt**
>
> If you've ever had a lily blooming by Easter or a baby forsythia shrub inside for an early breath of spring, you've witnessed—or bought the result of—flower "forcing." This kind of human-gardening project is done simply by manipulating the plant's photoperiod with plant lights or heavy blinds (as well as water and warmth).

Yet more orchestration is going on! Some shrubs flower before they leaf, and some leaf out before they flower, depending on the species. Some flower early enough that they can complete this stage underneath large deciduous trees that haven't yet leafed out and, therefore, block the sun from reaching the shrubs below. And shrubs that flower in spring tend to have set their flowers within their buds the previous fall (lilacs are an example), while those that bloom in summer placed their flowers on the launch pad just this spring (hydrangeas do this).

Who knew all this was going on out there!

How Do Flowers Do That?

All flowers have the same basic parts, as the following illustration shows:

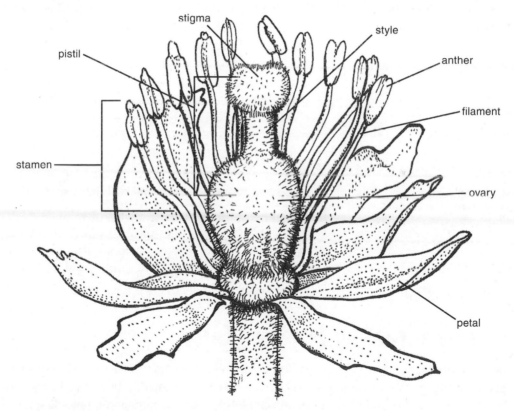

This cross-section of a simple flower shows all the floral parts.

Similar to many other creatures, flowers come in male and female versions. The males are called the *staminate flowers* because they have a *stamen*, and the females are called the *pistillate flowers* because they have *pistils*. A simple flower has stamen and pistil. Whatever the level of complexity, though, they use these body parts to ensure that the pollen reaches the *stigma* (the little cushion-y pads at the tips of the tiny stalks called the *anthers*). This happens as some of the pollen grains develop tubes that then find an opening in the pistil that leads to the *ovary*. Other pollen grains make sperm, which moves through these tubes into the ovary.

That's pretty much all it takes to start a "baby"—the new embryonic shrub in flower-land. For the next stages of this little drama, see Chapter 11.

This process occurs in flowering plants whether the male and female body parts are found on the same flower (if it is, the pollen doesn't have far to go), or in separate flowers on the same plant (which needs a bit more help from a pollination such as a honey bee), or whether the male and female are on separate shrubs of the same species (and that requires a longer "hike" by a pollinator). The second alternative might be occurring out in your yard today, depending on what species of shrubs you have. An example of this case, in which both the male and female flower are on the same plant, is the silver maple tree. The third choice, called *hybridization* or *cross-pollination*, occurs across your yard (and neighborhood) in the case of plantings such as cottonwoods and date palms.

When no pollinators are available or temperatures are too cold for them to move around, some plants can self-pollinate by altering the positions of their own stamen and anthers or pistils within a single flower. (For more details, see Chapter 2.)

Sprouts

Pollinators, who move pollen from one place to another, include many more creatures than the busy bee. Flies, ants, moths, spiders, and even small birds and mammals (such as the hummingbird and bat) do this. When motivated, humans are expert pollinators, too. We create new roses, tulips, and other cultivar treasures for the eye.

Flowering Shrubs by Zone and Color

Many homeowners think in terms of a shrub's color accents in their yard, so we've grouped our good-bet choices partly in this way. Zones have to be the primary consideration, but you'll notice that many shrubs of various colors are appropriate for a range of zones and plenty of overlap exists. To that end, we've deliberately grouped zones 5 through 8, zones 7 through 9, and zones 8 through 11 with overlapping. (Flowering shrubs are popular enough to have had cultivars developed in this broad a way.) As always, look for more detail in the tree and shrub grid in Appendix F.

In a book with a wide but overall scope such as ours, we haven't broken down our recommendations by the shape of the flower. Solitary, bunched, spike-y flowers—all are beautiful, and we aren't even going to force the technical names for these forms on you.

Remember, before you buy anything, check the tags for the timing of blooming. An "early spring" shrub could bloom in January or June, depending on when spring is for you. You might want all your new and existing flowering shrubs to bloom at once, or you might want to stagger them. This is easy to accomplish with a little planning.

The Real Dirt

We've provided the names of specific cultivars—shrub breeding is such an active field, and two cultivars of the same species could be and often are completely different in color. And some plantings are known by their Latin names only—in those cases, we haven't also provided the popular name because there isn't one. Just a few words to the wise!

Zones 2/3 and 4

Even in the northernmost part of the United States, beautiful choices exist, from whites, to yellows, to pinks, and more.

Whites

Serviceberry (*Amelanchier*). Blooms especially early, best at the edge of a woodland garden. Accepts most soils and either sun or partial shade. Also called Juneberry. Zones 3 through 8.

Mockorange (*Philadelphus*). Not picky as to soil, though likes sun. Zones 4 through 8.

Hydrangea (*Paniculata grandiflora*). Fist-size flowers, a late bloomer. Zones 4 through 8.

Sand cherry (*Prunus pumila*). Wide and bushy, needs sandy or gravely soil. Zones 3 through 7.

Chokeberry (*Aronia*). Early bloomer. Accepts almost any soil and partial shade or full sun. Zones 4 through 7.

Spirea (*Spiraea nipponica*). Many small leaves on branches cascading with flowers. The vanhouettei is similar, but its flowers bloom before the leaves. The amoena variety is also nice and fast-growing. Zones 4 through 8.

Dogwood, Gray (*Cornus racemosa*). Likes moist, well-drained soil but isn't too picky. The grayish-white blooming shrub tolerates sun or shade. Dicey for zone 2, though. Zones 3 and 4.

Sprouts _____

Alert readers might be wondering why so many shrubs bloom white. This is the most common color of shrub flowers naturally, and the farther north you live, the truer this is.

Honeysuckle (*Lonicera caerulea*). This creamy-white blooming shrub likes any soil and also likes the sun. (Not the same as the [low] bush honeysuckle.) Zones 2 through 6.

Heath (*Phyllodoce aleutica*). Mostly in Alaska. Small, dense bush with yellowish-white flowers shaped like urns. Zones 2 through 5.

Heath (*Phyllodoce nipponica*). Small, dark green leaves covered with pinkish-white bell-shape flowers. Zones 3 through 5.

Yellows

Honeysuckle, Clavey's Dwarf, and Emerald Mound (*Lonicera*). This shrub likes any soil and likes the sun. (Not the same as the [low] bush honeysuckle.) Zones 3 through 8.

Cinquefoil (*Potentilla potentilla*). Blooms over an especially long period, in white and pink as well as yellow. Accepts hot, dry conditions and needs full sun. Not picky as to soils. Zones 3 through 10.

Forsythia, Meadowlark (*Forsythia*). Blooms especially early. Needs full sun but accepts almost any soil. Zones 4 through 8.

Reds

Sheep Laurel (*Kalmia angustiflora*). Clusters of small starry-shaped flowers. Does best in eastern part of the United States. Zones 2 through 7.

Pinks

Spirea (*Spiraea japonica*). Small or dwarf. Not picky as to soil but prefers moistness. Has a long flowering period. Zones 4 through 9.

Hydrangea (*Hydrangea paniculata, grandiflora,* and *pink diamond*). Similar to the white hydrangea but turns pinkish purple after being white. Zones 4 through 8.

Bog Rosemary (*Andromeda polifolia*). Flowers are tiny bells. Likes damp soils. Zones 3 through 6.

Tamarisk (*Tamarix ramosissima*). Long blooming, large blooms. Doesn't like sandy soils. Zones 3 through 8.

Viburnum (*Viburnum trilobum*). This large shrub blooms well into the spring (if the first set is lost to frost, another will appear). Zones 2 through 8.

Purples

Lilac (*Syringa vulgaris* and *chinfensis*) are the classic lilac color. (Ameurensig is creamy.) Likes full sun but isn't picky as to soil as long as it's well drained. Zones 4 through 7.

Zones 5 Through 8

Across the United States' vast mid-latitudes, so many especially beautiful flowering shrubs are available in a great array of colors that we can't mention all of them, so we've selected enough in each color to get you going. When you shop online or even at a well-stocked nursery, you'll have even more choices available to you. Have fun!

Whites

Broom (*Cytisus multiflorus*). Prefers full sun and well-drained but not rich soils. Avoid windy areas or moving it after planted. Zones 6 through 8.

Enkianthus (*Enkianthus perculatus*). Deciduous evergreen shrub scaled for small gardens. Flowers shaped like bells, clustering and drooping down, white in early summer then blood-red in fall. Zones 6 through 8.

Magnolia (*Magnolia tripetala*). Yes, a shrub, not a tree. Likes moist but not boggy soil. Very large showy flowers. Zones 6 through 9.

Magnolia (*Magnolia stellata*). Slower-growing than *tripetala* but just as lovely. Zones 5 through 9.

Raspberry (*Rubus deliciosus*). Berry shrub with berries that are *not* delicious and often don't appear. Its flowers and leaves are large. Zones 5 through 8.

Flowering raspberry (*Rubus*). Low-spreading and evergreen for the shade. Leaves are shiny, dark green. Zones 7 and 8.

Flowering almond (*Prunus glandolusa*). Bushy springtime dwarf shrub in the almond family. Zones 5 through 8.

Spirea (*Spiraea arguta*). Easy to grow in a moist and fertile soil. Very reliable big bloomer with tiny flowers. For bigger flowers, try the Chamaedryfolia variant, and for perhaps even more graceful branches, check out the Veitchii. Zones 5 through 8.

Snowbell (*Styrax japonica*). Small flowers similar to snow-drops bloom all over this very large shrub. Zones 6 through 8.

Viburnum (*Viburnum dilatatum*). Easy to grow, not picky as to soils. Plant more than one if you also want berries. Zones 5 through 8.

Heath (*Phyllodoce nipponica*). A tiny shrub for a rock or a peat garden in cool places. Each stalk boasts dark green leaves and pinkish-white bell-like flowers, one per stalk. Zones 3 through 5.

Piersis (*Piersis floribunda*). Shrub is similar to the rhododendron. Dense, dark leaves set off small greenish-white flowers similar to those on a lily of the valley in this medium to large shrub. Zones 5 through 7.

Creams

Yucca (*Yucca filamentosa* and *recurvifolia*). Likes full sun, warm areas, and well-drained soils. Large blooms and gray-green leaves soften the spiky demeanor of this dry land plant. Flaccida is also a limper variant with even more conspicuous flowers. Recurvifolia is zones 7 through 9; the rest are zones 4 through 9.

Dogwood (*Cornus kousa*). Large shrub with flat branches that hold myriad tiny flowers. Zones 5 through 8.

Broom (*Cytisus kewensis*). Low to the ground and spreading, with simple leaves. Zones 6 through 8.

Elderberry (*Sambucus pubens*). Grows vigorously and sports tiny flowers in lacey clumps. Zones 4 through 9.

Enkianthus, redvein (*Enkianthus campanulatus*). The creamy tone is usually tinted with a bit of green, although quite a few varieties bloom in other hues. Zones 5 through 8.

Firethorn (*Pyracanthea atlantaniodes* and *rogersiana*). Not very picky as to sun and soil, even growing against walls. This variety is on the large side and with fewer thorns (spines). Small flowers bloom in large clusters. Zones 6 through 9 and zones 7 through 9, respectively.

Yellows

Dogwood (*Cornus mas*). Tiny flowers appear before the leaves, similar to stars on the branches. Quite large. Zones 5 through 8.

Camellia (*Camellia japonica*). Varieties include every flower color (not just yellow), blooming in spring on these large, glossy evergreen shrubs. Zones 7 through 9.

Weigela (*Weigela middendorfiana*). Prefers partial shade but otherwise not picky. Flowers have one orange spot. Zones 5 through 7.

Broom (*Genista pilosa*). Prefers full sun and well-drained but poor soil. Good in rock gardens. Boasts many blooms early in the summer. Zones 6 through 8.

Forsythia, spring glory (*Forsythia*). Can grow to 10 feet high. Flowers early, not picky as to soil or sunlight location but not as well shaped when under a big tree. Zones 6 through 9.

Broom (*Cytisus ardonii* and *beanii*). Loves the sun and well-drained soils. Tiny and bright with simple leaves. Zones 7 and 8.

Boxwood (*Buxus sempervirens*). Good bet evergreen for any well-drained soil in sun or shade. Many varieties exist, all on the large side. Zones 6 through 8.

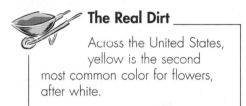

The Real Dirt

Across the United States, yellow is the second most common color for flowers, after white.

Barberry (*Berberis thunbergii, wilsoniae, Tom Thumb*), temolica, sieboldii, and rubrostilla. From spring through early summer, these dense shrubs boast various hues and types of yellow flowers. Also has excellent berries and autumn color. The Thunbergii, perhaps the most dramatic, is zones 5 through 8; the rest are zones 6 through 9.

Oranges

More Barberry (see preceding entry), the Darwinii and the Semperflorens both begin their show with bright red buds and then flame to orange. Medium-size and very popular varieties. Zones 5 through 9.

Quince (*Chaenomeles japonica*). Makes a nice dwarf hedge in a fertile, well-drained soil. Varieties have reddish-orange or brighter red flowers. (A red cultivar grows larger blooms earlier but does well only in zone 5.) Zones 5 through 9.

Zones 7 Through 9

This zonal range has plenty of colorful beauty available.

Reds

Glory Pea (*Clianthus*). Leaves are a bit grayish in contrast to the scarlet or rose-red flowers. Medium-size and blooms in early summer. Native to New Zealand. Zones 7 through 11.

Flowering Currant (*Ribes sanguineum* and *pulborough*). Tolerates most conditions but prefers the sun; grows rather large. Comes in many red varieties. Zones 6 through 8.

Fatsia (*Fatsia sellowiana*). Very unpicky as to light or soil, although it prefers sun. Blooms red/crimson in summer. Zones 8 through 11.

Fuchsia (*Fuchsia magellanica*). Likes any condition except large trees hanging over them. Most varieties are pink, purple, or crimson in hue. Slender flowers. Zones 8 through 10.

Pinks

Hibiscus (*Hibiscus syriacus*). This later-summer bloomer likes warm sunny locations and decent, moist soil. Varieties in pink are the Hamabo and Pink Giant. Zones 6 through 9.

Tree Peony (*Paeonia suffruticosa*). In spite of the name, these are shrubs that are fine in any soil that isn't boggy. Comes in varieties of any color, with the Spontanea a lovely pink. Zones 5 through 9.

Flowering plum (*Prunus blireana*). A flowering plum that has been crossed with an apricot, it's grown as a large bush. Profuse flowers contrast nicely with the purplish leaves. Zones 6 through 8.

Rhododendron (*Rhododendron chamaecistus*). Within a huge family with something for practically any yard, this variety is dense and small but with flowers the size of small plates. Likes the sun but not too much heat. Zones 7 through 9.

Wineberry (*Rubus phoenicolasius*). Blooms in summer. Stems have reddish-brown hairs that set off small flowers. Zones 6 through 8.

Weigela (*Weigela foliis purpureis*). Small grayish-green leaves with hints of purple set off first the reddish buds and then the flowers. Zones 5 through 8.

Hydrangea (*Hydrangea hortensis*). Very popular, likes moist but not wet soils and grows low. Zones 7 through 9.

Purples/Blues

Butterfly bush (*Buddleia davidii*). Grows best even in poor soils, late-flowering, quick-growing, large, and popular with butterflies. Varieties come in many colors. Zones 6 through 9.

Lavendar (*Lavandula augustifoli*). Pale and narrow grayish leaves set off dark purple, spiky flowers. Early flowering. Zone 6.

Magnolia (*Magnolia liliiflora nigra*). Early summer flowering with very vivid and long-lasting flowers. Many varieties. Zones 6 through 8.

Lavendar (*Caryopteris incana*). Flowers as late as early autumn. Small with downy leaves. Loves the sun. Zones 6 through 9.

Laurel, David's mountain (*Sophora davidii*). Blooms in early summer with small but very numerous flowers and tiny leaves. Likes hot sunshine and any soil. Zones 6 through 9.

Zones 8 Through 11

Those of you in this zone have many semi-tropical and even tropical choices. We're offering some mainstream good bets.

Whites

Rock rose (*Cistus aguilari*). This family, known as the rock roses, like lots of hot sun and poor (sandy) soils. This variety has large white flowers that bloom in summer. The medium-size Laurifolius variety is hardy with dark green leaves and does well in zones 8 through 10. Otherwise, zones 9 and 10.

Viburnum (*Viburnum clerodendrum* and *trichotomum*). Needs full sun and are very large—sometimes as much as 8 feet wide. Zones 7 through 9. The arborea variety, whose nickname is the lily of the valley tree, is a very large shrub with glossy, dark green leaves and blooms in late summer or early fall. Zones 8 and 9.

Spirea (*Spiraea arcuata*). Although this shrub is far more commonly planted north of this zone, this variety is more southerly. Its nice arched shape holds small flowers in clusters. Also comes in pink. Zones 8 and 9.

Hibiscus (*Hibiscus sinosyriacus*). Likes warmth and good soil for its trumpet-shape flowers, white with cherry/red/crimson centers. Zones 8 through 10.

Yellows

Broom (*Cytisus battandieri*, *grandiflorus*, *spachianus*, and *supinus*). This array takes you from early spring through late summer in a haze of yellow. The Battandieri is the most unusual with its large leaves on a broad structure, spikes of pineapple-scented blooms (zones 8 and 9, as is the Grandiflorus). The latter three look more like typical brooms. Spachianus (zones 9 and 10) has a long-lasting lushness, and Supinus is for the smallest places (zones 7 and 8).

Yucca (*Yucca whipplei*). Set off against its long, slender, spikey leaves in gray tones are hundreds of bell-shape flowers. Zones 9 through 11.

Sophora (*Sophora tetraphera*). This species, although often trees, includes this New Zealand native, a very large shrub. Flowers shaped like tubes appear in early summer, often after the plant has dropped its leaves. Zones 9 and 10.

Dogwood (*Cornus capitata*). Almost a tree with a profusion of creamy-yellow flowers followed by red fruits, followed by a lovely autumn color. Zones 8 and 9.

Caesalpinia (*Caesalpinia japonica*). Prickly, light green foliage. Likes lime-rich soils. Large, spikey blooms in light yellow. Zones 9 through 11.

Oranges

Flannel bush (*Fremontodendron mexicanum*). Not picky as to soil, but doesn't like its roots disturbed. Yellow-orange flowers are close to stars in shape. Large and blooms in late summer. Zones 10 and 11.

> **The Real Dirt**
>
> Semi-tropical and tropical flowers are more vivid in color, similar to the situation with tropical birds—think parrots. This is probably to make them stand out against all the lushness of this biome. (To us, the tiny wildflowers of the North are just as lovely!)

Reds

Tamarisk (*Tamarix truncata*). Not picky about soil, these love the sun. Dark green leaves accompany sweet-smelling flowers. Zones 9 and 10.

Abelia, glossy (*Abelia grandiflora*). Very dense with 1- to 2-inch-long, very bright flowers. Glossy dark leaves make an arched shape. Zones 8 through 11.

Fuchsia (*Fuchsia riccartonii*). A common variety, very hardy. Zones 9 and 10.

Pinks

Camellia (*Camellia reticulata*). Very large with dark green leaves. Some varieties come in crimson. Zones 9 and 10.

Rock rose, purple (*Cistus purpureus*). Purple rock rose. This member of the rock rose family loves the sun but accepts almost any soil. This purple variety, medium-size, features deeper pink areas, against the rosier tone of the rest of the bloom. A Silver Pink variety is a very hardy dwarf whose pink flowers are more of a salmon tint. Zones 9 and 10 and 8 through 10, respectively.

Purples/Blues

Mallow, Indian (*Abutilon ochsenii* and *vitafolium*). Full sun and with clusters of flowers. The first blooms in early summer, followed by the second in late summer. Both are large shrubs. The second variety is more of a lavender color and accepts even fierce winds. Zones 8 and 9.

Snowball (*Ceanothus rigidus*). Ceanothus. The other common name of these plants is "California lilac." This variety flowers early and is large, rather flat in shape, with dark glossy leaves. Zones 9 and 10.

Ceanothus, wavy-leafed (*Ceanothus foliosus*). Waxy leaf ceanothus. A dark blue, it is smaller and blooms a bit later than the following variety. Zones 9 and 10.

Ceanothus, Santa Barbara (*Ceanothus impressus*). This variety's season is in between that of the preceding two. Very hardy and a true blue. Zones 8 through 10.

The Least You Need to Know

- Flowers, in trees and shrubs and elsewhere, evolved to attract pollinators.
- Trees and shrubs flower at different times primarily to attract pollinators at different times throughout the growing season.
- The reproductive parts of a plant are inside the flowers.
- Fabulous choices for flowering shrubs exist in all areas of the United States.

Chapter 11

Fun with Fruit and Foliage

In This Chapter

- ◆ Why fruit and flowers?
- ◆ A look at foliage
- ◆ The plantings with the most appealing fruits
- ◆ Good-bet choices for color, season by season

As spring segues into summer, your trees and shrubs are busy transforming their flowers into fruits. Think cherry and plum trees as well as citrus, pineapples, and everything in between! But fruiting in the shrubs—their berries—is probably more of a factor in your decision of what to plant because so many more choices are available here. Some of these shrub berries are edible for humans, others attract wildlife, and even more are simply attractive, even after the flowering and fruiting season is over.

Tree and shrub foliage through different times of year is an important consideration when purchasing for your yard. Many shrub cultivars have been developed to feature yellow or variegated leaf color, grayish tones, or reddish-toned leaves to accent your yard year-round. Foliage changes in autumn may well guide your choices, too, in both trees and shrubs. After explaining a bit about the processes of fruiting, we'll offer lots of good-bet ideas here for all seasons. Although the fruiting sections tend to favor the shrubs over the trees a bit, the foliage sections focus on choices among trees as well as shrubs.

Fruiting Basics

With all their fruits and foliage, trees and shrubs almost seem as though they're trying to compensate for the yearly drop of their flowers! Many of them actually become their most beautiful in their fruiting and foliage stages. But how and why does it all happen? Let's take a look.

As the petals fall away, you can see a central area of the flower begin to swell. This means the tree has been fertilized and it's going to have a *baby*—a fruit or berry, which is simply a small fruit. Actually, the real baby—the seeds—are swaddled safely inside the fruit. The fruiting part is only the container that moves the seeds away from the parent so they'll have room to grow. It often serves as the temptation or lure for the creatures who transport them (more on the furry helpers coming right up).

The seeds are usually moved, but not usually by wind—as the conifers are—because most fruits and their seeds are too heavy. Rather, many of the flowering shrubs' and trees' seeds are transported via living creatures. Squirrels pick up and either eat or bury the acorn-encased seeds for the oak trees, cedar waxwings consume (and excrete) the berry-housed seeds for the mountain ash, and many animals carry seeds around without even knowing it—for example, small rodents might carry the sticky seed of the parasitic mistletoe in its fur. In fact, some seeds need to be scratched (called *scarified* because the scratches look like scars) in an animal's digestive system before they'll germinate properly. Insects also play a role in pollination as well as in seed transport.

People move seeds around, too, but unlike birds and other animals, we can't be counted on. We often unhelpfully toss the seeds into our garbage disposals, eat them, or even use the science of breeding to create relatively seedless fruits such as those of this variety of watermelon. Of course, we do plant a great many seeds also, even beyond the obvious grain and vegetable crops; this is, of course, how the wholesalers of the tree and shrub industry sometimes "make" their wares. So we are quite voracious consumers of the reproduction of trees and shrubs in many ways.

Huge amounts of plant energy are spent on the effort to propagate, but nature can seem wasteful. Vast numbers of seeds—sometimes thousands from a

The Real Dirt

Although most seeds are moved by creatures instead of wind, exceptions include lighter fruit/seed packages such as the "wings" of maple trees. A smaller number of trees and shrubs uses water as a vehicle, as in the case of the coconut, which may bob along on the ocean waves for hundreds of miles before reaching a new shore on which to sprout.

Sprouts

Some plants, including navel oranges, bananas, and pineapple, can multiply themselves without fertilization. They not only skip pollination and fertilization, but they also skip seeding, preferring to do it all on their own.

maple tree, for example—are created *inside* fruits, which develop *inside* flowers. Other plantings use the strategy of investing more into each seed, coddling it along—think the coconut, for example. All this just to get a new generation of trees and shrubs!

Understanding Fall Foliage

Trees and shrubs begin fall long before we see those dazzling changes in foliage color. Preparing for dormancy takes them weeks, during which they pull nutrients from their leaves back through and into the trunk. There, the nourishment is used to feed the roots—the only part of the tree that grows significantly in autumn. The tree drains the protein source for chlorophyll, which is what makes the leaves green, to provide root food, and the nitrogen is placed in storage for the next spring.

How do trees and shrubs know that fall is coming, even when temperatures may be quite warm and the rainfall ample? Mostly, they use the balance of daylight versus darkness, the reliable photoperiod, to launch these annual autumn adaptations.

As the chlorophyll in the leaves is withdrawn, and its green vanishes, the other pigments—which are there all along—become visible. A chemical called *anthocyanin* produces the red spectrum in fall leaves, from rosy pink through screaming scarlet. It exists in the leaves all year long as a natural antioxidant to promote the health of the tree or shrub. When an especially chilly fall occurs—the cold is a bit more stressful—the plant produces a bit more of the anthocyanin, leading to more brilliant red tones that year. Yellow and bronze autumn foliage tones come from other chemicals, which also becomes visible in the absence of chlorophyll. One is carotene, creating the yellow-orange palette (as in carrots, where it is especially predominant).

All this beauty and its delight for us is only a by-product of necessary autumn changes in your tree and shrub foliage.

Now on with the planting suggestions!

> **The Real Dirt**
>
> If the fall color of your trees and shrubs isn't spectacular in a given year, this is rarely the fault of the plant. It's probably because the fall is too warm or too dry—or too windy (and the leaves just blew away too fast).

Planting for Berries in Your Zone

Here we offer good choices for each of the three broad zonal ranges, focusing on color and general attractiveness rather than who can eat the berries when. Eating from the backyard, though nice, is not a necessity, and that's why we're stressing beauty here instead of dinner!

Zones 2/3 and 4

This area of the United States is rich in berries. They tend to be small, but very tasty—to humans and to birds!

Shrubs

Blueberry (*Vaccinium*). Tiny white flowers with a tinge of pink followed by edible, blue berries. Lovely fall color, too. Try the *Augustifolium*, a low-bush variety, or the *Corymbosum*, the high-bush.

Bilberry, kamchatka (*Vaccinium praestans*). This dwarf variety has nicely edible blue berries after the bell-shape flowers and before the autumn color.

Currant (*Ribes alpinum*). The flowers of this medium-size shrub smell sweet, and the leaves are yellow for fall. In between are the reddish berries, not particularly edible.

Snowberry (*Symphoricarpos albus*). A small shrub with light green leaves, it blooms pinkish in the shade but produces more white berries if planted in full sun. Not particularly edible. The *Orbiculatus* variety has pinkish-purple berries.

Trees

Sand plum, also called beach plum (*Prunus maritima*). Enjoy these fruits, which, depending on the cultivar, are red, yellow, or purple. If you don't live near a beach but have a sunny site, try the wild plum (*Prunus americana*), which tastes fabulous in late summer.

> **The Real Dirt**
>
> Southern regions tend to have larger, showier flowers, while northern regions get most of the fall color.

Rocky Mountain cherry (*Prunus bessey*). Add enough sugar to the fruit, and you can have a nice jelly.

Black walnut (*Juglans nigra*). Wonderful for its wood (very valuable), but also sample its nuts after the first frost. (Remember that nuts are "fruits" in that they hold seeds.) They'll stain anything they touch—so crack them open carefully.

Zones 5 Through 8

Here are some very tasty—or at least decorative—ideas for those of you in these zones.

Shrubs

Cowberry (*Vaccinium vitis-idaea*). You'll need plenty of sweetener for the dark red berries after you enjoy the bell-shape flowers.

Raspberry (*Rubus crataegifolius*). A large shrub with small flowers, large leaves, and red berries.

Raspberry (*Rubus ichangesis*). Large and prickled to keep the wildlife away. (Not you!) The red berries taste especially nice.

Trees

Peach (*Prunus persica*). Georgia loves them, and so will you.

Persimmon (*Diospryros virginiana*). This very tall tree produces fruit that's bitter by itself but great when made into jams, breads, and puddings.

Red mulberry (*Morus rubra*). Female trees, as usual, bear the dark red and mildly sweet fruit. The fruit's preferred more by birds than by us, but it's definitely edible.

Zones 8 Through 11

Go tropical! You can probably plant these in Florida now, as well as in Hawaii.

Shrubs

Berry bush (*Vaccinium duclouxii*). A large shrub with white flowers, often tinged pink. The purple, almost black, berries are edible.

Chinese prickly ash (*Zanthoxylum schinifolium*). A medium-size shrub with yellow-toned flowers and inedible red berries.

Viburnum (*Viburnum cinnamomifolium*). Large shrub with white flowers. The blue-black berries are edible.

Skimmia (*Skimmia japonica* and *confusa*). Small and medium with inedible red berries, respectively, these shrubs have fragrant foliage—if they're male—and like the shade.

Trees

Breadfruit (*Artocarpus*). The fruit can weigh 10 pounds, although the part you eat (after you cook it) is only the inner pulp.

Candlenut (*Aleurites moluccana*). Tall, tropical tree with kukui nuts that taste a bit like macadamia nuts. Roast them (they aren't tasty raw).

Date palm, Canary Island (*Phoenix canariensis*). This medium-size palm that grows to about 50 feet, yields—you guessed it—plenty of dates!

Planting for Spring and Summer Foliage Colors in Your Zone

In this section, we tell you about some great choices for foliage plantings, those with yellow-, grayish-, and reddish/purplish-toned foliage. All can add interesting color accents to your yard through most of the year—much longer, usually, than the visual displays from either flowers in spring or foliage in autumn.

Sprouts _____

Note that shrubs with yellowish leaves feature more or stronger yellow when the shrub is grown in full sun, and a more lime-green color when planted in full shade. Somewhere in between these light extremes is not only more visually appealing but can be better for the shrub because many have a tendency to sunburn in the full, hot sun.

Zones 2/3 and 4

An array of color is available for northerly yards.

Yellow

Mockorange (*Philadelphus*). Light yellowish-green leaves.

Raspberry (*Rubus idaeus*). Although the fruit is rather scarce, it has bright yellow leaves.

Viburnum (*Opulus aureum*). Yellow if in full sun; light lime color if growing in full shade.

Weigela (*Weigela looymansil aurea*). Light yellow-green in the sun; a lime green when planted in full shade.

Gray

Dogwood (*Cornus alba* and *elegantissima*). Grayish-green leaves with creamy-white edges.

Potentilla, abbotswood silver (*Potentilla*). Grayish-green leaves edged in white.

Salt tree (*Halimodendron*). Both the stems and leaves are grayish.

Sea buckthorn (*Hippophae rhamnoides*). Narrow leaves in a dark, silvery gray.

Red and Purple

Eastern redbud (*Cercis canadensis*). Not noted for its flowering, it has plumy-purple leaves.

Purple-leaf sand cherry (*Prunus pumila*). Has purplish-copper leaves. One variety of it, even darker, is Minnesota Red.

Spirea (*Spiraea japonica* and *goldflame*). A small plant with a long growing season, its leaves are orangey-brown and then move to orange.

Weigela (*Weigela florida* and *foliis purpureis*). Its small leaves are a purple tone of gray-green.

Sprouts

Reddish tones are common with autumn changes, but this section features shrubs that are reddish, purplish, or even copperish in spring and summer. The color often moves toward green for summer, but later these plants also tend to feature nice autumn color.

Zones 5 Through 8

The middle zones of the United States probably have the most choices of all!

Yellow

Boxwood (*Buxus sempervirens aurea pendula*, *aureovariegata*, and *argentea*). Creamy-yellow variegated leaves. The second two varieties are also variegated, with areas of both yellow and creamy-white on the leaves.

Butterfly bush (*Buddleia davidii* and *harlequin*). Creamy-edged leaves.

Dogwood (*Cornus controversa*, *variegata*, and *mas*). Creamy turning to whitish. The mas variety has bright yellowish-green foliage.

Golden elder (*Sambucus nigra* and *aurea*). Yellow-tinted leaves become more yellow as the summer comes. Shade leads light green foliage.

Gray

Barberry (*Berberis temolaica*). Unusually in this family, it has grayish twigs and foliage.

Cotoneaster (*Cotoneaster horizontalis* and *variegatus*). Small leaves edged with white add up to a grayish look.

Euonymus (*Euonymus fortunei* and *silver queen*). Its leaves start as bright yellow and then turn to a grayish tone with creamy-white around the edges.

Lavendar (*Lavandula lanata* and *Richard grey*). Light-colored gray-greenish leaves fill out this small, fragrant shrub.

Red and Purple

Barberry (*Berberis ottawensis* and *superba*). Its purplish-copper leaves are quite shiny. Note that many of the barberries are somewhere in this color palette, too.

Sprouts

By now, you've probably noticed that varieties with *purpureum, purpureis,* and such words as part of their names tend to have purple-toned leaves.

Winter hazel (*Corylopsis sinensis* and *spring purple*). Related to the witch hazel, this shrub has coppery-purple leaves.

Southern bush-honeysuckle (*Diervilla sessifolia*). This small shrub similar to Weigela greets spring as a bronzed-yellow haze of leaves.

Flowering plum (*Prunus* x *blireana*). A lovely coppery-purple foliage.

Zones 9 Through 11

In this zone, summer and autumn are really a continuum, with leaf color not so differentiated between the two seasons.

Yellow

Euonymus (*Euonymus japonicus* and *ovatus aureus*). Large leaves with yellow around their edges. The Microphyllus and Macrophyllus Albus are nicely edged in more of a white.

Sprouts

Whenever you see *Aurea* or *Aureus* in the Latin name, the shrub is yellow-toned. Those labeled *Variegata* are—you guessed it—variegated.

Fatsia (*Fatsia japonica, aurea,* and *moseri*). Golden yellow, variegated leaves.

Fuchsia (*Fuchsia magellanica* and *variegata*). Creamy-bordered leaves.

Laurel (*Laurel nobilis* and *aurea*). Yellow, quite noticeable leaves.

Gray

Broom (*Cytisus battandieri*). Silvery, silky, and also hairy in parts, on a dramatic plant.

Hebe (*Hebe albicans*). Several varieties have grayish leaves, as do Carnosula and Colensoi.

Pittosporum (*Pittosporum tenufolium* and *irene patersun*). Grayish and greenish areas on leaves that are almost white.

Rock rose (*Cistus albidus*). Has a whitish down, almost a fur, covering its leaves and other body parts. Varieties Parviflorus, Purpureus, and Silver Pink have less dramatic but still pronounced gray or grayish-green hues.

Red and Purple

Pittosporum (*Pittosporum tenuifolium* and *garnetti*). Its leaves have white margins then tinge with pink. Autumn and winter bring even more reddish hues.

Pittosporum (*Pittosporum tenuifolium* and *purpureum*). Shiny copper-purple leaves for summer.

Rhododendron (*Rhododendron ponticum purpureum*). Compact and dark purple in foliage.

Salvia (*Salvia officinalis* and *tricolor*). Small, it packs a lot of leaf color, first purple and then some gray/white/pink on a more greenish purple.

Planting for Autumn Foliage Colors in Your Zone

Fall is a glorious season. Although shrubs can be absolutely beautiful in autumn, trees offer more color because they're bigger. But with both shrubs and trees, the northerly zone groups are the most spectacular (the opposite is true with the flowers, covered in Chapter 10).

Zones 2/3 and 4

Here, some homeowners prefer reds, yellows, oranges, or purples—or all of them! And of course, some shrubs can be an orangey-yellow or a reddish-orange, in a blaze of beauty that summons all the colors of an autumn campfire.

Shrubs

Serviceberry (*Amelanchier*). This family of large shrubs in yellow tones tends to flame well in general for fall.

Barberry (*Berberis koreana* and *crimson pygmy*). Red berries on these small red-toned plants set off their fall hues.

Chokeberry (*Aronia melanocarpa*). Similar to the serviceberry group, its black or purple berries show off its yellow-toned autumn leaves.

Burning bush (*Euonymus alatus*). Known for its unique fall leaf color, a burning magenta.

Trees

Ash (*Fraxinus*). Here, many varieties are fabulous for autumn. Green ash and red ash turn a golden yellow, while the autumn blaze ash is deeper.

Aspen (*Populus*). These trees, which spread by rhizomes and are so present in large groves, have their yellow fall color set off by their light bark. Birch also tends to turn a lemony yellow for autumn, with the exception of the Crimson Frost and Purple Rain varieties, which have been developed for red.

The Real Dirt

Except for the many varieties of oak, almost all which turn brown—with the nice exceptions of the pin oak and red oak, which flash red for fall and the white oak, which is more purply—the North tends to feature a great deal of yellow and yellow-orange, as well as some reds and some purples.

Autumn blaze maple (*Acer*). This relatively new variety joins other maples—the paperbark, Henryi, Norway maple, and red maple, to name a few—in blazing red-purple tones for fall. The Amur maple and sugar maple are more of an orange-red.

Honeylocust (*Gleditsia*). Hardy trees in many varieties for many places, they grow throughout the entire summer and create an open, delicate shade. The Moraine and Skyline are an especially lovely golden yellow in autumn (and the Moraine lacks both thorns and pods, the Skyline lacking the thorns).

Zones 5 Through 8

Rich autumn color is characteristic of these zones and can last a bit longer.

Shrubs

Barberry (*Berberis thunbergii*). The scarlet berries on this compact shrub set off bright its red leaves.

Smoketree, American (*Cotinus coggygria*). Dazzling (and both developed and named accordingly) with red toned-leaves and faint flowers that look like a puff of smoke. Also fast growing.

Wintercreeper (*Euonymus fortunei coloratus*). A richly colored small shrub with purplish leaves in fall.

Maple, Japanese (*Acer palmatum*). Literally hundreds of varieties have been developed from this shrub, all grown for their red/coppery/purple autumn colors.

Trees

Cherry trees (*Prunus*). From the Sargent's cherry and Japanese cherry varieties to the Kanzan (especially hardy), these trees are known for their spring blossoms. We could argue that they are just as beautiful in fall in their orange and red tones.

Elms (*Ulmus*). Examples for this zone include the European field elm, the Louis van Houtte (very tough), and the dwarf elm and Siberian elm (for the colder parts of this zonal range). Many varieties are being bred that are resistant to Dutch elm disease, and the latter one is especially unlikely to succumb. They feature yellow tones.

Maples (*Acer*). Many of those mentioned for zones 2/3 and 4 are lovely here in autumn, too. But we can also add the Trident, which blazes yellow/gold/orange, and the Snakebark variety, which does a scarlet red in honor of the season.

Tulip tree (*Liriodendron*). Also called the tulip poplar or the yellow poplar, these trees bear tulip-y flowers in spring and then shine in yellow and gold tones for fall.

Zones 9 Through 11

Here, fall is a matter of summer leaf colors that last! Because this zonal range doesn't have what many people would call winter, its trees don't focus on getting ready for it by draining energy away from leafing at any one time.

Shrubs

Hoheria (*Hoheria populnea purpurea* and *foliis purpureis*). Large shrubs, they retain the purplish tones of their underleaves well.

Heavenly bamboo (*nandina domestico purpurea*). This variety retains its purple-crimson leaves all year.

False holly (*Osmanthus heterophyllus* and *purpureus*). Looks like a holly shrub but with a leaf—and branch—color similar to a copper beech's red and purple tones.

Photinia (*Photinia fraseri* and *robusta*). Large and wide, it holds its red color through most of the year.

Trees

Angelica (*Angelica*). Although these can handle zones 10 and 11, they do have a tropical look to them. Try the Chinese Angelica or the Japanese Angelica tree. The flowers and leaves add a light-colored touch with their white tones.

Birches (*Betula*). Medium-size and quite tough, they like the sun but not too much heat. Try the yellow birch in higher elevation areas, the cherry or sweet birch, and the Monarch birch elsewhere. All have yellow/golden tones.

Sprouts

Be sure to check Appendix F for trees covered in other chapters of this book that also have the colorful autumn look you're after.

Pistachio, Mexican (*Pistacia chinensis*). Slow-growing with great nuts, the pistachio can adjust to a wide variety of moistures and soils. The orange-red fall color lasts longer than that of a lot of trees.

Smoke tree (*Cotinus obovatus* and *grace*). These are medium-size trees for the more northerly parts of this southerly zone range. They're plum-colored in summer and dress up for fall in scarlets, golds, and oranges.

The Least You Need to Know

- Fruiting is the next reproductive stage after flowering, and tree and shrub fruits can range in size from delicate berries up to husky coconuts.

- Colorful foliage for spring and summer is quite common among shrubs.

- Foliage for autumn offers many choices and could even be the focus of your entire yard.

Designing Your Yard

In This Chapter

- Features for your yard
- Ten key landscaping styles
- Making design decisions
- Creating your final landscaping plan and calendar

Get ready to have a little fun. In this chapter, we walk you through a new or redesign for part or all of your yard. If you haven't read Chapters 1 through 7, it's a good idea to do that. You need to know your geographic zone and how your yard areas stack up on such issues as moisture, wind, light, soil conditions, seasonal extremes, and more.

To help you get a jumpstart on your landscape design, it helps to start with a "wish list." Jot down a few of your favorite trees and shrubs, perhaps 5 to 20, that you've read about in earlier chapters; that you found in Appendix F; or that you've seen in your neighbor's yard, a park, your parents' yard, etc. Include a mix of deciduous and conifer, large and small. Consider first the trees and shrubs native to your area. These natives have had 10,000 years to adjust to climate conditions. They can go with the flow, and they usually aren't invasive (they won't just take over). You can add to and subtract from your wish list as you go and as you discover more trees and shrubs that will work well in your yard.

But before you start buying plants and digging holes, you have some thinking and planning to do first.

How Do You Use Your Yard?

A big part of landscape planning and design is use of the area. Think about your yard. Do you want a considerable part of it to be an all-flat expanse of treeless, shrubless grass, or do you want to fill in yard areas entirely? Somewhere in between? Do you have growing—or shrinking—numbers of children onsite? Will you be selling your home in 2 years or staying put for the next 30 years?

Grab a notepad to jot down what you and your family members think on the following subjects. Go out and sit in the yard if it helps!

Movement and Flow

How do you need to move throughout your yard? Note the way everyone goes to the outside fire pit or the patio. What route do you use to get the lawnmower between your house and the neighbor's? Keep these areas open.

Who's Up for a Game?

Do you want to create, or keep clear, enough room in your yard for sports? Think about how much room it takes for badminton, catch, croquet, or even an ice hockey rink!

If you decide to move some shrubs or flowers out of the way for a sport area, keep in mind that not all will survive that uprooting, but the shrubs are more likely to. If you haven't planted yet, remember to mark off an area that you'll keep clear of any and all trees and shrubs when you do plant.

The Living Is Easy ... and Outdoors

Do you want to create an outdoor room? If so, you're not alone, as outdoor rooms are quite popular these days. Some people make outdoor family rooms by setting off an area with shrubs and hedges, often anchored by some trees, benches, or an existing deck or patio. Within this "room" might be a grill, a bird bath, statues or rock collections from vacations, maybe even a hot tub.

Other families create a private space outdoors by walling off an area from the rest of the yard with fast-growing shrubs, rocks, or perhaps trellises for vines.

Sprouts _____

When combining trees and shrubs with nonplant objects, remember to avoid conflict. Does that sprinkler splash the bench when watering the shrubs? Is the grill too near to dry or otherwise flammable plantings? Is the doghouse too close to a delicate shrub?

"I'd Like Some Privacy, Please"

Do you want to use trees and shrubs to establish more privacy from your neighbors or from the street? If so, think about something such as a "wall" of shrubs, small trees, or even medium trees in sections of your yard. Fast-growing plantings are good for this.

You can use hedge screening for privacy.

Trees and shrubs are excellent at blocking noise, too. Noise rises, though, so you need more than just some medium-size shrubs if quiet is your goal. Go up about 5 or 6 feet higher, and you will hear the difference.

A Yard for All Seasons

Do you want a four-season yard or one primarily focused on one or two seasons? Do you want springtime blooms all over your yard? Winter berries? Note this on your wish list.

Green Living

Do you want a green yard? An environmentally green yard, we mean. If so, choose long-lived trees that will soak up carbon dioxide for years, if not centuries. And for savings on your electricity bill, too, try a group of dense, medium-size trees and shrubs to help block cold winter winds and/or a group of tall shade trees near your house to block summer heat.

The Real Dirt

For families fully committed to going green, we've included Appendix E, about planting enough trees to create a "carbon footprint," and Appendix C, a list of top native trees.

Also consider shrinking or minimizing grassy areas as much as possible to cut down on gas-powered lawn-mowing, herbicides, and other ungreen "temptations."

A variety of new plantings for birds and other wildlife is a plus, too. And you'll probably want to focus on natural objects, such as rocks, for any nonplant materials, perhaps even making a bench out of a dead tree. (But no Technicolor plastic gnomes!)

Do You Have Something to Hide?

Do you want to block an eyesore or minimize the impact of something in your yard that's less than ideal? Sure, you can take down dead or dying shrubs if they're the culprit. You can also make your driveway less dominant by building a low stone wall around it—a two-sided one with soil in the middle—and planting shrubs inside. Be sure you know how tall and wide a plant species will grow before you buy and either do all one species for a more unified look, or a medley of the same three for a unified variety, for example. Boxwoods provide a more tailored look, and for a more free-spirited look, try a spiraea that cascades a bit over the edges of the stone.

Sprouts

Use a variegated-foliage shrub, a bench, or another unique visual feature to draw the eye in the direction you want it to go, instead of toward a less-than-lovely view.

Do you need a tool shed but don't like the look? Mask it with yew trees, sunflowers, or whatever!

Thinking About Your Design

Design issues are a matter of taste, of course, but there are some useful general ideas to keep in mind. This section is meant to help you brainstorm, so jot down everything

you think as you read. And nothing you jot
down here is set in stone (or green, for that
matter), so relax and have some fun. We help
you narrow your own specific style after the
following sections.

The Real Dirt

When thinking about
your yard design or re-
design, remember that all your
work will likely increase the
resale value of your house, too!

Shape and Size

When planning your yard design, keep in mind the size and shape of the plants as
well as their total mass. If you have a small yard, don't plant one sequoia; if your yard
is large, don't choose 10 dwarf evergreen shrubs. Keep in mind the future size and
shape your trees and shrubs will be, too. That group of three new trees you planted
this summer might look pleasingly balanced staggered in height, all placed in front
of a garden wall or circling around a deck, but if they grow at different rates, next
summer they might be unbalanced. So think ahead about what's to come for your
plantings.

Start by looking out the window at each
part of your yard—front, back, maybe the
sides—preferably when the trees and shrubs
are leafed out. Do you see any crowded
areas? If so, plan to prune or move some
younger plants (they're more likely to survive). Do you see holes? Consider adding a
small grouping of three shrubs. Where do
you tend to look, and should you leave that
line of sight the way it is, or add or subtract?
Where do you tend to walk? Go with the

Root Rot

Columnar trees are like
arrows for the eye, so
think twice about where
you place them. If you plant
such trees at each corner of your
house, for example, people will
hardly see your house; their eyes
will be drawn up to your roof
and up into the sky instead.

flow and perhaps emphasize that stretch of yard by lining it with low plantings or
putting down mulch. Roll these kinds of questions around in your mind and bring
them out for discussion with your family for a few days.

Next, start with an easy project. Look around your yard. Do you see an awkward-
looking or unlovely shrub you might want to replace? Or does your eye land on a
medium-size blank space between two shrubs or two trees? What might you put
there? How big should it be when it's full grown?

The Real Dirt

> Maybe a little strategic pruning is all your unbalanced landscape needs to come back to a more pleasant look. (See Chapters 16 and 17 for more on pruning.) And if you don't want a tree or shrub to grow as fast, as high, or as broad as the tag says it will, keep it "on a diet" of *slightly* less sunshine than it's supposed to need. But remember that the sweet little Colorado spruce you put up against your window will eventually become *three times as tall as your house!* You can't completely overcome a tree's or shrub's genetics.

Now it's time for a preliminary visit or call to a nursery or store or a check of a plant catalog or website to find out what they have in that size. You shouldn't buy anything yet; just make a list of what might work in the space.

Next, consider a slightly harder project: one that involves *three* new plantings. Do you have a place for them in your yard now? Should you get rid of something else to make room for the new plantings? If so, how large should these new trees and shrubs be? If a larger tree or a garden shed sits near your targeted area, put a piece of masking tape or duct tape on it loosely, just to experiment with what heights might work for nearby plantings. By now, you should be getting the picture on size and shape.

Sprouts

When you create a definite grouping of trees and shrubs, in any combination, it's best to plant an uneven number such as 3 or 5.

If you can't think of a planting that you like for an area, try picturing a bench, a mulch path, or a section of low fence there instead. Low objects seem to bring the height of the plantings down, or at least provide one more smaller-scale object to accompany them. The objects should not be exactly the same height as any of the trees and shrubs, though. You can also achieve better balance by having a single large tree on one side of your yard and three smaller trees on the other side. In general, a variety of heights and widths among your trees and shrubs is desirable.

Color and Texture

This part is easier, and not because trees and shrubs are all the same color—green—because they aren't! When thinking of color, you simply want to avoid monotony. All evergreens or all deciduous trees or all shrubs in the same color range could add up to a boring yard—not always, but sometimes. And one of each of a number of plantings can look odd, too, because that's not the way nature does it. Trees are naturally sociable creatures, thriving when near fellows of their species (but not too close), as well as interspersed with other species with whom they get along.

When thinking about texture, think about more than evergreen versus deciduous—although variety here is certainly a good thing to think about. Texture can be based on shiny leaves versus flat tones. If you live in a climate where winters are cold, think about leaves *and* twigs. And obviously, some trees and shrubs are bushier than others. Texture interest can come from different barks also—think about a river birch, a sycamore, and crape myrtle.

> **The Real Dirt**
>
> Bet you didn't know: shrubs with purple or yellow leaves tend to grow slower than ones with green leaves.

Repetition, Repetition

You want variety in color and texture, but you also want to have your yard "hang together." You can do this by repeating color and/or shape, maybe having three or more lighter-green trees in various yard places, or several shrubs with naturally cascading branches. The key is to not have them all close together but to place them where the eye can travel from one to another. Of course, you aren't restricted to trees and shrubs here—islands of blue flowers can pull together a look, too, as can the same or similar ground cover around all your big trees.

Another way to establish a strong, unified look is by *connecting* areas of your yard with fencing, edging, paths (stone, mulch, whatever), patios, and so on. These don't have to be in straight lines—a curving mulch path, for example is not only very pleasant to the eye (and foot) but makes your yard seem bigger. Line it with low shrubs or perennials, perhaps. And softer shapes, in plantings or other objects, feel more relaxing, while sharper ones feel more alert. (More on this coming up.)

> **Root Rot**
>
> Don't make any repetition obvious—don't plant one mulberry tree in each corner or dark evergreen shrubs in a line. Your yard should repeat the way a theme does in a piece of music—something such as a melody appears and reappears but in interestingly different ways each time here and there.

Sound and Smell

Sound and smell are two areas you can play with to make your yard more pleasing. And because these aren't visual features, you don't really need to think about balance or unity in this area.

Do you want to create a fountain for its sound of running water, or buy an ash tree that will "sing" in the wind?

Smells can come from many trees; good choices are cedar, azalea, linden, catalpa, black locust, and mountain laurel. (Also see Chapter 10 and Appendix F for more fragrance ideas.)

Hardscaping in Your Landscaping

Hardscape items, those nongrowing elements of your landscape, can add tremendously to your landscaping. Hardscaping ranges from decks, patios, and fountains to outdoor umbrella tables, arches (on which to train vines, perhaps), statues, fire pits/fireplaces, small or giant electric or gas grills, outdoor lighting (solar ones are nice), stone walls, swings, sections of trellising, planters and pots of all compositions, even tree houses.

def•i•ni•tion

Hardscaping includes all those landscape features that are not biological.

A tree house is an example of hardscaping in your landscaping.

In general, many people overdo their hardscaping—more than one or a very few such objects can easily make your yard seem small and cluttered, especially in winter when the plants have died back to some degree and the hardscaping stands out.

Deciding on Your Style

You've pondered the uses of your yard and areas within it. You've thought about your favorite trees and shrubs. You've begun to think how they might work together to create a dynamic unity of size and shape, color and texture, and perhaps sound and smell in a way that uses repetition without creating boredom. You've probably been considering your budget—without us even mentioning it! And you've been thinking about some hardscaping, too.

Before launching into a sketched plan, though, you have one more thing to think about: your style. Maybe you've been planning a tailored landscape while your spouse has been craving the wild abandon of an old English cottage garden with shrubs everywhere. You can work this out!

Here are just a few examples, some for a whole yard (because they wouldn't go well with other styles) and some for limited areas:

> **The Real Dirt**
>
> To save time and money, try out a website that asks you what tree or shrub you're interested in and then tells you where it will thrive: your local university extension's website.

Xeriscaped   An all low-moisture or water-conservation garden for a dry climate. Plant cactuses, rock paths, and one nice stone sculpture.

English cottage   A profusion of plantings, cascading over each other with lots of wild blooms, variegated foliage, every feasible height level. Think wisteria vines, chrysanthemums, London plane trees, and Japanese cherry trees.

Water-focused   Low shrubs, stone terracing at different levels (for water falls) anchored by a few trees in the background, pump and plastic liner. Or if you live on water already, a native plant barrier of flowers and grasses to absorb the run-off of soils or any lawn chemicals from your yard before they get to the pond or canal, river or lake. Water lilies look nice on a small artificial pond, too.

Japanese garden   Dwarfed shrubs, rocks, sand, small pools, and bridges. Make it all formal and contemplative and consider buying a bonsai tree.

Woodland   All shade trees with ferns and native wildflowers and perennials underneath. This is a good landscaping idea if you already have the beginning of a very shady area. Bracken ferns and trillium are nice here.

Ornamental   Formal all the way to topiary, very tailored with straight gravel paths, clipped hedges, and so on. Boxwood is only one shrub that can be shaped in these ways.

And if you just want to work on *part* of your yard, try these:

Color theme   Try an all-white shrub and flower garden along the front sidewalk, purple-toned shrubs and pink flowers out back, or variegated shrubs that set off the color of your house.

Native garden Include only the native plants, shrubs, and flowers of your area.

Food garden Fruit trees anchoring an area of vegetables, edged with small herb plants (or go all out with a trout pond).

Ethnic garden Based on a book you find about Scandinavian gardens, Italian groves, or whatever you like, as long as the trees and shrubs fit your zone.

You could also try one of the whole-yard styles, but in a set-off area where it doesn't stylistically conflict with other areas.

Putting It All on Paper

Now it's time to take pencil to paper and draw your landscaping plan. First, finalize the list of the tree(s) and shrub(s) you'll be using in your design. Add any and all hardscaping elements that you plan to add.

Second, go outside and measure the dimensions of the yard area involved in your project. Outline that area, to scale, on graph paper, maybe one square on the paper for every square yard of yard. Now draw in the location of your driveway, shed, and any other permanent features. Make 5 to 10 copies of your plan. You're going to mess around with different locations for the new plantings!

Sprouts

If you're feeling ambitious when drawing your landscaping plan, you can even draw your house onto the plan and include lines for walkways among your yard areas.

For the next step, you can probably get your kids involved: cut out several small, medium, and large green circles for each new tree or shrub you *already* have. Make the little ones, about the size of one or two squares of graph paper, for the bushes; medium ones, two or three squares, for large bushes and medium-size trees; and larger ones four or five squares and up, depending on how much yard space they take up, for your big trees. Using another color, cut out circles for any hardscaping items already onsite, again creating several identical versions of the paper objects. Then cut out lighter or darker green circles for the *new* plantings and another color for any *new* hardscaping items.

Now place your existing and your new items on the graph paper. Look out at your yard and try to picture it actually looking the way you have it on paper. Move everything around as many times as you need to until you get it just right. You might want to take your top two or three final designs to each window that faces that area of yard. Try to picture what the new yard will look like from each vantage point. This might give you an idea of what to remove, if necessary, and help you narrow down the finalists. If the whole plan is still a bit hard to picture, take some sort of sticks out into the yard and put them in place for each separate design you're pondering.

The Real Dirt

For more elaborate planning beyond trees and shrubs—re-grading your yard; building walls, patios, fences, sheds, paths, gates, and other hardscaping features; installing an underground watering system; or adding flowers, vines, and groundcover plants—consult a good landscaping book or make an appointment to talk with a specialist at your local nursery or garden center.

Finally, be sure you know where your property line and any city right-of-ways are located before you finalize any plans! Your city probably also has a list of approved and/or forbidden trees for these areas—so check with them first, too.

Once you start making your yard more wonderful, it can be hard to stop, so be sure to plan, plan, plan—and save your pennies!

The Least You Need to Know

- Before you purchase or plant anything, think about the way you'll use your yard and your favorite landscaping styles.
- Trees and shrubs in groups of three, five, or another uneven number are especially pleasing.
- Shape and size, color and texture, even sound and smell, are top design considerations.
- Hardscaping can be a nice addition to your yard, but don't overdo it.

Chapter 13

Buying Trees and Shrubs

In This Chapter

- ◆ Personal preferences
- ◆ Large or small?
- ◆ Where to shop and buy
- ◆ Tree and shrub packaging

Are you ready to purchase your new trees and shrubs? You've come to the right place, because this is the chapter that goes with your credit card. In the following pages, we cover everything you need to know when buying your new plants. First, it adds some final preferences to consider before buying, followed by advice on what size to get to where to buy, including online sources. We also share tips on inspecting your plants before you hand over the money and the best times to plant.

A Few More Preferences

We've had you do a lot of thinking about your yard, your design, and some favorite trees and shrubs you've seen and would like in your yard, but you have just a bit more thinking you can do before you purchase your new plants (see Chapter 13 for more on purchasing).

Street Issues

How close to the street is your house and your planting area? If your yard has an area quite near the street where you'd like to plant a tree or shrub, read on:

◆ Shrubs are better to buy for this area because large trees have large roots and they may break into and plug a sewer line or bend a sidewalk, making it unsafe for walkers and bikers.

Root Rot _____

Placing a tree or shrub too close to the street might get you into real legal trouble and you may have to move the tree or shrub. See Chapter 13 for more on where to plant, including issues connected with permission to plant near the street.

◆ A plant may die slowly from road salt or because the roots aren't strong enough in this encounter with pavement, especially a large area such as a driveway's. So save your money.

◆ Both trees and larger shrubs can quickly grow to block street signs, conceal fire hydrants, interfere with utility lines and property, even drop tree limbs on the heads of passersby. Again, not a good way to use your credit card.

Allergens

If you or a family member has plant allergies, you'll want to figure these out before pulling out your wallet. If tree pollen is the problem, you might not want to add conifers or male trees because they reproduce by making their pollen airborne, carried by the wind to find the cone. And the bigger the plant, the more the pollen!

It might be better to plant smaller deciduous trees and shrubs—and on the leeward side of your house, opposite from prevailing winds.

Sprouts _____

If you prefer to grow grass and flowers under your trees, remember that they need light. Avoid buying trees with large, overlapping leaves, such as the mulberry, catalpa, and Norway maple. Choose instead "open" trees such as the honey locust, silk tree, or acacia.

Invasiveness

Trees that spread by rhizomes underground, such as the quaking aspen, black locust, and white poplar, as well as the Norway maple and certainly the buckthorn, can spread, creating an area of saplings and eventually a whole clump of trees in your yard. Some bushes, such as the creosote and sumac, do this, too. Maybe you welcome these extra (free!) trees; maybe you don't.

Other trees have invasive roots, invisibly taking over the underground areas around them. Willows and silver maples are known for this kind of interference. Don't choose them for areas near underground pipes or utility lines. Plant shrubs there instead.

Still other trees are invasive through no fault of their own. Not native to the United States, such trees have been introduced from elsewhere and with no natural enemies here to keep them in check, they go wild. For this reason, we recommend you buy native trees, which have found a reasonable role for themselves in the local ecology. You'll find fewer native shrubs because more cultivars have been developed for shrubs than for trees, but some of these work very well.

Sprouts

You might fall in love with a tree or shrub but can't find it in a store near you because it's not among the most popular species. Now what? Several months or even a year before your purchase/planting date, contact a local nursery, university arboretum, or native plant society. They may have been considering growing this plant from seed and might now do so if you ask. Or they may have seeds you can buy and start yourself.

Large, Small, or Somewhere in Between?

You considered the size of what your new trees and shrubs would grow into in the planning chapter (Chapter 12). Here, now, we're talking about the size of the new tree or shrub you're purchasing. Basically, you can buy a tree or shrub in a variety of sizes, either one as a seed in a pack, as a sapling, or as a mature plant. You can buy a "baby" pear tree or one that's already 4 feet tall. You can choose a sapling pine, a 6-footer, or a 20-foot, too-big-for-Christmas version ready to fill up your entire front yard. Prices vary accordingly, although *seedlings* are often *given* away or sold for almost nothing by public-minded groups such as the National Arbor Day Foundation.

Root Rot

If you happen to vacation in the rain forest or tropics, beware the strangler fig. One kind is the banyan tree, which begins as a vine, snakes its roots down the trunk of its "host," and can even drop other roots 90 feet or more through the air to the ground. Eventually, the root system strangles its host, hence the name. You don't want to mess with this plant, and you certainly don't want it in your yard.

Tiny trees, however, often die, whether you have a green thumb or not. Larger trees have shown that they can live for awhile, and no one is going to mow one down by mistake. Of course, large trees have issues, too. They're harder to plant, perhaps involving a couple hours of digging on your part or forking over major dollars to a nursery company with its tree-planting machinery. These trees need more watering and watching the first year as they adjust to their new home, too. They may not even be able to adapt, especially if they're top heavy from too much fertilizing at the nursery (see Chapters 14 and 18). But they sure do look a lot better!

The Real Dirt

> Jeanne met a guy at a party who had a sad tree story to tell: he loved oak trees and, about 5 years ago, planted a bur oak near his property line, which also happened to be near his neighbor's house. He watered the tree, mulched it, and fertilized it. The tree grew the way bur oaks do, and by its sixth year, it was scraping his neighbor's house so he had to dig it up. Unfortunately, it didn't survive the transplant.

Medium-size trees have some interesting psychological benefits. They seem to comfort us and even enhance creativity and mental health functioning in children. People recovering from surgery get better faster if they have a view of trees and shrubs outside their hospital window. Prison inmates who can see trees use fewer medical services. And they'll make you feel better, too!

A Look at Natives and Cultivars

In this book so far, we've emphasized the native species as good bets whenever possible. They've been growing successfully in your area for thousands of years, seeing weird winters, strange springs, droughty summers, etc. They aren't delicate "hothouse" plants. These trees each have *two* Latin names: *Quercus rubra* for red oak, *Quercus macrocarpa* for bur oak, and so on.

Cultivars of native trees can be excellent choices, too, and you should be able to buy your regions' cultivars locally. Some native trees have had no cultivars developed from them; others more than 100. Fruit trees and those noted for beautiful flowers or foliage tend to have the most cultivars. Cultivars are especially numerous among shrubs. Cultivars have *three* Latin names on their labels. The first word is the genus name and then on down to the name of the cultivar itself.

Cultivars differ a great deal. One may have red flowers instead of white flowers, another may be more resistant to one of the native tree's characteristic insect invaders, yet another may be twice—or half—as tall. These cultivars have been developed by grafting the roots of one tree with the trunk of another. Cultivars aren't exactly the same tree as the native tree from which they were bred, so be sure you know that a given cultivar has the features you want. Or buy the native if it's available.

Introduced trees and shrubs can be fine, too, provided they aren't invasive. Some were brought to this country by early settlers, and the ones that have survived since then are good bets. Some may be more delicate but serve a special purpose—think about the Japanese cherry trees in Washington, D.C. Some came over on their own, courtesy of birds and their droppings, floating (something such as a coconut with seed), or hitchhiking as seeds on a ship or plane.

Where to Shop for Trees and Shrubs

You have lots of choices of where to buy your new trees and shrubs, from catalogs to garden stores, plant societies to big box stores, tree consultant companies to online vendors.

Catalogs

If you're like us, plant catalogs often fill your mailbox and e-mail inbox, even during the winter. Many are careful about describing which trees and shrubs fit with which zones. Some aren't so careful—or they simply want to dazzle you with blooms you *wish* could grow in your yard. Catalogs vary a lot price wise. See Appendix B for some of our favorites.

Garden Stores

More good places to check out are the small, medium, or large all-garden stores in your area. These are as good as the people who own them. These stores tend to offer lots of advice at their help desk, by phone, in handouts, and among the plants for sale. They're sometimes more expensive, but you more often get better service and information.

The Real Dirt _____

Smaller garden stores sometimes specialize in one kind of plant, offering many cultivars. They usually sell all flowering plants, or all hostas, and the like.

Plant Societies

Plant societies are another good place to buy. These include groups such as nonprofit plant societies, local/regional/national garden clubs, university arboretums, botanical gardens, etc. They often have a great deal of local information available and run annual or semi-annual plant sales. Prices and quality tend to be especially good because these plantings have been a labor of love and an outlet for creativity. You can also find trees and shrubs beyond the typical.

> **The Real Dirt** _____
>
> Trees and shrubs make nice memorials. Planting a tree or shrub in your yard can be a nice way to commemorate someone you love who has died or honor the birth of a little one. Or a volunteer group you're associated with could plant a few in a city park in honor of civic-minded citizens. In both cases, you could even make or buy a plaque with the dates (but don't tie it around the trunk because that could kill it).

Large Retailers

Big box stores, from The Home Depot and Lowe's to whatever is near you, are other good tree and shrub avenues. These stores generally have a good number of the most popular tree and shrub choices, and the prices are often excellent.

It's possible that the real price of trees at a big box is about one-third higher than what shows up on your receipt because about a third of them will die, at least in Jeannie's experience. Shopping here can be worth it if you know exactly what you want, what to do with it, and have no questions to ask the employees. And that one-third more expensive might still be cheaper than other sources ….

Tree Consultants

We like tree consultant companies because Josh works for one! These are the companies you call to prune a large, high, dangerous dead branch off your long-time oak tree, or to tell you what's wrong with that weird-looking maple. They also really know their trees and shrubs and can give you some good advice on a few things you might plant to replace something that's dying or dead. They will also plant your new tree or shrub for a fee.

Online

Of course, it's always convenient to check online sources. As long as you know your zip code (not hard!) and what you want to plant (easier now that you've read this far in the book), you can just plug in the information and find what you're looking for. (See Appendix B for some of our favorite e-places.)

Tree and Shrub "Packaging"

Who- or wherever you buy from, you'll find the tree or shrub somehow rooted and packaged for sale. Usually, it's in either a container or balled in burlap. Sometimes it comes as bare roots (with the tree attached). Each packaging method requires a little different treatment.

Containers

The containers, generally dark plastic pots, come in various sizes, and the plants therein are often priced according to the size of the pot. Plants can live quite a while like this if given light and moisture and their roots are kept cool, so you can usually find containers available over a longer season.

Container trees may be especially thirsty when you plant them because they might have been a bit overfertilized before they came to you. Smaller trees tend to recover faster from this kind of stress than larger ones do.

Balled or Bagged

Balled-in-burlap trees' roots have been able to "stretch" out a bit more without the sides of that plastic container in the way. These trees and shrubs should be planted before spring (any time when the ground isn't frozen).

Fabric bags aren't common, but you might see them. These porous bags were planted right with the tree, either above or below ground. They easily allow water to reach the roots and the roots to expand as though the bag weren't there because they can poke right through it. Trees sold this way have been able to breathe and expand a bit better, too, so they might have more of the smaller absorbing roots intact.

Root Rot

When planting balled or bagged trees, don't let the whole root system get damaged or even fall apart when you remove the metal container.

Bare Roots

Sometimes trees and shrubs are sold with bare roots, although this is a relatively uncommon way for them to be sold. You might see this if you buy them (or get them free) through a nonprofit group that got them at little or no cost. You might also see this if you purchased quite a few plants at a time and got professional help planting them. Found via the garden store nurseries, these trees and shrubs come right from the field and are to be planted fairly quickly, within a few days or a week or so. What these trees and shrubs lack in convenience, they make up for in cheaper prices.

> **Sprouts**
>
> Planting techniques for your new tree or shrub varies a bit, depending on whether it came in a container, balled-in-burlap, or as bare root stock. These are detailed in Chapter 14.

Believe it or not, bare root trees do fine. They don't have to adjust to two different soils, after all—both that new soil in your yard and the old soil they were packed in. There wasn't any of the latter, after all. Also, they haven't experienced any damage to their finer roots by being pulled out, or cut out, of any container. And they are lightweight and easy to handle.

"I'll Take *That* One!"

Before you carry your tree or shrub to the cash register, take a few moments to inspect your potential new tree. A few easy checks now might save you coming back next year to replace your now-dead tree or shrub.

First, check for moss growing on the soil. You don't want to see any because that indicates that the tree or shrub has been in the pot too long.

Next, the roots. Roots are perhaps the trickiest to diagnose, but they're also the most important. You won't be able to see everything, but carefully take hold of the trunk where it meets the soil and pull up slightly. Everything should hold together inside the container while it rises about 1 or 2 inches off the ground. When the tree and soil, together, do leave the container, be sure the root ball isn't girdled. Also look to see that the main roots aren't in kinks, with, say, 90-degree turns. And be sure the main, large roots are within about 1 inch of the soil's surface.

> **def•i•ni•tion**
>
> **Pot bound** or **root bound** refers to a tree or shrub whose roots look all mashed together similar to a huge meeting of white threads. They may straighten out fine, but the tree or shrub has been stressed.

Don't worry if the smaller roots look shoved in a bit—that's inevitable. In fact, you should be able to see a lot of these little white roots, similar to threads. You should see about the same number of them all around the root ball, and the tree shouldn't look *pot bound* or *root bound*. If you do see such roots, quickly and carefully put the plant back in the pot because it is alive! Trees are much cheaper in the fall. Be sure you get a healthy one and laugh all the way to the bank!

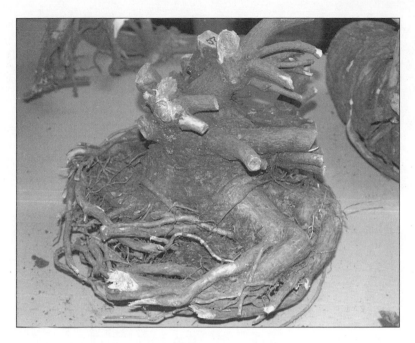

Pot-bound roots are confining and restrict the tree's growth.

(Sample courtesy of Gary Johnson and Dave Hanson)

The Least You Need to Know

◆ What are your preferences for tree "litter," street proximity, allergens, and invasiveness? Decide before you finalize your plan.

◆ Remember to keep tree or shrub size in mind when planning. You don't want a large plant near a street, sidewalk, driveway, utility pole, or neighbor's property.

◆ Native trees are less-often invasive nuisances, and some cultivars and trees introduced from elsewhere can be fine in this regard, too.

◆ It's easier to do a quick but important pre-buy check whether the tree is in a container or comes as a bare root.

Chapter 14

Planting Tips

In This Chapter

- ◆ Discover the best time to plant
- ◆ Planting trees and shrubs like a pro
- ◆ Preparing the soil, the tree, and the hole
- ◆ Hole-digging tips and what to do after the tree's in the hole

Congratulations! You've made it through all the important preliminary planning stages and you've bought the perfect new tree or shrub for your yard. Whether you've chosen one new planting or a dozen, it's almost time for your shovel to hit the dirt.

We said *almost*. Before you start digging, we need to cover a few key techniques and tips to ensure the most successful future possible for your yard companion(s), including when to plant and where to plant your new tree or shrub in your yard; preparing the hole; properly filling in the soil around the plant; and the initial watering, mulching, and dealing with any grass and weeds in the area. We cover transplanting in this chapter, too, so you can make a new plant part of your yard as trauma-free as possible.

When to Plant

When the first warm weather hits in the spring, garden shops and big box stores fill their nursery sections with tons of flowers, trees, and shrubs, and that's when many people buy and plant them. And that's fine, but you can plant a tree or shrub in any season except for winter (in the northern states).

Planting in the spring is more fun, in our opinion. The birds and the bees, fresh air, tra-la-la, and all that. This is when you want to plant shrubs that flower. If you plant in the spring, though, you'll probably need to water your new tree or shrub quite often. (See more on watering in Chapter 15.)

Fall is great for planting trees, too. The tree knows it doesn't need to provide nutrients to its leaves in autumn and doesn't need to really grow at all aboveground. (Roots continue to grow all year long.) Also, you don't need to water a fall-planted tree as often—nice for all of us who have plenty of other things to do!

Readying the Soil

It's best to start soil preparation where your new tree will be planted about 30 to 90 days before the plant date. But don't worry if you didn't do that, especially if you have average soil, some recent rainfall, and have chosen trees and shrubs that aren't soil-picky. (Check Appendix F for some nonpicky plantings.)

Before you do anything, especially digging, call your utility company to find out where any electric, gas, phone, or water lines and pipes run under your yard. Some run parallel to the street and some run from your house out to the street.

 Root Rot _____

Just adding soil as a new top layer without mixing the layers (such as ladling some potting mix on) doesn't really help—tree roots and even shrub roots go down deeper than this. And the loose material might wash away in the next rain.

Removing and Adding

If you do have some lead time, it's a good idea to remove the grass layer in the immediate area and then, using a shovel or hoe, break up the soil about 1 foot down into the ground where the hole will eventually be dug. Cut in some organic mulch, using at least half as much mulch as the soil you'll be removing when you dig the hole. Work it in, mixing the soils together very well. (For more on mulching, see Chapter 18.)

A Helping Hand

No matter how careful you are—and also how careful the people at your plant store were—trees and shrubs always experience some root damage or even death when they're moved or planted. They need this little bit of help from you!

But you're not finished yet! Here are a few other things to consider:

If you think you need to raise the pH of your soil for your new planting (based on testing along the lines of information from the soil chapter), work in some fallen pine needles (from a neighboring park or woods, perhaps, or a chemical equivalent discussed in the mulching sections of Chapter 18) and mix well. Repeat the process as often as you can for at least several years in order to see results, mixing the material outward from the base of the tree.

If you need to improve drainage for your new tree or shrub, fill in the low area with mulch and dirt to raise it up. Be sure to mix well.

Also, pull up all competing weeds (roots and all) in the area where you plan on planting.

If the spot in your yard where you've chosen to plant your new tree or shrub needs improvement but none of the earlier recommendations are feasible, your best bet is to choose a different part of your yard to plant in. The same is true if your preplant activities hit an area that you just can't dig through at all, be it a large rock or just an impermeable soil layer, perhaps of clay. If that's not a good reason to plan ahead when you design your landscape, we don't know what is!

 The Real Dirt

The best season for planting trees is fall (if you live in a four-season area) because that's when plants are programmed to build their root systems (unlike in spring and summer when they use their energy to grow above ground). The soil is warmer and trees are usually cheaper in the fall, too.

Readying the Plant

Okay, now that your soil is in good shape, let's look at your new plant. The process of preparing your new tree or shrub for planting differs, depending on what form it's in (see Chapter 13). But in all cases, water your new tree or shrub right after planting it.

Root Rot

Avoid planting trees and shrubs from seed, or even from cuttings, unless you're pretty good at gardening in general. It's hard to know what the plant will look like, genetically speaking, when it grows. And tiny plants are too easily wrecked by lawnmowers, dogs, or kids.

Container Plants

Before planting a container tree or shrub, lay it on its side and gently shake and tug on the container—not the plant—to remove it. If the roots are in a tight spiral, loosen and separate them by hand if possible. If this doesn't work, use a knife to slice partway into the small outer roots to relax the circling. Also, make a small criss-cross cut across the whole bottom of the root ball to sever the nested roots there. If done in moderation, this cutting actually stimulates the roots to grow better after the tree or shrub is planted.

Balled or Bagged Plants

For a balled or burlapped tree or shrub (only the larger ones tend to be available this way), eventually you'll use scissors or a knife to carefully remove the twine, burlap, and any wire basketing around the root ball, without letting the root ball crumble. But before you remove the wrapping, you need to dig the hole to the right depth first. If you think the root ball might fall apart, you can leave the burlap partly held around it spread open; you can "plant" this material along with the tree or shrub because it's biodegradable.

Bare Root Plants

Keep bare root trees in their wrapping and in a cool place up until the time of planting, preferably not more than two days. Then prune away any dead branches as well as any branch or root that appears to be diseased. Use a misting hose or just sprinkles of water to keep the roots moist, but not wet, during the pruning. After any pruning, soak the roots—not the whole tree—in a bucket of water for up to 12 hours.

Be especially careful handling and caring for bare root plantings; they've already lost some of their root system.

Digging the Hole

You might think that anyone with a shovel or spade can dig a hole, but it isn't quite that simple. You'll need a yardstick or tape measure along with a pen and piece of paper and maybe a piece of masking tape (you'll use this to mark measurements on the shovel you're using). Keep your new tree or shrub in the shade, especially its root ball, during this process.

Taking Measure

Before you dig, you need to take some measurements. Begin by finding the *soil line*, the place on your new tree or shrub where the trunk met the surface of the soil before you unpacked it. Measure the distance between this line and the top of the place where the roots spread out (called the *root flare*), as you spread the roots out a bit like a skirt around the trunk. Write down that measurement. Now look at the roots and measure how wide they are in extent and record that measurement. Now you have the two magic numbers that indicate the depth and width you need to dig the hole. This way, you don't have to stop and measure the hole every time, you can mark the measures on your shovel with masking tape.

Measuring for the correct planting width (left) and depth (right). Note the masking tape on the shovel handle.

Now you're ready for the tree to hit the dirt, right? Not quite. Before digging the hole, shovel or spade up a few inches of the top soil. Go below the grass roots, if grass is present. If the soil is predominantly clay or otherwise compacted, dig a hole a couple inches shallower than your soil line number but a bit wider than the width of the roots (you might want to jot this down) so the roots can spread out in the less-compacted top soil layer.

The overall dimensions of the hole need to vary slightly depending on whether your new plant was bought as bare root, containered, or balled and burlapped.

If it's a container plant, the depth of the hole needs to be the root line and its width at least twice the width of the container it came in. The root flare point should also end up being 1 or 2 inches above the surface when it is planted. Again, plan ahead. If you dig too deeply, you'll just have to refill and tamp down.

The Real Dirt _____

> A common cause of death in newly planted trees and shrubs is being planted too deeply. It's like burying them alive! You'll soon see that even the roots should be a bit above the surface to keep water from pooling around them. Don't worry, they'll settle in. And the width of the hole is just as important as the depth. You don't want to strangle the roots or give them the huge task of pushing through solid dirt on their very first day in your yard.

If it's a balled-and-burlapped tree or shrub, it's planted more shallowly. About one-sixth of the soil ball should end up being above the surface. The width of the hole should be 2 or 3 inches wider than the extent of the roots in their still somewhat curled-up state. The depth allows more oxygen to reach the roots, which is best in this case.

If it's a bare root tree or shrub, it will be planted very close to the level where it was growing (the soil line on the little trunk) and with the root flare an inch above the surface in the new hole. The hole should be about the width of the root system. With bare root plants, the holes tend to be shallower and wider than for container or balled-and-burlapped plants. You can also flare the roots around a small mound in the middle of the hole. Plan before you dig!

Taking Shovel to Soil

Check your notes, know your measurements, and then grab your shovel or spade. Dig down gradually, measuring both depth and width every so often. While you work, keep these things in mind:

The new tree or shrub will settle down into the hole after it's planted, so the hole doesn't have to be quite as deep as it otherwise would need to be. The hole should not narrow as it becomes deeper, though—in fact, it should be a bit wider at the bottom than at the top, sort of bowl-shaped. Again, this helps the roots. When you've finished digging, roughen up the sides of the hole so they don't look like solid, smooth walls of dirt, which would make the roots have to work to get through it when they're already a bit stressed by the planting.

Don't add anything now to the hole such as mulch or fertilizers or other soils. You don't want to alter the soil this fast because your new tree already has two new soil situations to contend with immediately—the soil around its roots when you bought it and the soil of your yard.

Use your garden tool or your feet to slightly solidify the soil at the bottom of the hole so water doesn't drain out too fast. Now, also for root health, and especially for bare root trees, make that small mound or cone of soil at the bottom of your perfectly measured hole. The bottom roots can then flare out around this dirt.

Next, create a little ridge in a circle about 2 or 3 feet out from the center of the hole in all directions. This makes a little blockade to keep moisture and mulch securely near the tree, but not up against the trunk.

Sprouts

If your new young tree has smooth bark and you live in an area that has cold winters, but with occasionally warm afternoon sunshine and hungry deer and rabbits, you might want to wrap its trunk for its first winter. Be sure it's loose enough to allow air in but tight enough to keep out water. Try corrugated white drain piping, which reflects the sun. (For more on combating deer, rabbits, and other wildlife, see Chapter 23.)

To Stake or Not to Stake?

Staking is a controversial subject among arborists, but in general, we don't believe you should use stakes to stabilize your new tree. It's useful mainly for trees planted as bare root and in an open, windy area, and even then, the stakes should not be left on for more than a few months, preferably less. Stakes are kind of like casts for a broken arm—they support the structure but also weaken it by taking over that job!

However, if your soil is sandy, the wind is stiff, or vandals are active near the location of your new tree, you might need to stake it for a few weeks until the roots are firmly established. This is especially true if the new tree is substantial in girth compared to the size of its root mass. If you decide to do this, use two stakes, well spaced around the tree, and get some professional advice. And don't forget to dismantle the staking system as quickly as possible. A few weeks, perhaps.

Using *guy wires* to prop up your new tree is potentially even more damaging to it, no matter what size the tree. The wires cut into the bark and trunk, even when covered with protective material. If you think you need to prop up the plant, you might want to hire a professional who can install compression springs. Regardless, remove the system as soon as possible, at least after several months.

If you have to do *something* to keep your new tree or shrub from tipping over, you have a couple options: you could prune off a few branches to reduce the aboveground weight of the tree. (Please check Chapters 16 and 17 first!) Or you could use 2 or 3 short fence

def•i•ni•tion

Guy wires are metal wires extending out from the tree trunk like spokes that are anchored to short stakes buried in the ground.

stakes, each maybe 4 to 6 inches tall and an inch or so thick. Position them 4 or 5 feet away from the tree, the first one on the side where the predominant wind hits

Root Rot _____

Don't use fishing line or wiring of any kind on your tree, even if it's rather loosely looped. Wind could move it enough that it cuts into the bark. Ouch!

the trunk and the other(s) on opposite sides so they aren't significantly shading the trunk. Pound them securely into the ground so only 2 or 3 inches of stake is visible above ground. Use fabric or nursery grade webbing around stakes and trunk, _loosely_ tying the line to the tree about 6 inches below the point where the tree bounces back in your hand when you grab the trunk. The tree should still be able to blow in the wind.

It's Time to Plant!

Yes, it's finally almost time to plant your tree or shrub! Before placing the tree or shrub into the hole, though, get ready for your tasks _after_ the planting. Be sure your garden hose or sprinkler is out and attached to its water source.

1. Insert Tree in Hole

Set your new tree or shrub gently in the hole, and check to be sure it rides high enough (as described earlier in the chapter). If your soil is so sandy that the tree wobbles, add soil a bit above this level. If not, remove it, fill back in, and tamp down some dirt. Place the tree or shrub back in the hole, making sure it's oriented in an eye-pleasing way, spreading out the roots slightly around your little dirt mound inside the hole and removing any girdling roots. If it settles down too low, pull it up and add more dirt to the bottom of the hole.

Sprouts _____

Don't fertilize new trees or shrubs until they've been in your yard for one year. They will have already been fertilized sufficiently at the nursery or garden store you bought them from. The plants will grow vigorously, anyway—first mostly below the surface. If you can't resist a little fertilizing, use a bit of a low-nitrogen product and a dash of vitamin B_1!

Pruning encircling roots is easy to do and increases your tree's chances of survival.

potential girdling root pruned before planting

2. Fill Hole

With your new tree or shrub in the hole, now it's time to fill the hole. First fill it with water and then let it drain. Next, use the same soil you dug up to backfill the hole around the plant, loosening it if necessary so it isn't in large clods, and gradually shovel it in on all sides. When it's about one-third of the way up, tamp it down slightly with the blade of your shovel or your foot to gently remove the excess air in the soil.

Continue tamping down the soil in stages, adding a small amount of water in the outer circle of the hole each time, until the soil layer is at the correct level. If the plant is settling too low, gently grab the trunk and pull it all up a little (this only works if the difference is small). Be careful not to hit the roots or allow the trunk to lean to one side or another when you tamp down the dirt. Now check the ridge blockade you made to be sure it's intact.

The Real Dirt
About now, a neighbor might stop over with some unsolicited advice and tell you that you should place sand or gravel at the bottom of your planting hole. Smile—but don't do it! Instead of improving drainage, this "old guys' tale" actually directs too much water away from the roots.

Next, mulch. Leave a 3-inch circle completely bare right around the trunk (that keeps it from rotting). Spread the mulch everywhere else to a depth of about 2 or 3 inches. The mulch can be any organic material from wood chips to leaf litter, even gravel in this aboveground location. But do not use peat because it becomes too easily water-logged. (See Chapter 18 for more on mulching.)

3. Water

The key with water is not to overdo it, as most people do. Too much moisture can rot the plant or, short of that, make it unstable. Think about having to balance on squishy soil yourself, and you'll understand. Mulch helps retain the moisture, allowing it to drip down toward the roots slowly and thoroughly.

But how much water should you give your new tree or shrub? Of course, this depends on how much it's rained lately! Water enough to make the soil feel damp but not wet when you stick a finger in it. After watering, tamp down the top layer of mulch around the tree slightly to eliminate any remaining air pockets.

Root Rot

If you have an automatic watering system, don't use it with any new trees and shrubs planted in heavy clay soils. And don't position any water source near the trunk—a few inches out, or even a foot, is good.

After the first day, check twice a week before watering again. Burrow your hand down through the mulch and through the first few inches of soil. Water again only if all these layers are dry. If it is fall, you might only need to water a couple more times before the ground begins to freeze. (At that point, it doesn't do any good anyway.) If it's spring, rainfall might do the job for you, at least some of the time. Just keep up the weekly checks for several months.

4. Keep It Clean

Your next and final step is a grass and weed check. Dig up anything that's trying to grow back under your tree up through the mulch. Although grass might seem like a trivial thing, your young tree or shrub will grow much better if nothing else grows within 12 inches of its trunk. The grass's roots could actually interfere, or at least compete. And the lawnmowers and weed whackers used to control the grass are even worse for the tree. Shrubs are usually better at covering their territories.

The Least You Need to Know

- Being shoved into a new place is actually hard for a young plant.
- Planting methods vary depending on how your tree or shrub came "packaged" from the store.
- Measure and then dig to avoid planting your new tree or shrub in a hole too deep but not wide enough.
- Staking your new tree or shrub usually isn't a good idea.

Part 3

Tree and Shrub Maintenance

In Part 3, we tell you how to keep your new trees and shrubs alive and healthy through their life cycle. You'll read about watering tips, pruning advice that will enhance your courage and success in this department, and info on mulching and fertilizing in the best ways for your plants. We even offer advice on end-of-life issues for your trees and shrubs.

"Woody? You awake? I had another nightmare about the electric trimmer."

Chapter 15

Cool, Clear Water

In This Chapter

- ◆ It's simple: plants need water
- ◆ How much water and when?
- ◆ Tools and techniques
- ◆ Wind? Drought? No problem
- ◆ Water-conservation tips

Except in special circumstances (to be described in upcoming pages), well-established, mature trees that are growing well in your yard don't need to be watered much if at all. Nature takes care of it for you. Young trees, shrubs, and plants under special circumstances do need water, however. In this chapter, we *hydrate* you with information on proper watering—how much, when, for how long, etc.

And if you haven't already, we recommend you read Chapter 18 in tandem with this chapter because the subjects are so closely related. Don't see how? You will.

Why Water?

Water is a primary component of your trees' and shrubs' "bodies," just as it is in your body. Your plants constantly process water, drawing it from the soil through their roots, trunk, leaves, and branches and then exhaling it into the atmosphere where it comes down again as rain or other precipitation.

Trees and shrubs need water to conduct photosynthesis, which, as you learned in Chapter 2, creates their food and cools their bodies. Water helps transport nutrients around their roots, trunk, branches, and leaves. And they need it for their root tips and buds to swell, necessary in their growth process. Needless to say, your plants love a rainy day!

The Real Dirt

Trees and shrubs use so much water that they run a deficit nearly every day and replenish their supply every night.

Too much water can kill your plants, though. Excess water interferes with their breathing through their pores (stomata) in their leaves and can overwhelm the oxygen they need to pull from the soil through their roots—all the little pockets of air get flooded with water. And if the water doesn't drain well through the soil, your plants can be damaged by excess fungal growth and buildup of salinity. (Water has natural salts in it, to some degree.) Too much moisture can also erode or even compact the soil in your yard, attract insects such as mosquitoes, and lead to the arrival of "pioneers"—trees that grow where you didn't plant them and don't want them.

Mature trees, long inhabitants of your yard, often get plenty of water without you dragging out a hose, and most can endure a couple weeks or even months of drought by drawing on their own considerable water storage capacity, closing their stomata, and pulling in more moisture from the soil. Older plants require water only during severe droughts and during prolonged high wind conditions, which can really dry out a plant's leaves.

The Real Dirt

Some mature trees survive drastic circumstances such as droughts and excessive winds by dropping all their leaves. They often regrow next spring but, in the meantime, the tree looks alarming and unattractive on an otherwise lovely summer day. All this stress does weaken the tree.

Younger trees and shrubs, particularly newly planted ones, need some help filling their water needs. Not only are they growing much faster, but they also lack the canopy that keeps their surrounding soil from drying out.

In general, trees with larger leaves and those with broader crowns tend to need more water. Those with thickly waxy and hairy leaves can get by with less because the coverings tend to keep the water from evaporating.

What's Soil Got to Do with It?

Plenty. By volume, soil is about half air and water and about half solid material. If your soil has a good balance of textures from fine to coarse, it will drain well and hold moisture well. Your new trees and shrubs can never use more than about half the water the soil holds, though, because some of it clings *too* hard to the soil particles and some of it drips down too deep. A deeper soil and a more extensive root system, one not interrupted by sidewalks, streets, or even your house, is better at the kind of drainage that works well for your plants.

Trees and shrubs have problems getting water when the soil is too compacted. Construction equipment can easily compact the soil around their roots so severely that the air and water pockets are collapsed—smashed into the soil. Arborists call this "bulldozer blight." Root systems of mature trees extend about two or three times farther out than the size of their canopies, with younger trees and shrubs much more restricted. So you need to keep that heavy machinery quite far away from your plants.

Root Rot

Trees can't grow in pots outside during a cold winter because the pots don't provide enough drainage. What moisture there is evaporates quickly right out of the soil. Gravel in the bottom only makes things worse—their roots just freeze to death.

Sprouts

Your plants need *more* water if your soil is cracked. And if you can squeeze water from a handful of soil, if you see standing water on the soil, or if algae (or any kind of scummy-looking stuff) appears on the surface, you need less—let it dry out!

Watering 101

Before you plunk down a hose or waterdrip and let 'er rip, stop and read this section first. How much you should water—when the rain isn't enough—depends on several factors:

- The age of your trees and shrubs
- The size of their roots and canopies
- How hot and/or dry it is
- How your soil drains in the immediate area of a given planting
- Rainfall

Root Rot _____

If a tree or shrub wilts completely, no amount of water can bring it back! Arborists call it the *permanent wilting point*. You can call it dead.

Your trees and shrubs also need much more water in the growing season than they do in fall and winter, when the soil is less absorbent. And on sunny days and windy days, a great deal of water evaporates before it sinks into the soil. Cloudy, calm days are a good "rest" for the plumbing of your plants.

Where Do I Aim the Sprinkler/Hose/Waterdrip?

Young trees and shrubs—those planted in the last 1 to 2 years—need an *average* of 5 to 7 gallons all at once every 4 to 7 days, applied where it will reach the root ball. No, you don't have to drag a 5-gallon bucket to each of your plantings; that's not the best delivery method anyway. A sprinkler or waterdrip works fine, and here's a trick for ensuring your plant gets enough water: set a can or bowl near your plant where the sprinkler will hit it; 5 to 7 gallons is about the equivalent of an inch of water in the can. The water should drip or trickle into the ground slowly, which is why waterdrips work so well.

Sprouts _____

When using a sprinkler to water your tree or shrub, be sure the water doesn't hit the trunk or leaves, where it could encourage fungal rot and bacteria invasion.

Older trees and well-established shrubs need more water but less frequently, and rain can be enough to satisfy them. If you do need to help out, about 1 or 2 inches per week should be enough. A few cautions, though: don't water close to the root ball because their root tips aren't anywhere near there anymore. Be sure that any mulch around your trees doesn't touch the trunk because rotting mulch can rot the trunk. And don't let water get into your tree's cavity if it has this kind of open area at ground level. The water should seep into the outer area of the tree's or shrub's *dripline*. And don't give your trees and shrubs smaller bursts of water at irregular intervals because that encourages them to develop shallow root systems, less protection against drought.

Here's a time-saving watering trick for young trees: when the tree is quite young, build a basin around it, a lower area that extends about 2 feet out from the trunk. Build up the edges at this radius with the dirt you dug up. Place your watering equipment so this inner area is well soaked. As the tree grows, you can dig an additional basin a few more feet out in all directions and water more there as your tree matures and its roots grow.

If your area receives heavy rain regularly, cut a few pathways *out* of the basin for the excess water to drain. Or dig a shallow trench in a circle around the tree, about 6 feet out in all directions, 1 or 2 inches deep. This is where you want some of the water to land when the tree's roots have grown out that far. You'll be encouraging them to do so.

def•i•ni•tion

The **dripline** is the circle around the tree where the outermost leaves would drip naturally during a rain.

Sprouts

As you can see, this kind of watering plan is *not* the same you'd typically use on your grass. If your watering has to work for both grass and trees/shrubs, at least get rid of the grass under the trees, as far out as the canopies stretch. Then you won't be encouraging grass to grow under the trees, creating root competition. Or just stop watering *all* your grass as often.

Shrubs tend to need more water because their root systems are much less extensive and a greater proportion of their "bodies" is leaves. Leaves are and need to be damper than trunks. Also, they should be watered closer to their trunk mass, a few inches out instead of a few feet as with trees.

How Often Should I Water?

Young plants need water often, especially during the growing season, but as your plants age, their water needs change, depending on your climate, weather, and soil conditions.

Younger trees (those not yet a year old) haven't developed an extensive, efficient root system, so check the soil for moisture down several inches and if it's dry, water. Very young trees—those younger than 6 months old—need water every week. During the rest of their first year, water deeply once a month. After that, do your watering weekly unless your yard receives 1 inch of rain. Water more often in summer.

Through the growing season, water your young trees about every 2 days and your new shrubs every day. When they pass their 2-year birthday, you can water the trees every 3 to 7 days and the shrubs every 2 to 5 days. If your soil is sandy, water them more often but in smaller amounts.

Watering costs money, but so did your new tree or shrub. Don't be pennywise and pound foolish and let your plant die young from not enough water. Also, your trees will grow thicker and taller faster if you water them in their first few years. Older trees usually get enough water from rainfall, your grass watering, or both. If these don't add up to an inch every week or so, do a long, slow, deep watering about once a month.

When Should I Water?

Sprouts

If you live in an arid area and have just a few trees, especially ones that are either aging or very young, you might want to install a soil-moisture sensor. Some can be attached to turn on a watering system, and others give short-term readings.

The best time to water is early in the morning. Your trees and shrubs can then work on a good day of growing, and a noonday sun won't burn their leaves if any water gets on them. Morning watering also reduces the chances of fungal infections and is more efficient because less of your water evaporates in the sun before your thirsty friends can slurp it up.

Never water at noon or in the afternoon. Even before dawn—for those of you with an automatic method— is better than late in the day or in the evening.

Watering Tools and Techniques

You *could* carry buckets of water out to each new tree and shrub every time you need to water, but water is heavy! Unless you're looking to build up your muscles, let some watering tools and techniques help you out. Try waterdrip hoses, those with holes in them to drip out slowly, any regular sprinkler, or a water bubbler. The latter, installed underground, bubbles out the water at a medium rate of speed.

Dealing with Droughts

Whether you live in Arizona or Maine, you'll experience a drought at some time. Sudden droughts are worse than gradual ones, and unusual ones are harder on plants than an annual "dry season." Trees and shrubs can get used to the latter, but they still suffer when they're dry. Their leaves steadily become smaller and thicker, woody areas within the plant shrink (affecting the circulatory system), breathing and photosynthesis to create food slow down, and the balance of growth hormones becomes disturbed. The stress can be such that 2 or 3 years later, your tree or shrub can die from an infection or infestation that was established when it was in this dry, weakened state.

Of course, plants try to adapt. They restrict their water loss via the leaves and pull in more from the soil. And trees and shrubs native to your area tend to do much better during a drought or even a couple years of any other adverse condition. They even grow more during the typical wetter periods, taking an acceptable break during a drought. Cacti, for example, have bodies designed primarily to store water—like camels. They also tend to be light in color and have rough and/or waxy exteriors.

Your whole community will be experiencing the drought at the same time, so watering restrictions might be in place. So water less often, focus on the younger plantings and those with buds ready to open, and skip all lawn chemicals (they make your plants thirsty).

> **The Real Dirt**
>
> Winds, particularly fierce, can dry out your trees and shrubs considerably. And if your tree or shrub is near a hard surface such as pavement or a side of your house, heat that bounces off that surface will further dry out your plant. Add water!

A Note on Water Conservation

Water is becoming a more valuable "commodity" all the time. World and regional populations are increasing, livestock quaffs water by the gallon, as do agricultural crops as well as vegetables and fruit. Yet no amount of rainfall alone can balance this demand. You might be wondering how to balance your plants' need for water versus feeling as though you're "wasting" it by watering. If you live in an arid part of the country, plant native trees and shrubs. Group them for efficient watering. Also add nonplant materials to further beautify your yard, such as rock gardens and garden sculptures.

The Least You Need to Know

♦ Most people water too much, blocking soil oxygen and *encouraging* root rotting.

♦ Plants younger than 2 years old need water daily during the growing season.

♦ Water daily for about 6 months, then weekly, then generally only during dry periods.

♦ Water close to a shrub but several feet out from a tree's trunk—and deeply or not at all.

♦ The best time to water is early in the morning.

Chapter 16

Pruning Deciduous Trees

In This Chapter

- The importance of pruning
- Proper pruning approaches
- What *not* to do
- The tools and techniques you need

You've probably heard about pruning, but maybe you haven't mustered the courage to attack a whole yard full of trees and shrubs to get them in shape. You're not alone. Pruning can be an intimidating part of caring for trees and shrubs. It takes sharp tools, and the thought of chopping on a plant might give you flashbacks of someone chopping on your hair as a kid—and the resulting less-than-ideal haircut.

Never fear. After you finish this and the following chapter, you'll have the guts to go forth and prune. And you'll also be happy to hear that your plants prefer your tools to the wilder ones wielded by the wind!

Pruning Basics

Why *prune?* Why spend a precious evening or weekend day to influence the shape and the growth of a tree or shrub in some way? In a sense, it's like training your plant. Some of it's aesthetic, but it's also important for the health of the tree or shrub. The trick is to do it without damaging the plant along the way!

Pruning for Structural Training

Young plants, similar to their human counterparts, can be a little wild, maybe throwing an extra branch toward the sunlight, shoving against the garage, scratching a window, growing a little crooked, or perhaps even developing a split trunk (when they're not supposed to have one). At the very least, a young plant can look enthusiastically lopsided! And maybe the nursery didn't prune them perfectly either.

Every tree has a basic genetic shape—some are more like a cone, or an upended broom, or a lollipop, whatever—so they have tendencies that you need to work with. You're not starting from scratch and inventing the tree's shape. (In fact, if you have to prune ordinary yard trees more than every 3 to 5 years, that tree probably shouldn't be in that location at all.)

def•i•ni•tion

Pruning is the removal of part of a plant, not only a shoot or branch, but sometimes also its buds, roots, flowers, or fruit.

Sprouts

A plant's growth becomes more focused after pruning. Wounds from dead branches seal more quickly.

Here, the training goals are basic. The first, which requires removing branches as necessary, allows the younger tree to focus its energy on strengthening its trunk so it will grow to be well tapered and sturdy. You may also want to train it by pruning to reduce the shade a bit in that area, keep branches out of the way of structures, or guard against wind damage.

It may be somewhat surprising to hear that losing a limb by pruning can be good for a tree, but it is. Not only will the trunk and roots be able to use more of the available energy, but all the remaining branches will get a boost, too.

Pruning for Tree Health

Many pruning projects involve removing dead, diseased, and broken branches; those interfering with each other (by being crossed or rubbing together); or those interfering with your house or other structure. As long as you prune properly and don't remove more than 25 percent of the aboveground mass, you aren't likely to hurt the tree.

Besides pruning the horizontal or lateral branches, you can also prune the more vertical ones, thinning the tree's canopy a bit. This allows more light to reach the rest of the branches, enhancing the tree's growth—and any plantings under it. It also improves air circulation within the canopy, reducing the chance of fungi and/or insect infestation.

Root Rot _____

When pruning, remember "not too much." A tree might not bounce back from a heavy pruning.

Pruning for Safety

Safety issues can emerge when an older tree's large, heavy branches extend over decks, kids' play areas, roofs, and other areas where _our_ own limbs might be at stake. You don't have to take the whole branch off in these cases, but you should reduce its mass, as we'll see later in the chapter.

Safety also comes into play with utility lines. No one wants a stiff wind or snow load to knock down a tree, taking a utility line with it, where it could harm passersby. Utility companies spend millions of dollars pruning around power lines. To help them, and maybe yourself, don't plant any large new trees under lines. And watch out for the ones already planted there. If pruning seems necessary, call the utility company to do it.

If you do your own pruning, please be careful with ladders—have a "spotter" with you to watch both ladder and limbs. It's also best to hire a professional for high-up jobs. And if you have plant allergies, check out the tree species ahead of time. Sensitive people have become temporarily blinded from pruning a sycamore tree in late spring or summer.

Pruning for Aesthetics

Pruning for beauty is probably the most common reason. You may want a more symmetrical tree. (Trees usually "want" that, too.) Even aging trees can look like beauty-contest entrants if they're shaped even just a bit, removing their weaker limbs. At the same time, pruning can compensate for difficulties such as crowding with other trees, loss of a limb to disease, winds that have affected their shape, interference from urban structures, and the like. A pruned tree simply has more vigor.

> **The Real Dirt** _____
>
> You may be wondering why trees need such "star treatment." What do they do in a natural forest without us pruning them? In forests, many trees are crooked, lopsided, and decked in dead branches, but still make do somehow. You may or may not want your yard to look that way! But by domesticating trees, we've actually made their lives harder, making them adapt to streets, lawnmowers, patio construction, and more. We don't think it hurts to show them a little love now and then.

When to Prune

Before you grab any tools, a bit of prepruning planning is necessary. The "when" of pruning is an issue that includes when during the year as well as when during the life cycle of the plant.

Pruning During the Year

Hawaiians need not ponder the calendar much because their trees can be pruned anytime, while Minnesotans—at the other extreme—can safely prune some of their trees only in the fall, and others only in the spring (both the nongrowing or *dormant season*). And pruning in both late winter and summer is advised in some places and under some circumstances.

def•i•ni•tion _____

The **dormant season** is when the tree isn't growing. This is usually late fall, winter (unless yours is very cold), or very early spring.

If you're not sure when it's best to prune in your area or zone, check with a local plant store. A few things are certain anywhere, though:

- If a branch is dead, you can lop it off anytime— but be sure to take off only the dead part.

- If a tree is smaller than 2 inches across, timing is also that flexible. You can prune it anytime.

- If you want to prune a 2-inch or more living part of your tree or shrub, you should focus on the dormant season.

- Summer is usually the worst time to prune, especially if you're pruning more than this year's growth, and especially on a rainy or humid day—insects and fungi that attack trees are really out on the prowl.

- Early spring and fall are bad, too—fungi spores are on the loose!

- It's best not to prune any individual tree more than once a year.

Now let's refine our thinking a bit by treating the dormancy of three kinds of trees a bit differently. Conifers can be pruned anytime, as you'll learn in the next chapter. The dormant season is still the best time—they will produce less sap and resin then. Trees that don't have showy flowers, or those *with* obvious flowers but that bloom in summertime (as opposed to springtime) should also be pruned in dormancy. Flowering trees that are springtime bloomers, however, should be pruned right after their flowering (which is a lesser kind of dormancy, but still falls within that category); otherwise, they may become exposed to a bacterial invader called fire blight. (More on bacteria in Chapter 22.) Flowering plums, magnolias, and shrub versions of them fall in this category. If you prune in fall, winter, or early spring by mistake, you'll lose this year's flowering period.

Root Rot

Infectious organisms are in their prime during warm and hot weather, so be very careful about pruning during this time.

Within the dormant period, late winter is the best time for most deciduous trees. The next spring's growth seals off the wound more quickly. And don't worry if sap flows from the wound for awhile. It doesn't hurt them—it's even the way that trees can form their own sticky traps for insects.

Sprouts

If you want to encourage dwarfing, prune at the *height* of the growing season. Or buy a dwarf cultivar to begin with.

Pruning During a Plant's Life Cycle

Trees can—and should—be pruned regularly, but lightly, for strength and other features during their first 3 to 5 years. Remember that a "stitch in time saves nine"—it's just easier to prune trees at earlier stages of their lives. Although trees can be pruned for dead branches at any time in their lives, mature, mid-life trees (a period that can last for decades up to hundreds of years) generally need no such radical or regular pruning. (See the following "Types of Pruning" section.) Aging trees can and should be pruned to boost their vigor. Just like a hip replacement surgery in an elderly person, it can provide a new lease on life!

Types of Pruning

The most common types of pruning are removing material to clean the tree's crown, thin it, raise it, reduce it, or restore it. We discuss them one by one in a second, but keep a couple things in mind: don't take off more than 25 percent of any tree any one year, and start at the highest level in the tree for any pruning project. That way, if a falling branch crashes too hard into a lower one, you can revise your overall pruning plan and get rid of the damaged branch if you have to.

But do not cut until you read this entire chapter! You'll need to hear about the tools to use and do some detailed planning.

Crown cleaning is removing dead or diseased branches anywhere on the tree. The remaining branches will get more sunlight and gradually fill in the gaps.

Crown thinning involves pruning away living branches to let in more light and air while still maintaining the natural shape of the tree. Plan first to get rid of branches that are crossed over each other or are spindly. Then focus on any narrow V-shape branch pairs where they seem to be growing together. The two branches are almost always only weakly attached. You'll prune some of the small horizontal branches off one of the pair to weaken it and encourage the other one to take over as the trunk.

Next, find pairs of roughly parallel branches where one is over the other and both are about 2 inches in diameter on a tree of say, 40 to 60 feet tall. Mark the branches in these pairs with string, ribbon, or tape; you'll prune them later. But step back and check for symmetry again. You may need a last step of marking some of the smaller laterals on the remaining, main branches.

Root Rot

Mature beech trees and birch trees should *not* have their crowns thinned. They are liable to die from it.

With *crown raising*, you remove branches from the lowest levels, which makes the crown look higher. People often prune this way to make room for people or vehicles to move under the tree without getting scratched by low branches. It can also be done to improve a view. A tree's lower branches are often droopy, but unless it is really a safety issue, leave some of them until they naturally die. If your tree is still fairly young, leave a few of the lower branches on to encourage the tree trunk to grow thicker there and then taper nicely toward the top. Plan to take off the stronger rather than the weaker ones. You'll prune these weaker ones in subsequent years.

Crown reducing is done when the entire tree is too large. Here, you take off whole branches at a time. However, it should never be done on a pyramid-shaped tree or, in general, unless absolutely necessary. You might take this approach to pruning when the tree is shoving against a building, another tree, or another structure; shading your solar collector; or something significant along those lines. Or it could also be because you—or more likely an earlier homeowner of your property—didn't prune years ago.

Crown restoring is reshaping a tree to its natural shape if it's been damaged by a storm, vandals, or previous inexpert pruning. If the trunk and the main scaffolding branches are still healthy, this can work. It can even be fine to do this kind of pruning during the spring/summer growing season, unlike most pruning, because it will keep remaining branches from growing back spindly, instead of vigorously, on their own. You might want to undertake this project over 2 to 4 years if a significant proportion of the tree needs to be removed. But check the tree carefully each year to be sure it isn't apt to collapse from its previous problems.

> ### The Real Dirt
>
> Big trees take pruning a bit hard. They need longer to recover, all the while displaying necessarily larger and unattractive wounds. In the process, they are prone to decay—and paradoxically, they are also *more* likely to regrow part of the unwanted branched. And you may have to contemplate this possibly dangerous work during a period of several years. Today might be the day to get some professional help.

Sometimes it's better to remove a whole tree instead of pruning a damaged one or separating a pair of them. This is most likely when the trees were planted too close together to begin with and one of them has become misshaped. (Of course, we're going to blame those previous homeowners!) The remaining tree in the former pair will, over a couple years, fill out nicely to take over the space. You can remove the designated tree in stages if you like, too, which may make the "hole" in your yard less obvious as the filling in occurs.

Your Pruning Toolbox

At pruning's basic level, you need at least one saw, set of shears, and set of loppers. Some of these you may already have, some you can borrow from neighbors and friends, some you can rent from hardware stores, and some you'll need to buy. If you're going to learn to prune, you won't be doing it just once—trees require regular maintenance—so you might want to purchase at least one of these tools rather than rent or borrow.

You'll need a *saw* for branches larger than 2 inches in diameter, one that has three blade surfaces per tooth, cuts as you pull (not push), and has coarse teeth (about 5 per inch) arranged in V's. Any single-bladed pruning saw that fits both your hand and the spaces among the tree's branches will work. (You want the blade on only one side so you don't accidentally damage any nearby branches with the other blade.)

Sprouts _____

Remember to clean any and all tools after each use. This is especially important if you think a to-be-removed branch is diseased by fungi or bacteria. In this case, have some bleach available—a 5 percent solution is good, as is a 70 percent solution of denatured alcohol. You'll need to immerse the tool for 1 or 2 minutes after wiping off all wood material. Bleach is corrosive, so be sure to clean it off and re-oil the tool afterward. Also, keep your tools sharp. And it's important not to use a tool so small that you'll need to strain and possibly make a ragged cut.

You'll use *shears*, or hand pruners, for branches up to ¹/₂ inch in diameter—a size likely to cover many or most of your pruning projects. Your shears should either operate as scissors with both handles held in one hand, or as a wire cutter, where one blade pinches the branch against the tool's other, broader surface. Called a by-pass (or bi-pass), this tool is less likely to crush the tree's remaining tissue.

Root Rot _____

It's best not to use a chainsaw because when you're doing a crotch cut (see the next section), the heavy blade is liable to end up too low in the crotch and damage the tree.

Pole pruners, or *loppers*, are best for use on branches up to 2 inches in diameter but too high to reach. They're basically pruning shears, but larger and mounted on a handle at least 6 feet long. A lopper works similar to scissors except that you operate the blade by pulling on a rope. Some have extension handles and telescoping poles.

Pruning Techniques

These tricks of the trade differ a bit depending on whether you're pruning a living branch, pruning a dead branch, or doing a crotch cut.

For each living branch, first find the *collar*. This is the area where the bark looks different from the trunk and makes a sort of wide mouth around the whole branch. The upper part will have some sort of ridge, too. You can also think of this zone as the area just before the branch becomes uniform, as a kind of suture zone. This is the area you want to leave *on* the tree.

def•i•ni•tion _____

The branch **collar** is the area of protective cells, slightly raised where the branch meets either the trunk or a branch larger than itself.

Now you're ready to prune your first smaller branch. Grab your shears, placing the cutting blade on top if you have that type, or both blades of the scissors type around. Position your tool so it's just outside the branch collar/ridge and angles down, away from the trunk or main branch you're removing the smaller branch from.

Be sure you don't leave a large stub, or else an entire branch might die. You can leave a very small lateral with a small stub. Cut quickly and hard, without twisting your tool (that damages it). Your "report card" will arrive by the next growing season, where you should see a *whole circle* of solid woundwood. If the shape is more like an oval, then you probably cut in too close.

For a larger branch, more than about 1 inch in diameter, take up your larger shears or your saw. Carefully hold your hand under the branch to support it slightly as you shear or saw. Remember if you're sawing, the motion is pulling *toward* you.

For even larger branches, those larger than about 2 inches across, you'll need to make three—quite different—cuts. The first one is just a notch on the underneath side of the branch, about 12 inches out from where the branch attaches to the trunk to about one-third of the way in from the branch tip inward. (This cut is made to keep the branch from ripping off because of its weight.) The notch should penetrate about $\frac{1}{4}$ of the way through. The second cut is outside the notch you made but goes the whole way through the wood. And the third is to cut off the remaining stub, again outside the collar and ridge. If necessary, you can cut partway in from the bottom and finish from the top. Do not treat or disturb the wound—it's up to the tree to do that.

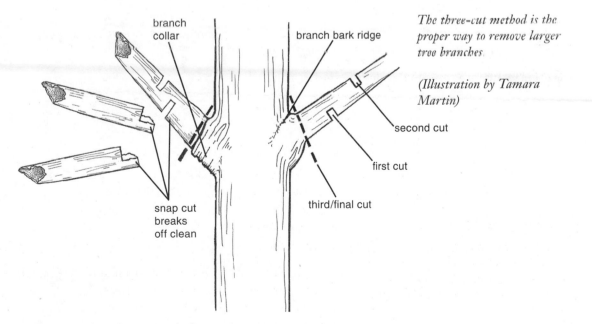

branch collar

branch bark ridge

snap cut breaks off clean

second cut

first cut

third/final cut

The three-cut method is the proper way to remove larger tree branches.

(Illustration by Tamara Martin)

For dead branches, the process is about the same except that the collar and ridge are usually easier to see. It's still often best to use the three-step method, even when the branch isn't particularly huge, because bark is more likely to rip in this case. And the older the tree, the more careful you need to be with a living branch collar.

For a crotch cut—a cut into the area where a branch nearly as large as the trunk is weakly attached in a narrow V—you also need to make three cuts. The first is a notch a few inches above the crotch—on the branch you want to remove. The second is lower down but above the bark's ridge—cut all the way through the branch. And the third step is to prune off the stub just inside the ridge and parallel to it. (This removes the inclusion, or shared bark area that was weakening both of them.) This helps you avoid the strange-looking "water spouts" (from latent buds).

Keep in mind that older trees may not be able to tolerate a crotch cut and the two trunks/large branches in a V may have to be cabled together to prevent sudden detachment.

The Least You Need to Know

♦ Pruning can actually be good for trees, as well as for your yard and your safety.

♦ You can do the pruning yourself when high branches aren't more than about 3 inches in diameter. Otherwise, call a professional.

♦ Prune a given tree no more than once a year, removing no more than 25 percent of it.

♦ Pruning in the dormant period is usually best.

Chapter 17

Pruning Conifer Trees and Shrubs

In This Chapter

- Conifer pruning tips
- Conifer branch issues
- The importance of flowers (or no flowers)
- Finding your pruning style

Pruning for conifers and especially shrubs is different from pruning your deciduous trees (which you learned about in the preceding chapter). After all, you don't want to thin the crown of a conifer because it grows in a cone shape. And you wouldn't saw off a tree down to the ground over a couple years to boost its blooming, but that's perfectly fine sometimes with some shrubs.

It's important to know how, when, and where to prune these plants to ensure their successful growing and their beauty. Read on, dear pruners!

Pruning Conifers

Pruning conifers might be the easiest pruning you do, especially if you're used to pruning deciduous trees—and some conifers don't require any pruning at all! You do need to prune some evergreen trees, though, for a few simple reasons:

- ◆ To get rid of dead/diseased/structurally problematic branches

- ◆ To control branch density

- ◆ To shape a misshapen tree

- ◆ To trim the total size of mature trees

The latter can be done quite radically if you like—up to 30 percent of their crowns can safely be removed in one season. Do keep in mind that most conifers don't have the same type of hidden (latent) buds in reserve. If you want a branch to grow back, leave some foliage on it. The buds will be there, though not elsewhere.

A big difference, within the conifer family, one that affects how you tackle them, relates to their branching—are they whorl-branched, random-branched, or columnar? Let's look at each.

Whorl-Branched Conifers

Whorl-branched conifers feature branch groupings on the same horizontal plane all around the trunk. The effect is like very loosely stacked green pancakes with space in between them. Look around: most pine trees are whorl-branched, as are some spruces and firs. This whorled branching creates less competition between branches and trunk and doesn't weaken the trunk.

You don't need to prune whorl-branched conifers except if you want to. If you do want to shape your tree, or reduce its breadth, you can prune the small branches as far back as the bigger branch they grow on or prune the bigger branches as far back as a bud (however undeveloped).

Random-Branched Conifers

This is the larger group among the conifers, and it's characterized by *not* having the whorled pattern. The branches grow from the tree's trunk in a random pattern, more similar to deciduous trees. And they have partly hidden buds that can spring to life if you prune off a branch's outer length. Random-branched trees include the larches, cedars, redwoods, sequoias, bald cypress, yew, and arborvitae.

With these trees, you have a choice of pinching or shearing. As with the whorl-branched conifers, you can pinch the new shoots, or you can cut off their tips. Be sure any branch you want to continue to grow still has foliage on it. (They grow from the tips of their foliage.)

If you want to control the size of these trees, try this: find pairs of branches (not exactly paired but roughly so), in which the ones above would hide a shortened branch below if you pruned it off. Shear the lower of the two back just far enough so the upper one still conceals the cut of the lower one. If you end up with several lighter areas (arborists calls these "white eyes") after pruning, rub a little dirt onto each one to make your tree look natural.

The Real Dirt

Some conifers grow in more than one active period each year (you'll be able to see the new growth). You can pinch or trim during any or all these growth spurts, but don't do it in between. And to be safe, avoid the height of summer. (Insects!)

Columnar Conifers

You don't want to prune columnar evergreens too much. You can, however, prune away any branches that curve up and out, not matching the column's shape. If you cut them back to the fork farthest out from the trunk, your tree will still look natural.

Sprouts

Help your columnar conifers shed their dead needles by taking a garden hose to them. No pruning shears needed, and you've done your watering!

Pruning Shrubs

Too often, we think of shrubs as generally short plants, often forgetting how tall—and how broad—they actually can get. If a shrub supersizes, we're tempted to overprune, ruining its natural shape and even preventing it from flowering. Most homeowners make three key mistakes with their shrubs:

◆ Placing them in a site they will quickly outgrow. Pruning needs can then become drastic!

◆ Waiting too long in the life of a shrub to begin pruning.

◆ Pruning from the top only, resulting in an odd-looking shrub.

The Real Dirt

By "shrubs" here we mean deciduous shrubs because evergreen shrubs tend to take on a rounded form on their own and don't require much, if any, pruning. Evergreen shrubs with broad leaves grow quite symmetrically. Some might need annual thinning to keep their shape and to prevent them from becoming very large, but only if those are issues for you.

Sprouts

Always, *always* read the tag to determine the size the tree or shrub will get before you buy it.

Shrubs are versatile little growing machines with lots of easily visible (and usually pleasant) branches and also lots of buds. New shoots readily grow from lower on the base of the plant, too, from latent buds there. The growth readily branches out from those buds, at their tips and those dotting the sides of the branches. These buds can create leaves, branches, or flowers depending on the kind of bud. And to a great extent, the buds make the shrub self-perpetuating, renewing itself easily.

But before you go out and start hacking on your shrubs today, stop. First, your tools: scissors-style shears with small blades are best. And shrubs need to be pruned mostly by thinning them rather than by removing entire large shoots (as you do with trees), even if what you want to do is make them appear smaller. You don't want to damage or disrupt the flowers by pruning at the wrong time of year. Only dead branches can be removed at any time.

Shrubs Without Major Flowers

Prune shrubs that don't produce notable flowers in the dormant season, after the shrub has moved through its whole aboveground growing cycle. You'll get better wound closing, less sap flow, and less chance of disease from insect invaders and bacterial infections. Also, you're better able to see the shrub's structure at that time.

As you prune, remember to keep a natural look by pruning all around, not just on the top or in one area.

Early Flowering Shrubs and Trees

For early springtime bloomers such as dogwoods, redbuds, crabapples, some spiraea, cotoneasters, forsythia, serviceberry, and magnolia, prune immediately after their blooming period to get it over with, from the plant's point of view. Shrubs that flower early in the spring actually set their buds the *preceding* summer, and you want them to have time to do this again vigorously *this* summer.

To prune, remove old stems at or near ground level and thin out any new ones that look weaker. Prune the others back from their tips so they only have one or two side branches left.

Late-Flowering Shrubs

Prune summer-bloomers such as mock orange, potentilla, and hydrangea either in early spring before growth begins or during the dormant season. Don't prune in late summer or early fall because that will encourage them to grow back at a time when they should be going dormant.

Foliage Shrubs

Prune shrubs you've chosen mostly for their foliage, such as burning bush, honeysuckle, sumac, elderberry, and smoke tree, in the spring before the plant starts growing. This boosts their foliage later, instead of interfering with it by pruning too close to their own "prime time."

> **Sprouts** _____
>
> If you have a much-overgrown shrub, you might be able to turn it into a very nice small tree by removing the small and medium low-growing branches, creating a trunk. Do this across 1 to 3 years, depending on the size of the shrub. And if you pruned poorly (oops!) and the plant really looks ugly, don't fret. You can cut off most healthy shrubs close to the ground to start over. (Just don't damage their roots!) But do this over a period of more than 1 year—and consult your local garden store first to ask about the habits and needs of that particular shrub.

"Heading" cuts on a privet help reduce and rejuvenate the shrub.

Root Rot

Heading most shrubs damages their health. Although it's quick, it's not a good idea unless you have a particularly aggressive shrub such as the privet.

For overgrown shrubs, leggy or otherwise unkempt, you can prune radically, but do it across 2 to 3 years, doing about half or a third of your eventual pruning goal each time. Just after the plant finishes blooming, cut some of the thickest, woodiest stems back to the ground and lightly prune the tips of the other branches. Do the same the next year and the year after that. If you're tempted to do it all at once, in one year, your results will be a spindly shrub that won't bloom vigorously for years. Though it can be sad, because you don't get nearly as many flowers during these years, this radical technique can rejuvenate a bush for years. It's as though you bought a brand-new one!

In addition to being beneficial for the plant, some pruning can be beautiful, such as this bonsai pruning.

(Pruning by Kevin Oshima)

The Least You Need to Know

◆ Conifers generally require less pruning than deciduous trees, palms, or shrubs.

◆ Shrub pruning is timed to when the shrub flowers.

◆ Palm trees need a lot of pruning, mostly for safety.

◆ Shrubs can sometimes be pruned down to the ground to rejuvenate them—just do it over more than 1 year.

Mulching and Fertilizing

In This Chapter

- ◆ Why—and why not—to mulch
- ◆ Which mulch is for you?
- ◆ Feeding your trees and shrubs
- ◆ Tips for fertilizing your plants

Mulching and fertilizing can do wonders to boost the health and appearance of your trees and shrubs. Mulching and fertilizing are not new-fangled ideas. Natural forests have been mulching and fertilizing themselves with needle and leaf fall for as long as conifers and deciduous trees have existed. And even early people understood the benefits— remember the story about the Native Americans showing the Pilgrims how to bury a dead fish with their seeds at planting time? You can still fertilize with a dead fish!

Mulch Basics

Besides looking nice spread evenly around all your plants, *mulch* shelters your plants' roots against temperature extremes And dramatic levels of rain or drought. Mulch protects roots from competing plants and makes the soil more porous, more stable, and a better home for friendly fungi and other soil microorganisms. It also reduces the amount of watering you need to do, and it enables you to mow farther away from your trees and shrubs.

Materials such as gravel, polyethylene weed cloths, shredded plastic bags, various papers and nut hulls, even pavement are all considered mulches. Shredded newspapers are partly organic—the paper comes from trees—although the ink (unless soy-based) and other chemicals probably do not. When using newspaper, avoid the color inserts because of the inks, and shred some of it to go under a woody mulch. Gravel never needs to be refreshed and deters squirrels from digging, but it's virtually impossible to rake up leaves or other materials that litter it, and it can hold too much heat.

Natural, locally fallen leaves, needles, and twigs—the all-natural, original mulch—provides about half the nutrients your plant needs. (The rest may or may not be in the soil.) But many people rake up all this natural mulch and get rid of it. Keep some of those fallen leaves, mix a bit with features from a few other plant species, and then cover this with a layer of organic mulch. This homemade mulch is quick, is inexpensive, and looks good!

You also could shred local leaves with a mulcher and maybe throw in a thin layer of grass clippings, if you like (and if it isn't contaminated with lawn chemicals). Avoid soggy composts or wet peats. And be sure the leaf pieces aren't too small, or they'll blow away.

Why Mulch?

Some beneficial effects from mulching appear almost immediately; others show up over a longer haul. What can you expect? Early benefits—those occurring quickly up to a few months—include …

- Root system growth, which strengthens the tree or shrub.
- Protection of clay soil from dry cracking.
- Dilution of the salt content of salty soils.
- Reduction in sogginess *and* the conservation of moisture.
- Moderation of temperature extremes.

◆ Prevention of weed development, provided the layer is at least 2 inches thick.

◆ Reduction of organic wastes in landfills—you're using it!

◆ Elimination of the weight of vehicles (and even people) from the space over the roots because people steer around mulch patches.

Nice longer-term effects include …

◆ Savings on your water bill.

◆ More nutrition for the plant as the mulch leaches out and decomposes.

◆ Soil evolution toward a rich soil.

 The Real Dirt

> Mulching can occasionally create nitrogen deficiencies, but those can be corrected by fertilizing. If you suspect a nitrogen deficiency because leaf color and vigor are anemic in your tree or shrub, a small amount of fertilizer either under or over the mulch might fix the problem (see Chapter 21). More often, mulching can protect the plant and the top soil layers where its root system is growing, so fertilizing isn't necessary.

Why *Not* Mulch?

Mulching can be a negative in certain situations, though:

Don't mulch if the soil around your plants doesn't drain well now. Mulching will make it even soggier.

If your area experiences extreme cold or extreme heat, don't mulch. Mulch in winter chills the air above it and heats the air above it in the summer. However, mulch increases the soil temperature by about 5 degrees in winter and decreases it about 3 degrees.

Mulching isn't a good idea if you're concerned about the initial hardiness of your tree or shrub. New plants that are mulched begin their growth a bit later in the season because the mulch prevents the soil from warming up quite so quickly.

Too much of anything isn't good, and that's true for mulch, too. The organic component of a soil should fall between 1 and 6 percent; usually 2 percent is about right for a yard. You also want your soil to be pretty uniform so roots don't encounter abrupt changes as they grow.

Root Rot _____

Don't put a solid plastic layer under mulch. It can suffocate roots.

Mulch up against the trunk can cause trunk rot and girdling roots and also provides a hideout for rodents. Never mulch trees that already have some fungal root rot or collar rot. And don't mulch any closer than 4 to 8 inches from a tree's or shrub's base.

If you create too thick a layer or too small an area, you'll weigh down all the roots. About 3 or 4 inches is good for the coarse organic, wood-based mulches; go with 2 inches for the inorganics. A 3- to 6-foot-diameter circle around an average-size tree is ideal; a couple feet less for shrubs. One "recipe" that can easily become too clogged is grass clipping + dead leaves + shredded bark.

Mulching isn't necessary if your trees and shrubs are mature and well established and if you live in an area with adequate rainfall where moisture evaporation isn't a big issue for your plants.

Types of Mulch

Quite a few types of mulch are available:

◆ Peat moss

◆ Wood chips

◆ Bark pellets

◆ Manures

◆ Solid waste

◆ Compost

◆ Biostimulants

◆ Vermiculite

Most of these are organic; biostimulants and vermiculite are the exceptions. No one type is best for everything and everyone, and each has pros and cons, as you'll see in the following paragraphs.

Peat moss is sphagnum moss, which grows organically in northern wetlands and is dried out for sale. It tends to be acidic (high pH) and to hold water especially well—these qualities may or may not fit your soil's needs. Peat can be flammable, so it's best not to use it too close to the house. And it's not an easily renewable resource.

Wood chips are probably the most common, good-bet mulch, but its speed of decomposition depends on the plants it came from. Conifers release their nutrients into the soil quickly, within a few months, and conifer mulch is moderately priced. Redwood, cedar, and cypress mulches decay over several years and cost more. These are also quite rot-resistant. The smaller the pieces of any wood, the faster the decay.

Sprouts

Freshly planted trees need more mulch, but they can more easily be affected by less-than-ideal mulch materials. If you want to use fresh wood chips and barks, go with a layer about 1 inch thick on new plants. Spread this first to allow the very top layer of soil to deactivate some of the carbon-destroying nitrogen in the mulch. You can also place a thick layer of it somewhere away from plants and from drainage into a storm sewer and allow rain or a sprinkler to leach out the nitrogen across several months. Or you can compost it. Mature trees and shrubs can accept several times this amount of the fresh wood.

The rounder shape of *bark pellets* means they're less likely to become soggy and compacted than other wood materials, although bark pellets have a greater tendency to become matted than wood chips do. These pellets are inexpensive but often so small that they blow around.

You probably wouldn't want to work with the fresher vintages of *manures*—and that could actually burn trees and shrubs anyway. After it's decomposed for awhile, manure can be fine as long you don't use too much and don't see any weed seeds.

Solid waste? Like from the sewage treatment plant? Yes! If you buy organic fertilizer in bags, you might be getting this product, although in a dry form. When combined with wood materials, it can make a mulch fit for a fancy recipe book (well, maybe). It's best to use more of the wood than the "organic fertilizer" in the mix.

The raw materials in *compost* are usually plant materials—from wood chips to paper to vegetable peelings, and more—with manure perhaps added. When allowed to mix in the naturally warm environment created by the pile of debris and by the

The Real Dirt

Some communities or companies provide household paper wastes, or other such material, often composted. Just be sure you're not getting shredded car and truck tires, or wood from the demolition of buildings or decks, which can release heavy metals into your soil. And the waste should be somewhat aged—raw-looking wood chips can pull nitrogen out of your soil.

microorganisms within it, the nasty components—bad fungi, weed seeds, even many pesticides—are neutralized, resulting in a good chemical (pH) balance.

If you'd like to try composting yourself, it's easy to do, and many online or local sources can guide you on how to do it. The only drawback is that it might be decomposed enough that it disappears quickly right into the soil. So does *compost tea*. Your mulching advantage can be short-lived.

Biostimulants include various acids, vitamins, and plant hormones. We don't think they work well and don't recommend them. Likewise, we don't recommend *vermiculite*. Some forms behave a bit too much like asbestos.

> ## def•i•ni•tion
>
> **Compost tea** is a highly nutritious (not to you but for your trees and shrubs) brew of biological organisms from compost plus water.

Why Fertilize?

Believe it or not, the first rule of fertilization is … skip it whenever you can! Trees and shrubs can usually live without it, especially as their root systems grow and more of their needs are met by the soil—and especially if you've chosen plantings that do well in your type of soil.

> ## Root Rot
>
> Dousing your trees and shrubs with nutrients can be very damaging to the environment. Phosphorous runoff from an overfertilized yard into the nearest storm sewer or waterway is the dream scenario for algae growth. One pound of phosphorous in the water equals, very soon, 500 pounds of algae! Plants almost never need it either.

But fertilizing can be a good idea to correct a deficiency in your soil (perhaps only noticeable because the tree or shrub lacks vitality), especially a highly alkaline or sandy soil or one with lots of moisture. It's also helpful to boost fruiting, flowering, and foliage. It also helps improve the health of an older tree that may have gradually depleted the soil and also is now infected with a wilting fungus.

The top three things your trees and shrubs need to thrive are carbon, oxygen, and hydrogen—and these come free, thanks to nature. Minerals are what *might* be needed, as you'll see in the following sections.

Major Nutrients

The major nutrients, the ones your trees and shrubs might need most, are these:

◆ Nitrogen

◆ Phosphorous

◆ Potassium

◆ Calcium

◆ Magnesium

◆ Sulfur

Nitrogen is the substance most likely to be in low concentration in your soil, especially the farther north you live in the continental United States or if you live in Hawaii. It's also the one your plants are most responsive to when you give it to them; their leaves, shoots, and roots just perk up.

The Real Dirt

Your established trees and shrubs can easily adjust just to slight and even moderate mineral deficiencies. If the leaves look nicely green, don't worry!

Nitrogen develops naturally from organic material such as leaves, grass clippings, and other plant debris decomposing and being incorporated into soils; from animal wastes leaching in; and from bacteria, other microbes, and even lightning, which can draw or burn it out of the atmosphere and change it chemically within the soil to nitrates. Any disruption of this, from removing all plant debris to having soils stripped during construction, reduces the amount of nitrogen available to your trees and shrubs.

Grass, weeds, and microorganisms in the soil also use nitrogen, which means less for your trees and shrubs. It also can be partly volatilized and/or partly leached away in rainfall. (Readers who live in areas with ample moisture experience a lot of this leaching.) The warmer it gets during the growing season, the faster nitrogen chemistry moves, too, just as your new plantings need it most.

Different formulations of nitrogen are available. Slow-release organic nitrogens, although more expensive, are time-effective. When used in late summer or fall, they will still be working for you the next spring. They are also better in sandier soils. Heavier soils generally need less nitrogen of any kind. Inorganic nitrogens, labeled as such at the store, are cheaper; some use ammonia and some use plastic and sulfur.

Root Rot _____

Be especially careful not to give fruit trees too much nitrogen. You'll cut into the fruit production and also increase the risk of fire blight disease.

Nitrogen needs vary with the age of your trees and shrubs. Newly planted ones can benefit from a little of the slow-release variety, but not too much and not the quick-acting types. That would encourage the aboveground parts of the plant to grow at the expense of roots—and the roots are most stressed during planting. In their second stage, rapid growth, your plantings can benefit from a bit more, provided no dwarf or slow-growing species are involved. And mature trees and shrubs need little or no supplemental nitrogen.

Phosphorus levels are usually fine in trees and large shrubs suited to the temperate zone, although some homeowners use it in combination with potassium for fruit trees and smaller shrubs. However, Hawaiian soils as well as especially acidic soils and poorly drained soils in general do sometimes require it. And because phosphorous concentrates in the upper layers of soil, disruption or removal of that layer in construction projects can create a need for it. Younger plants sometimes benefit from phosphorus once during their first 3 to 5 years of life. But any excess pollutes our waterways and water supplies (in the form of phosphate).

Potassium levels in the soil are generally adequate for most trees and shrubs. Any leaves left on the ground leach it out in ample supply, and any reasonably rich soil contains plenty just from its own organic content. Soils with lots of wind-blown sand might require potassium; even here, though, most plantings do fine without it. Potassium concentrates near the surface, so projects that regrade a yard can disturb it, as can excessive watering. Wood ashes, or "potash," are a well-known potassium source. Have a soil test done before adding potassium.

You rarely need to worry about providing *calcium* for your trees and shrubs. Deficits occur mostly in highly acidic soils and in sandy soils from areas that experience very high rainfall. Use a soil test first to check for its levels. And to correct any deficiency, add calciticor dolomite lime to acidic soils and gypsum or elemental sulfur to alkaline ones.

The Real Dirt _____

A tree or shrub that looks low in vitality might not be lacking any minerals in the soil; it might be suffering from an insect infestation, disease, damage, lack of enough water, or even poor pruning. See Chapter 21 for more on diagnosing problems.

Magnesium is another soil constituent you seldom need to add to trees and shrubs except in isolated circumstances. Only acidic sandy soils and calcareous soils can require it, usually by injection once a year.

Sulfur is in ample supply—often too ample a supply—from air pollution alone (it's a byproduct of coal-fired power plants). Trees and shrubs pull some of it out of the air for us—yet another reason to love them!

Types of Fertilizers

More than one type of fertilizer exists, and selecting the right one for what you need can be a challenge. These are the fertilizers most relevant to trees and shrubs:

◆ Complete

◆ Simple

◆ Special

◆ Organic

The "complete" in *complete fertilizers* refers to the fact that they contain nitrogen, phosphorous, and potassium—the three biggies. On bags of fertilizer, you'll see a number such as 22-5-1. The first number (22) is the percentage of nitrogen, the second (5) is the percentage of phosphorus, and the third (1) is the percentage of potash (the form of potassium typically used). They usually also have some other nutrients, although these may not be specified.

Simple fertilizers can be all nitrogen—in the form of ammonium sulfate—in which case the bag label will indicate 21-0-0, for example, or in the form of urea (e.g., 43-0-0). Phosphate-only formulations are usually called "superphosphate." And "KC1" or "muriate of potash" is potassium chloride.

Special fertilizers are for a single type of plant, such as orange trees or azalea shrubs. Usually acidic, they are labeled according to the type of plant they help.

Sprouts

Remember, you almost certainly need only the nitrogen, if that, unless you're working with fruit trees and berry shrubs, in which case you might want to use some phosphorous and potassium.

Organic fertilizers vary a great deal but are usually less strong and act more gradually. Sometimes inorganics are added. The same numbering system exists. Synchronity and Milorganite are two we recommend if you want to fertilize.

Most homeowners use the *dry fertilization* method, with one of the preceding fertilizers. These fertilizers come in a big bag, are the least expensive, last a couple weeks, and generally work fine unless it's windy.

Liquid fertilizers such as Miracle-Gro are best only for your vegetables and annuals—it washes away (and down) too quickly for your mature yard companions.

Spikes and tablets are fertilizer solids that you pound into the ground or drop in holes you've dug. They usually affect only a small part of the root system and so might not be worth the money.

Root feeders, or tubes with liquid, are portable; you move them around every so often to different plants. They come in long tubes but still should only be placed 6 inches into the ground. As liquids (inside), they act for only a short period of time.

Applying Fertilizer

We recommend dry fertilizers if you must fertilize. It's easy to apply by either "broadcasting" (widely spreading) the nitrogen, phosphorous, potassium, etc. or by digging it in. You'll need to use work gloves when handling the fertilizer.

You can easily determine how much fertilizer you need: use about 1 pound of nitrogen (in the form of urea, for example) for approximately 1,000 square feet of yard. If a bag says urea 45-0-0, it's 45 percent nitrogen, so 1 pound ÷ .45 means you need 2.2 pounds of the bagged stuff for your 1,000 square feet.

Sprouts _____

To apply dry fertilizer (wearing your gloves, of course), you can either scatter it around yourself or use a mechanized spreader (they're inexpensive, and some hardware stores rent them out, too). Your goal is to get the granules into as many places as you can!

Choose a dry day for the project to keep the fertilizer from clumping. Mark a place on a circle that's as far out from the trunk as the dripline. Scatter the fertilizer beginning just inside this circle and extending a few feet out from it in all directions. This is where the roots are. Sprinkle the area afterward to move the fertilizer down into the ground. Repeat this the next day unless it rains.

When to Fertilize

The best time to fertilize is just before the growing season. In Minnesota we have one growing season (the spring), Hawaii has three, and you're probably somewhere in between. If necessary, you can also add more fertilizer in the late fall while the ground is still warm.

New trees and shrubs should get water with perhaps a bit of a fertilizer such as Start-Up. Fertilizers can be like steroids at this stage—potentially dangerous—because the plants don't have enough roots to absorb it.

Trees and shrubs from 1 to 5 years old are in their rapid (teenagerlike!) growth period, so unless they're dwarf varieties or otherwise slow-growing, or live in a dry, compacted soil, you can give them some nitrogen starting about a month after the growing season begins. Do about 5 to 8 pounds per 1,000 square feet, or, even better, test your soil to see what you might or might not need.

Mature trees and shrubs, if healthy, need fertilizer every few years—or none at all. Fertilizing in summer isn't a good idea. Your trees and shrubs have less excess water and so may experience a dormant season—and should be allowed to kick back!

Root Rot _____

Ever heard the expression "a rug on drugs"? Even if you haven't, it's good advice: don't use much, if any, lawn chemicals on your grass "rug."

Fertilizer Cautions

You've probably picked up on the fact that you need to exercise some care when fertilizing. Here are some more points to keep in mind:

Don't overdose, especially with nitrogen and especially when the soil is dry. It can attract some insects, run off to pollute the nearest waterway, and seep into the underground water supply (the aquifers from which many communities draw, or will draw, their drinking water).

Don't wrap your trees and shrubs tightly with burlap-type cloth. It protects them from sunscald, but it's too confining.

Be especially careful with your young plants, whose roots can easily be burned from too much nitrogen.

Skip the fertilizers that include herbicides and those with too much nitrogen—or many of your flowering trees and shrubs will grow lovely green leaves but have very few flowers (flowering requires phosphorous).

Don't use so much nitrogen that you burn your grass.

Never add phosphorous without conducting a soil test to see if it's actually needed. It can increase the saltiness of your soil.

Winter Care

For winter, your trees and shrubs might need a little extra care. Starting in early fall, be sure to take the following steps:

Decrease your watering to allow dormancy to begin and then increase it in late fall up until the time the ground freezes. This will help your tree or shrub avoid winter dry-out.

Avoid relying on snow cover to make a cozy blanket for your tree's and shrub's root systems. Instead, after that last bout of watering, add an organic mulch layer 3 or 4 inches deep. This can be shredded brown leaves (green ones need to use too much nitrogen to decompose) or woodchips.

If the bark splits, remove the dead pieces without hurting what's left. Let the tree repair itself in the spring and summer.

With this little extra care, you help your tree or shrub avoid stem frost cankers (also called sunscald) and bark cracks, browning, stem death, bud death, and of course, total death! The cankers and bark cracks occur usually on the south, west, and southwest sides when a late-winter sun, reflected bright off snow, quickly raises the temperature of the tree's "skin" after a cold night has chilled it. (This can even cause it to start spring growth, hardly a good idea.) The cracking happens to trees that ran low in water last fall and were also damaged by a lawnmower, a chewing rabbit, or an imperfect pruning. The warm-cold cycles can then cause further damage. Browning, especially of conifer needles, can appear any time from late winter through the beginning of summer. Wait until late spring (after new growth is in action) to prune off the dead areas.

The Least You Need to Know

◆ Mulching a few inches deep with organic mulch is good all year long, especially in autumn.

◆ Most trees and shrubs need only nitrogen fertilizer, if any at all.

◆ Fruit trees and berry shrubs may require some phosphorus and/or potassium, but conduct a soil test first.

Everything Ages

In This Chapter

- Examining structural problems and defects in branches, trunks, and roots
- The dangers of wind, ice, and urban life
- Prolonging the lives of your plant
- Proper disposal of dead trees and shrubs

Trees age and die for many reasons, although the last straw is usually a stiff wind. We're not including extreme events such as volcanoes, avalanches, and earthquakes in this chapter; instead, we cover common causes for tree failure and discuss some ways you can prevent tree death and the possible subsequent damage to your car, your house, or worse. We also give you tips on the best way to dispose of dead trees and shrubs if it comes to that.

Note that in this chapter we focus mainly on trees because their collapse is far more serious.

Branch Problems

Your trees' branches are usually pretty easy to see, depending on the season and how many leaves remain on the tree. If you see a large, obviously dead branch that stretches out over your roof or otherwise threatens to damage something, you need to prune it off. (See Chapters 16, 17, and 21 first.)

Other issues are a bit harder to see, such as inner decay of a tree branch. Here, the bark might be in place, although the branch is rotting from the inside. At some point, leaves won't grow at all on this branch, which *will* become noticeable. But for now, if the decay seems to be incomplete, you can prune the branch of all its smaller branches and shoots. This reduces the weight on the branch and can prolong its life. (Using wires or cables does not work for this branch problem.)

Another structural problem with branches is weak attachment in trees with a single trunk (we're not discussing those with several trunks, each growing up from the ground). Here, one large branch sticks out from the trunk several feet or yards up from the ground, creating a narrow V-shape angle. The branch looks substantial enough to be almost a second trunk, or *double-leader*. This situation creates too much mechanical stress on the trunk—after all, this kind of tree is designed to have only one base. If the thick branch and the trunk have bark between them, as though they were sharing a bandaged area, that means even more stress—probably worsened by the beginning of cracking. (This might or might not be easily visible.)

The tree may have developed this structural problem because of genetic problems or because of too little sun from one direction. Now it could become an ideal site for decay and even for misplaced roots to sprout out. The two branches already look as though they could someday just split apart—and this could indeed happen.

Poor branch attachment occurs where the angle between the trunk and a large branch is too narrow.

(Sample courtesy of Minnesota Shade Tree Short Course, Tree House of Horrors)

branch bark ridge

with branch
inclusion
or no real
attachment

Your choices here are to gradually diminish the growth on the poorly attached branch, remove it completely, or create a brace with cables. For the first two solutions, be sure to read the appropriate pruning chapter first. For the latter solution, you need a professional arborist. (Take a look at Chapter 14 for more on this issue.)

Maybe the most unusual partial failure of trees is called *summer branch drop*. This can happen in a mature tree during the summer, which is usually a good time for trees. It can even happen on a windless day to an apparently healthy tree. The branch that suddenly crashes down may be up to 3 feet in diameter, though the break usually isn't at the trunk attachment. It usually happens to a long, horizontal branch on an especially hot day. And if it has happened to one, it can happen to another on the same tree. Some tree species seem to be more susceptible than others. Watch out for the elm, beech, ash, cedar, eucalyptus, oak, olive, pine, poplar, silk oak, silver maple, and sweetgum, among others. Unfortunately, arborists and researchers aren't completely sure why this happens.

Sprouts

Inspect all your yard trees every 1 or 2 years. The best times are during the dormant season, after a major storm, or anytime you notice a leafless or needleless branch, perhaps in damp weather (if you're looking for fungi), and maybe in spring after the deciduous trees' leaves have emerged. You might decide to fix the problem yourself or hire a professional.

Although you might be tempted to wait before dealing with these problems, don't wait more than a season or two. If the problem is caused by insects, they are likely to spread to other parts of the tree—and maybe to your other trees. If the tree is close to your roof, is over your driveway, or impinges on anything else important, you should act more quickly or a brisk wind or heavy precipitation load might "prune" the branch for you—with unfortunate results.

Trunk Problems

Problems can also develop in your trees' trunks. Fortunately, these are usually visible—if it looks like the tree is suddenly leaning over significantly, is rotting out near the ground, or has a fungal mass attached to its base, it's probably time to consult a professional. (For more on fungus problems, see Chapter 22.)

The good news is that problems such as these can take a long time—often years—to actually kill your tree. In fact, fungal problems are far more likely to weaken a tree structurally, by rotting it out from the inside, than killing it outright. The bad news is that issues such as these don't look very attractive—and there's not much you can do after the situation is an advanced stage, short of taking down the tree when necessary for safety reasons.

The Real Dirt

A healthy tree is a finely honed natural system. It must actually *encourage* death of its leaves or needles, flowers, and fruits every year yet keep the hormones that accomplish this from killing the whole tree.

Let's take trunk decay first. If it looks to be mild or moderate—less than a third of the mass of the trunk, perhaps—you can try pruning the tree's whole crown. This reduces the effort the trunk needs to expend to keep a larger structure alive. For this extensive pruning, you probably need to hire a professional, and you need to repeat this pruning in a few years as the crown grows back. In the case of more extensive trunk decay, you probably should have the tree cut down.

Some trees naturally develop hollowed-out trunks at their bases as they age. Here, the area should look clean and not rotty. This is fine, and you need do nothing about the cavity. Trees with tendencies in this direction include the linden, red oak, and hackberry.

You might also see a tree leaning away from the vertical—the tree might even be almost horizontal! Sometimes you can see that the tree is gradually correcting itself by angling back up to vertical growth. You don't need to do anything in this case, and probably couldn't anyway. But if the angle is moderate, you can prune to reduce the weight and extension of its crown and help your tree get back on the right track by itself. You could try propping it up next, but you should hire a professional to create this Y-shape support to help it stay up.

Root damage can cause a tree to lean.

And if your tree has just recently begun to lean significantly and you can see cracked soil or a mound of soil on the side of the trunk opposite from the lean, have it taken down completely because it's ready to crash.

Rotting roots can cause tree failure.

Root Problems

Most root problems are hard to spot (unless you're a mole!). You can probably observe a girdling root before you buy a tree or monitor it in your yard. Girdling roots circle around the base of the trunk, gradually restricting the flow of nutrients and water to the upper part of your tree. If you see a girdling root, you might want to consult a professional, although there's probably very little that can be done and the tree will slowly die.

To figure out if a girdling root is beneath the soil surface of a tree that you're pondering buying, look for moss or lichen on the soil's surface—that's a sign that it may have been in the pot too long and developed a girdle. And you don't want to see a root of any significant size growing out of the holes in the bottom of the pot, because that indicates the kind of pot-crowding that leads to girdling.

Also visible and a sign of root decay is a smooth bulge in the trunk the whole way around and well above ground level. Pruning is unlikely to work here because the tree is no longer young.

A smooth bulge on a shade tree is a reaction to injury.

(Courtesy of Minnesota Shade Tree Short Course, Tree House of Horrors)

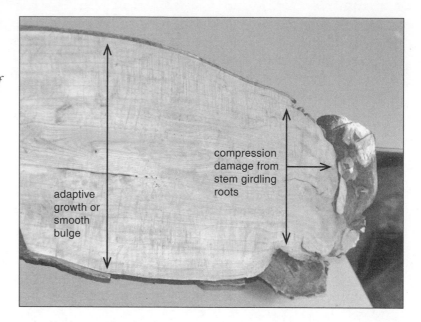

compression damage from stem girdling roots

adaptive growth or smooth bulge

You can suspect root problems if the main roots are visible because the soil around them has eroded or they're just growing now too close to the surface. The tree might not be able to access enough nutrition from the soil. If the tree has grown large and is close to a curb, street, driveway, or other impermeable structure, it might not have enough room for the roots, although they might extend out well enough in the other directions to solve the problem. (Roots grow out in five directions if nothing is in the way.) Root problems can also become extreme if excavating equipment comes near the tree.

The Real Dirt

Root problems are most likely to cause tree failure when the soil is poor; the aboveground tree is particularly heavy or asymmetrical; the plant is exposed to the wind; or if the species generally has shallow roots, such as the blue spruce or ficus.

In this race with decay, practice a little watchful waiting. You don't want to get rid of a tree before you have to—as long as it's not presenting a danger. If the roots have been severed anywhere near the trunk—the result of a city sidewalk project, for example—you could prune throughout the crown to reduce the weight and extent of the tree's body, although this is a pretty risky process. But if this unfortunate tree is in a windy place and/or one where its failure could be dangerous or damaging, you should probably call a professional to have it removed.

Some trees do a pretty good job of repairing mild to moderate root damage from any cause. But the new roots often don't develop to be strong enough, soon enough, to hold up the tree during stressful conditions such as too much water in the soil, too much ground cover under their canopy, or fierce wind.

Soil Problems

If the soil your tree lives in was sufficient for its needs when it was planted, it can still become insufficient later. Maybe too many other trees have grown up around that tree, hogging the nutrients. Or water flow may have eroded the soil around it. Sogginess can damage the root system, too. Arborists say that about two-thirds of the time when an entire tree fails, it's because the soil was too wet all along to allow the roots to grow deep enough to stabilize the tree. Often this soil was poorly textured to begin with—it may have been fill from a road or home construction project, even one long ago. Now that the tree's larger, these problems can become more threatening to the tree. There's not a lot you can do here.

Tree Competition Issues

You might have already noticed: grass and flowers just don't grow under some of your trees. Most people conclude that it's just too shady there and choose to spread down some mulch and forget the problem. More likely, there's some criminal activity going on out there. Many of our seemingly sweet and peaceable trees and shrubs are engaging in chemical warfare with each other—with chemicals they manufacture themselves—called *allelopathy*.

The reason for this sabotage is so the dominant tree can spread out its roots and enjoy the full cafeteria of soil nutrition, soak up all the water and air it wants for dessert, and drink in its fill of sunshine. The Chinese tallow tree of the southeast and southern United States does allelopathy well but isn't

> **Sprouts**
>
> Some problems can be hard to diagnose by yourself. If you see birds, tree mammals, bees, or insects such as carpenter ants living in (not on) a branch or trunk, you can guess that the tree has decayed in that area. But if you're not sure, you might want to have a professional inspect it with you.

> **def•i•ni•tion**
>
> **Allelopathy** is the process in which plants release their own chemicals onto or into the ground to prevent the seeds and seedlings of other plants from setting down roots and growing too near to them. It comes from the Greek word for "mutual suffering."

malicious—it just doesn't want to share space with that willow or bald cypress. Black walnut trees are also well-known alleolopathists.

Larger tree species tend to be best at allelopathy, because that's one of the reasons they *are* larger species. Native trees also tend to be better at it because they've had thousands of years to evolve the best chemical arsenal for their ecological niche. And imported plantings, called *exotics*, often seem like allelopathy experts because the native trees nearby haven't had time to arm themselves against the wiles of the new invader. The previously mentioned Chinese tallow tree is an exotic.

Allelopathy is a complex phenomenon and not well enough understood by scientists. They do know that a natural forest is more likely to have finished most of its allelopathy battles, at least until the next disturbance comes. What you see is what has won out. After a disturbance such as a forest fire or a logging, though, the first group to take over is fastest to get itself started in general—but may also be very good at allelopathy. An excellent example is the American chestnut tree, which once dominated our eastern forests for centuries (before a fungus mowed it down). It kept black birch, yellow birch, and eastern hemlock from becoming established. (They now are, but huge efforts are also being made to bring back the chestnuts.)

At your yard level, you might be pitting two species against each other unwittingly, spoiling for a bright green fight.

Where do our sweet yard companions get these conveniently fierce poisons? They metabolize them from the minerals in the soil, which are often attached to clay particles (many of these heavy metals are also used by the tree to discourage animals from eating their body parts). Many of the relevant chemicals are tannins (very prominent in oak leaves but also present in teas), humic acids, melanins, and quinines.

The Real Dirt

About 100,000 chemical weapons have been identified across the whole plant kingdom. One, for example, prevents any birch seedling that pops up near a black walnut from being able to photosynthesize at all. Some of these allelopathic chemicals might be developed into natural, well-targeted herbicides.

Trees pack this power into their leaves, their twigs, their cones, and, most often, into their roots. Rain and melted snow gradually wash the chemicals into the soil. Trees whose leaves decay quickly and those that thrive in areas with large amounts of rainfall can't be as good at allelopathy because the chemicals wash away too far or too fast. The eucalyptus plays an interesting twist on this: when it endures the stress of drought, it moves into allelopathy to get rid of its neighbors that would be competing for water.

The dry land mesquite tree mentioned is conveniently fast-growing and planted extensively so it makes for an interesting common example. Do you want a mesquite tree *and* a Bermuda grass lawn? You won't get both. Also disliking this grass variant—remember that grass roots are surprisingly extensive and so competitive with trees—are the sycamore, white oak, northern red oak, hackberry, and some eucalyptus trees.

This battling chemistry doesn't just apply to tree-to-tree competition either. Pine cones, at least of the Japanese red pine, won't let some weeds grow near them. And bilberry shrubs won't let Norway spruces thrive nearby. More David and Goliath battles emerge as the lovely but small heather plant beats out the Sitka spruce tree.

But the king-of-the-hill prize probably goes to the black walnut tree. It emits a chemical called *juglone*, with concentrations that can be strong enough to kill quite a few species of oak, birch, pine, and several other conifers. It allows red oaks to live—nice guy.

> **The Real Dirt**
>
> Tree chemistry goes even beyond blocking out other plants. As you'll see in Chapter 24, trees can communicate among themselves well enough to mount a group attack on insects, emitting the same chemical at once.

Extreme Weather

Although trees can be quite tough, weather extremes can be tougher. A load of snow, for example, can weigh hundreds of pounds when its moisture content is high. An aging or weakened tree can fail under all that weight. Ice is worse; encasing every branch in a thick swaddling, it can increase the weight on a branch by 30 percent, snap off branches, and take down many whole trees at once.

Unusual wind might not seem like it fits in this category, but if your tree has withstood significant winds from the prevailing direction—often out of the west in the United States—it has built up more trunk mass on that side. Believe it or not, a wind from the *other* direction can knock it down. So can a "straight line" wind, or an extremely horizontal one, because the tree's not used to dealing with that.

If lightning strikes your tree and strips off too many branches, or if it burns too widely around the trunk, the tree can fail. Lightning superheats the water and sap inside the trunk, which causes the tree to endure a fast expansion of its tissues— sometimes fast enough to kill a lot of the plant's cells. Trees can repair themselves after less severe strikes, but if they're too misshapen as a result, they can die later from structural problems.

> **Root Rot**
>
> Lightning strike wounds are an open invitation to insects and fungi infestation.

Root Rot

It might be common sense, but we have to say it: do not place your grill or picnic table under an elderly or impaired tree.

Urban Lifestyle

Living in an urban area is hard on a tree. In a natural forest, trees shield each other from wind. They can also stretch out their roots more amply, grow shoots and suckers at will, and hope that insects or deer pick on other trees in the group. Our yard trees, no matter how many, are more like only children, standing out there all by themselves.

Disposing of Dead Trees and Shrubs

As trees age, they develop problems that they had a better chance of surviving when they were younger or healthier. We've offered some ideas for extending their lives in this chapter, but don't feel guilty if your tree dies. Decays and weaknesses are part of their life cycle. Usually the final straw is a stiff wind. Unless you have removed them before this, they finally just topple over. It may not happen for 1 or 2 years after their death, but it will.

When a tree dies, you'll be faced with what to do with the "corpse." You can let it stay in place until it falls down on its own (depending on what might be in the way). You can hire a tree service to remove it. Or you can remove it yourself. Be very careful if you remove it yourself; large upper branches, perhaps partly rotted, can loosen and fall unpredictably. Of course, the trunk can, too! If it looks like a good idea to play "Tin Woodsman," saw or chop through the trunk at a comfortable arm level, maybe 3 or 4 feet up from the ground. This positions you best to run away if necessary. Then saw or chop the trunk again down to within a few inches of the ground. The stump can either be left to decay naturally over a few years or you can call a stump removal service (they'll chew up part of the root system, too).

Now you have several additional choices. Mulch/chip/compost it in place. Or build something out of the wood. Or send it to fill up the landfill, but please only consider that as a last resort.

Sprouts

The best time of year to remove a tree is winter in the north and the dry season in the south.

It costs to have your trees and shrubs processed and hauled away. The amount is based mostly on the size of the tree and how far it is from a driveway or street. Sloped backyards can require a crane to lift the tree over your house. Shrubs are pretty easy, of course.

The Least You Need to Know

◆ Your tree's branches might suffer from decay, poor attachment, bad tapering, stress from snow and ice, and summer drop.

◆ Trunks can rot, lean over, be knocked over, and be slit by lightning.

◆ Roots can become girdled, rotten, crowded, severed, or weakened in soggy soil.

◆ Some problems can be dealt with by pruning, but metropolitan life is hard on trees.

◆ Wind is usually the final blow that causes a tree to topple over.

◆ Inspect your trees and shrubs once every 1 or 2 years and after major storms.

Part 4

Tree and Shrub Diseases and Damages

Trees and shrubs can get sick or encounter accidents. The more you know about these pitfalls, the more likely your trees and shrubs are to survive them in good shape. In this final part, we explain how to prevent some major problems entirely, offer tips on diagnosing those that do occur, and share lots of information about the major illnesses and attackers of your trees and shrubs from tiny bacteria to big old deer.

Also included are plenty of examples of trees and shrubs that tend to be resistant to problems.

"Don't look behind you just now, but I think I heard something."

Chapter 20

Preventing Major Problems

Many problems your trees and shrubs encounter are preventable. Trees, with their size, extensive root systems, and, we hope, longer life spans, are more vulnerable, but shrubs require watching and care in some of these regards, too.

Problems can loom. Trees can become newly stressed—by crowding, by their own great growth, or by new street or sidewalk construction or utility work nearby. And of course, something those neighbors are doing may affect them, such as driving their heavy equipment over your trees' roots (which, yes, may have sidled into their yard)! Shrubs can become completely trampled.

In this chapter, we take a look at ways you can prevent or lessen some of the problems that plague trees and shrubs.

Construction Problems

Construction presents several issues for your trees and shrubs. The most obvious is that they may be severely wounded or chopped down in the excavation process. Even smaller wounds can be invitations to insects. Also, excess soil from a "big dig" can end up dumped over the root system of the nearby trees, reducing their access to water and oxygen by collapsing the pores of the soil. And the original soil layer over their roots can become compacted when repeatedly rolled over by heavy equipment and supplies. The roots of existing trees can't breathe in these situations, and new trees and shrubs often can't even be planted for years in such solidified soils.

Brand-new home construction isn't the only challenge. Problems can easily arise when building a patio or deck or expanding your house or when sidewalks, curbs, and gutters are added. Street widening and utility ditch digging cause problems, too.

And remember that your larger trees' roots, especially those near your lot line, might have snuck into your neighbors' yards, so they're vulnerable to what's going on over there.

In a construction project, sometimes trees are removed while others are left. The decision-making might not be up to you, but if it is, remember that mature trees are the most impressive, but younger trees will be with you for more years into the future. These younger trees—up to 40 years old—can cope better with the stress of a construction project. Those older than 70 adjust the least well, and the middle-agers are in the middle. You might even be successful digging up a tree smaller than 8 to 10 feet tall, placing it in a pot, and planting it somewhere else after the disruption is over. In fact, soil and other changes during construction are almost the same, from a tree's perspective, as being picked up and moved anyway. Just don't expect certain success.

To protect your trees near construction, install fencing around any tree in a vulnerable area, including its root system. Remember that the roots may easily extend twice as far out in all directions as the dripline.

Root Rot

If a tree or large shrub is deliberately taken down, the stump can suffer some of the same problems, inviting in, perhaps, carpenter ants or termites. Be sure to remove it, particularly if there is more than one affected stump or if any stump is near your house. Unless you have special grinding equipment, hire a professional to do this.

The Real Dirt

You might be able to persuade your city to replace all the trees and shrubs destroyed in construction projects. Try to get them to plant 3 to 5 times as many as they take down, because not every tree planted will live. You might even persuade your community to make tree and shrub protection and/or replacement part of every city construction project.

Roots Versus Construction

A healthy, mature tree can lose the function, or the entire existence, of up to one-third of the outermost areas of its root system and live to tell about it. It might be able to tolerate more loss than that because the roots gradually regenerate. That's the good news.

The bad news is that not every tree in your yard is this healthy and mature and that it's easier to exceed this one-third limit than you might think. With most of the roots lying in the top few feet of soil, machinery can cut them off. Also, construction often requires excavation and regrading. A pile of dirt can be dumped over the tree's roots, tamping down the air pockets in the soil, suffocating your trees and altering the flow of water in your yard. Also, if all the roots on one side of the tree happen to be compromised, the tree will lose stability. And it is also hard to know if the tree has more of its roots on one side than another, because there are many individual differences based on a variety of growing situations.

Fortunately, you can tell if the result is just too much for your plants:

Sprouts

To determine where you will and won't disturb roots, dig down just 1 inch with your hands in the area where you expect excavation. If you encounter no root thicker than 1 inch, that tree can probably survive the project.

- Are the newest leaves on the trees and shrubs in the construction area smaller and yellower?

- Do they look scorched in summer or fall off too early in autumn?

- Are twigs dying, or the new spring shoots short?

- Can you see evidence of new insect attacks?

If you see two or three of these symptoms during the first year after a major excavation, your tree may well be dying. Ponder whether you should take it down now or let it experience a slow death before toppling over.

The Real Dirt

Some research came out a couple years ago on city trees versus country trees. City trees seem to double their aboveground mass compared to those in small towns and rural areas in the same amount of time, given the same soil and other such conditions. The reason? The city slickers get extra warmth and more carbon dioxide, which help them compensate for ozone. That ozone, though, blows out especially easily to the countryside, overwhelming the seemingly more healthful conditions out there.

More Tree-Protection Tips

In addition to attention to the previously discussed preventative details, you can still do more to prevent construction damage to your trees and shrubs. Here's our top 5:

1. Designate a parking area for construction vehicles and zones for supply storage and debris containers. Bulk up that area with thick mulch or double and overlapping plywood sheets to help redistribute the weight of what's going on above.

2. Add a 12-inch-thick layer of woodchip mulch over any tree root areas where heavy equipment might pass.

3. Don't install hard surfaces under any trees, or at least have them lifted up off soil level on small footings, as with a deck.

4. Get your city to require tunneling under (not through) roots larger than an inch in diameter if encountered during utility trenching.

5. Have the city construct their sidewalks out of material that requires shallower excavation—reinforced concrete, for example, and with a geotextile fabric underneath it—anywhere near a tree.

Tree and Shrub First Aid

Tree wounds and cavities—caused by construction accidents, wind or storm breakage, aging issues, less-than-perfect pruning, cabling, or even diagnosis and injection of a "medicine"—need to be cared for as immediately as possible to prevent decay and disease from becoming established. You'll have help because the tree will try to heal itself—more like sealing itself—by developing *woundwood* or *calluses*. The wound remains, unlike a cut on your finger, but it's enclosed by the new wood. This is often called the *closure* or *compartmentalization* of a wound.

Repair occurs from the outside perimeter of the wound in, from some or all sides. Although the end result might be smooth bark, the wound is still inside so it can continue decaying—if the decay was allowed to get out of hand initially. The more vigorous your tree is, the better it repairs its wounds and prevents decay.

Root Rot

Fast-growing trees tend to decay faster because their lives are shorter.

The shape of the wound and its position on the tree don't seem to make much difference, except wounds to the trunk above its strongest roots are repaired faster. You can bandage torn bark (see the later "Lightning Strikes!" section).

Unlike with people's wounds, you want to be very careful about trying to sterilize a tree wound because that kills the *good* microorganisms that often move in to consume the decay-causing fungi. And wounds from the injections can become compromised, too. Repeated Dutch elm disease treatments with harsh chemicals, for example, can cause internal damage to trees (although some of the plant-growth regulators used do not). Trees can generally cope with an injection every 3 to 5 years, but not more often.

Cleaning and Dressing the Wound

Leave the living bark in place, but remove the dead bark. This gives insects less area to hide in.

Despite what product labels might say, nothing chemical (as opposed to mechanical) is available to encourage faster repair without side effects, so save your money! The only acceptable step is to cover the wound. This keeps it from drying out or freezing and allows the tree hormone ethylene to remain nearer to the wound to do its work.

Replacing Loose Bark

Replacing loose bark helps, but only if you do it quickly. Get rid of the shredded pieces, fit the old bark back on, and hold it down with a small amount of duct tape or small tacks. Cover your handiwork with a moist cloth, peat moss, or even damp paper towels, and wrap it all up by tying plastic around the trunk or branch. Check in a week or two. If the bark hasn't begun readhering, remove everything, allowing light and the tree itself to take over. If your doctoring is starting to work, wrap everything back up and check in another week or so. You'll be able to see by then whether your efforts have worked.

If you haven't discovered the bark wound quickly, remove all the loose pieces, clean the wound, and cover it very loosely and only with plastic. Don't allow the plastic to touch the wound; tape a kind of loose pouch around the wound. Secure everything with duct tape, but not tightly. You want the wound to dry on its own.

Root Rot

Don't use clear plastic to wrap the bark back on the tree because that won't protect the wound from too much sun.

Buttressing Your Trees and Shrubs

Mechanical strengthening methods can help keep your trees from toppling over in a storm. These are all best done by a professional. Buttressing can be done to prop up large limbs, and cabling a weakened two-part trunk together is also possible. These measures are usually necessary and suitable only for large, mature trees that you really, really want to save; that have a good prognosis if you do; and that could create significant damage if they were allowed to fail. But if serious damage could occur to property or people from a weakened tree, it should be removed.

Lightning Strikes!

Trees are quite often hit by lightning. Most city trees seal off the wounds and live. In a natural forest, though, this is often how forest fires get started. In settled areas, access to fire trucks is easy, and so we're not going to address the fire aspect of lightning here. Instead, let's look at how to prevent lightning from harming your trees directly and what to do if it does.

Sprouts

If your trees tend to be shorter than those of your neighbors, if you live on lower ground than the yards surrounding yours, if your trees are primarily young or middle-aged and vigorous, and if you live in an area of the country with relatively few lightning storms, you might not have to worry about lightning.

Lightning and thunderstorms pack a huge punch. Some storms last much longer than others, and some have more lightning than others. Every thunderstorm has some lightning—10 million to 100 million volt strokes, scorching fast through the atmosphere—but not all lightning travels down to the ground. Quite a bit is cloud-to-cloud lightning and within-cloud lightning. And even when it hits ground or jumps over from where it does hit, it doesn't always "find" a tree.

To boost the chances of escaping lightning damage, remove decaying trees and ponder planting trees that are less susceptible than others.

If your tree is hit, it may lose one branch or be sliced in two vertically. It may have its crown killed or trunk split. Sometimes one large branch or trunk looks as though the bark had been whittled off by a giant knife. And sometimes it gets burnt black.

If you live in a significant zone for lightning and have susceptible tall trees near your house, you might want to mount protection by installing one or more copper (not aluminum) wires from the top of the tree down along the trunk, to about 25 feet away from the trunk. Ground the wire (or two or three wires if the tree is large) to a copper rod that you then bury 10 feet underground at that outer level. This "grounds" the lightning through the copper instead of solely through the tree. The exact ways to do this depend on your soil, and the thicknesses of wire and rod vary with the size of the tree. The system needs to be inspected every couple years during the dormant season, too. Thinking of using a reputable professional? Good idea.

> **The Real Dirt** _____
>
> Note that this protection doesn't completely prevent lightning from attacking your tree—nothing can really do that—but it does direct the lightning into the ground after it hits, instead of into the whole body of the tree.

Cold Weather Care

There are some remaining considerations that focus on the dormant season—late fall and winter. *Winterburn*, a kind of sunburn that occurs in winter because the tree is less accustomed to hot sun then, is just one example. During this time, your trees and shrubs are, in a sense, hibernating. They receive less-intense sunlight, so they gradually conduct less photosynthesis. Without that energy elixir, a lot of what else they do slows down or stops. Your trees and shrubs seem to need more help from you in this season, especially the younger ones—and no stress, at the very least.

Here are some suggestions to help your plants through the dormant season:

> **def•i•ni•tion** _____
>
> **Winterburn,** or *sunscald*, can turn some trees' boughs brown, permanently dead.

- ◆ Shovel or mop up road salts and other street chemicals, including gasolines and oils from vehicles, if they encroach within the dripline of a tree or near a shrub.

- ◆ Don't drive over any roots by mistake, even if it's hard to tell where the edge of your driveway is with all the snow! (Totally frozen ground, though, is okay.)

- ◆ Shake the snow off any delicate shrub, leaving a little on for insulation. (By delicate, we mean one where you might have given in to temptation and pushed your zone a bit.)

- ◆ Consider chicken-wire fencing for the plantings especially attractive to winter-roaming critters.

- ◆ Don't let the dog toilet near the same few trees and shrubs all winter long.

◆ Ponder installing a temporary wooden-slatted snow fence.

◆ Don't allow any tree or shrub to overwinter outside in a pot, even if it's a large pot.

Of course, your trees and shrubs don't really need to be totally babied, especially the mature ones. Jeannie has a white pine at least 200 years old that can support a couple thousand pounds of wet snow in quite comfortable grandeur. And a neighbor has a cotoneaster hedge that, in a different storm, became encased in a huge, rectangular ice box—with no harm done.

The Least You Need to Know

◆ Construction can kill trees and shrubs, and the process can take several years to become evident.

◆ Root systems are especially easy to damage.

◆ Some aboveground wounds can be "bandaged" successfully.

◆ Winter brings challenges, but they can often be met.

Chapter 21

Making a Diagnosis

In This Chapter

- Diagnosing problems in your trees and shrubs
- Discovering what is and what isn't a major problem
- Is the culprit biological or nonbiological?
- Knowing when to call in a pro

Not every problem can be prevented, and sometimes your trees and shrubs do get damaged. Whether it's during a home expansion, a civic project such as a new sidewalk, difficult weather, poor soils, pollution, critters, or another culprit, this damage can take its toll. Younger trees and shrubs tend to be better able to withstand sudden changes, but older trees are more vulnerable to the sheer accumulation of a lifetime of onslaughts.

But don't worry, there's a lot you can do after you see the problem, understand it, and learn some remedy tips.

Tools and Supplies

As with most jobs, you need tools and supplies to do the job well. That's true with diagnosing your tree and shrub patients, too. Here are the basics you'll need before you head out into your yard:

- Notepad (electronic or paper) to sketch the location and record issues you see as you walk around your yard.

- Camera to record special problem issues so you can show the images to an expert (a free one at the plant store or botanical garden, perhaps).

- Binoculars to observe problems high up in trees.

- Small hand magnifier to look for insect or disease evidence.

- Plastic bags with blank, sticky labels to scoop up any offending insects, a sample of a small gall, an infected-looking twig, a diseased or unusual-looking leaf, etc. Label anything on the spot, with the species and location of the relevant tree or shrub written on the sticker. Also, if you don't know what kind of tree you're dealing with, add enough leaves to the bag so the expert can identify it. (That helps with diagnosis because many specific afflictions are associated with specific species.)

Root Rot

For the general home-owner, we don't advocate gouging into trees with chisels, augurs, or saws—or equipping yourself with an electron microscope or even a soil tube. Leave that to the pros.

- Your smallest pruning tool to clip off a problem twig to store in one of the plastic bags. Remember to disinfect the tool if you're clipping from more than one tree because it might be evidence of a transmittable disease.

Take a Look Around

It's hard not to assume the worst when you see signs of stress on one of your trees or shrubs, but don't jump to that conclusion right away. An otherwise healthy tree or shrub could lose all its leaves, be chewed into green lace, or turn a strange color and still survive. Remember, deciduous trees and shrubs survive the loss of *all* their leaves every year and conifers drop their needles within 2 to 9 years, depending on the species—and they live to green up again!

But do note the following information for each situation you find unusual as you inspect your yard dwellers:

- Where on your tree or shrub does the situation occur—leaves, bark, above-ground roots, stems, or trunks?

- What's the pattern of the problem? Are there spots only on leaf edges? Do the smaller shoots look warped? Is the bark disturbed on one side?

- ◆ What's the extent of the problem? Does it affect the whole plant or its lower branches only?

- ◆ Did this happen gradually or suddenly? (If you know.)

- ◆ Does the problem occur on all your (and nearby neighbors') trees and bushes of the same species, or just on one tree or shrub?

- ◆ Where within your yard is the problem? On the slopes only? Next to the street?

- ◆ Have you recently pruned, watered, fertilized, or mulched this tree or shrub?

The reasons behind some of these questions emerge as you continue reading. For now, we'll just point out that living creatures (from a fungus to a termite) tend to pick only on their favorite species of tree or shrub—and do their damage over a period of a few years. A weather issue, however, causes more widespread damage. And soil and herbicide damage may affect a group of trees or shrubs of the same age.

Now it's time for a closer examination. You're still in the information-gathering stage here, though, because a given symptom can be from several different causes. (Where it is most likely to be from one cause, we've specified that. Otherwise, you'll need to read the rest of the chapter to better link symptoms with causes.) Record these conditions and photograph any special situations, in case you need professional advice.

Sprouts

The more you know about past conditions around your patient, the better you'll be at diagnosing. And remember that symptoms often don't show up for several years after an injury.

Leaf Yellowing

Discoloration of green leaves can take several forms:

- ◆ Mottled or blotched

- ◆ Yellowed leaf tissue but green veins

- ◆ Stippled or dotted with yellow

The causes include insects, too much soil moisture, too little nutrition, pollutants such as herbicides in the soil, too-cold weather, and too much or too little mineral content in the soil. (Pin oaks and sweetgum trees are prone to iron deficiency, for example.)

The result of this condition is poor growth. Look for insects first and then don't water for a while. Next, skip the herbicides and then perhaps send out some soil to a local agricultural extension service, university, or garden store to be tested for mineral content. Allow enough time in between to really rule out—or in—each possible cause.

Leaf Scorch

Here, parts of the leaves have turned light or dark brown and dried out enough that they look scorched by fire. Basically, the leaves have dried out dramatically.

Sprouts

Leaf scorch is certainly unattractive but, with attention to the chemical factors—and hope for a better season next time—an otherwise vigorous tree will usually survive to leaf out next spring.

This partial leaf death can occur at the tip, along the margins, or in scattered interior areas. Or the entire leaf may have died. Or the leaves may be healthy in certain areas of the tree while other areas such as the canopy are completely brown. Causes include drought; a sudden increase in the amount of sunlight after a very long cloudy period; too-hot weather; too much wind; frozen soil; too little potassium; or too much boron, chloride, or sodium.

Other Leaf Irregularities

In addition to scorching, the leaves may have blistered areas, generally caused by insect activity. They may have a powdery, mildew-y look thanks to a fungus. And they may have irregular dead areas—sometimes a whole branch, a few shoots or twigs, leaf edges only, or whole leaves. This probably comes from anthracnose, a fungal infection that looks bad and is bad, although it can take years to kill the tree. It can be treated by a fungicide spray on the leaves or an injection into the trunk.

Wilting

Here, the leaves have collapsed from lack of moisture in their cells. Your soil might be too dry, but it also could be flooded or too salty. The roots may have been damaged in some way, including by girdling, which can strangle the tree. It might be too hot for the tree. Or a fungus may have attacked.

You can probably try watering (and enough to dilute any salt) and check for insects, considering pesticide if they appear to be the cause. If girdling is the culprit, consult a professional—don't attempt to cut that root yourself.

Leaf Drop

This one you'll really notice if it's spring or summer and suddenly one of your deciduous trees has no leaves at all. If your yard has endured a very dry period, that's the most probable cause. Water the tree, but expect no new crop of leaves until next spring, if you're lucky. Only about 25 percent survive a *complete* leaf drop.

Other causes include leaf yellowing, leaf scorch, and leaf wilting over the long-term as well as rootloss from soil toxins and too-cold or too-hot temperatures. You could also swear off lawn chemicals if you think that might be the cause.

The Real Dirt _____

Brown leaves, on which the dead areas edge the leaves or run between the veins, are often evidence of drought, especially in trees you've recently planted or transplanted.

Needle Drop

If conifer needles have spots that seem to be coalescing until the needle dies, this is a fungal infection. White or orange blisters, created by insects, can also cause them to drop off.

Conifers usually are less likely to lose all their needles to disease than deciduous trees are to lose all their leaves because needles represent 2 to 9 years of growth and then shedding, a major investment by the tree, which tends to have become protected by evolution. Leaves are the investment of 1 year.

Twig and Branch Dieback

With this condition, the evidence starts at the tips and moves in toward the trunk. If you suspect this is your problem, think back: did the outermost leaves start to die first? If so, check out the previous leaf problems. Otherwise, consider blaming fungi, bacteria, scale insects, and boring insects. The dieback could also be from drought, too-cold weather, soil that isn't draining properly, and lawn chemicals.

Sprouts _____

Herbicide can travel far, and invisibly, on a hot day, even when there's no wind. A neighbor many houses away may have sprayed a chemical that affects trees and shrubs in your yard. If several of your trees and shrubs develop twisted or curled leaves, that might be the cause. But there's good news: they will probably recover.

Lion's Tail Shoots

Lion's tail shoots look as though a fluffy lion's tail (leaves on a small shoot) is growing out of the top of a branch, the stub of a branch, or even a stump—similar to a hand, without enough arm, stuck to a body. Have you pruned too much? That could cause it. Is the tree surrounded by impervious pavement and is so starved that it's releasing buds in desperation, in the wrong places? If not, the cause is probably old age or a slow-progressing disease that has been affecting the tree for a long time, weakening its growth.

Witches' Brooms

Witches' brooms are similar to lion's tail shoots but grow out of the end of twigs. Here, salt spray from winter road treatments is often the culprit, as are insects and genetic conditions. The result looks like a broom. Watering the tree can help.

Cankers

Cankers are lesions in the bark deep enough to kill a layer of phloem, cambium, and some xylem (see Chapter 1). They come from an infection on trunks, branches, twigs, or even roots, by a microorganism of some kind, usually a fungus.

What Is or Isn't a Worry

The good news is that some features of your trees and shrubs that might look weird to you are actually normal. We give examples here, dealing with leaves, bark, flowers and fruit, growths (swollen areas), and various harmless tree "decorations."

Unusual Leaf Coloring

Some shrubs and trees are actually supposed to start the spring with coppery or reddish leaves. The apricot tree and Chinese photinia are such examples. No problem—the green will come! Check with a plant store when in doubt about a given species.

And quite a few shrubs start their growing year with yellowish leaves if the spring is wet and cool. They'll fix themselves.

Among evergreens, sometimes the oldest batch of needles (here and there around the trees) turns yellow or brown before dropping off. The white pine does this, for example. Remember that conifers lose their needles across several years.

Root Rot

Check regularly for rotten mulch or mulch too close to the trunk, which provides a breeding ground for fungal spores.

And both summer and fall weather conditions, which naturally vary from year to year, can cause any tree's or shrub's leaves to turn from green to their autumn color at different times within fall. Everything should start over fine by the following spring.

Unusual Leaf Drop or Retention

Some trees and shrubs deliberately dump all their leaves to cope with even a moderate drought period. The California buckeye is one of these. Southern magnolias can get rid of that year's leaves in almost any season, no matter how unvarying the conditions

seem to be. And some trees keep some, most, or all their dead leaves all winter, shedding them only as the new buds push them off.

Sprouts

The beeches, chestnuts, and several oaks such as the cork oak are known for dropping their leaves in a drought.

The beeches, chestnuts, and several oaks such as the cork oak tree qualify here.

Bark Oddities

Peeling, cracking, and furrowing bark are not necessarily bad. Your paper birch, river birch, plane tree, or Russian olive is not sick! And that furrowed skin on the trunk of your black walnut, black locust, or mulberry is really just stretch marks formed as the tree fills out.

No Flowers *and* No Fruit?

Young shrubs, especially those whose flowers form on spur shoots, usually don't flower until they are 3 or 4 years old. Again, don't worry! And some shrubs just display a kind of natural energy efficiency, creating a large crop of flowers and fruit one year and then almost none the next year. Crabapples and apricot trees often do this, often to outwit predators.

Growths (Galls)

These swellings, called galls, can occur on any part of the tree, not just the trunk; they can even look like tumors. Sometimes they're signs of a fungal or bacterial infection, but sometimes they're actually something you *want* to see.

A gall can be a reservoir of latent buds (ready to spring into action if the tree loses too many branches); the redwood does this. Or a gall may be the compartmentalization, the sealing, of a wound on any tree, from lightning, pruning, insects, or other causes. (See Chapter 22 for a discussion of crown gall.) Or it might be housing good bacteria that help the tree fix nitrogen from the soil to grow; examples of this phenomenon occur in the silk tree and the black locust.

The Real Dirt

Pale green lichen such as "grandfather's beard" festooning a northwoods tree, not only is especially beautiful, but is also a sign of extremely fresh air. Like that lichen!

Tree "Décor"

Décor is our word for the lichen, moss, and algae that might decorate your tree or shrub, especially in shady, damp areas near a large body of water or in quite warm climates in general. The Spanish moss of the southeastern United States is a good example of a plant that doesn't hurt the tree at all. (Find more on these tree companions in Chapter 22.)

Diagnosing Biological Causes

Don't expect to be perfect at diagnosis. The causes of the symptoms we described earlier in this chapter can be multiple, and one cause can mask the evidence of another, as well as capitalizing on any tree or shrub previously weakened. Weakening can come, too, just from being recently planted or transplanted, or from aging—it doesn't have to be a major drought or powerful storm, or anything else you've been around to notice.

And not every problem needs to be dealt with. Almost every tree and shrub in your yard has some sort of minor wound—and will be able to overcome it. But for troublesome symptoms, let's look at some possible culprits, in the context of general diagnosis and advice (Chapter 22 offers more information about specific organisms).

Fungi

Fungi are the most common cause of infections in your trees and shrubs, although most of the fungi worldwide do no harm to us or our plantings. The only part of them we can see are their reproductive parts—the mushroom, molds, and growths (the rest is underground or inside the leaf or twig).

With so many possible fungal diseases, let's look at one very common example that you might diagnose: does your oak have a growth on the trunk at ground level? Check for armillaria root rot, especially if you also see irregular dying of some but not all the leaves. This is incurable, although new leaves will emerge to replace the dead ones over the next few months or in the next growing season. It does help to water the tree. Death could come quickly or could take decades.

Bacteria

These tiny organisms can make their way into your tree or shrub whether it has a wound or not, but more easily if it does. Fortunately, most of these bacteria are harmless—and quite a few are beneficial. The bad ones, though, can cause a huge variety of symptoms from blackened leaves to cankers and galls. Our general advice here is to disinfect your pruning tools to halt the spread every time you prune.

Viruses

Even smaller than bacteria, these organisms need to highjack some of the host cells of your trees and shrubs to reproduce. Typically, they spread via a sucking insect such as an aphid, a leaf hopper, or a scale insect. What you'll see as a diagnostician is diminished or distorted growth in your tree or shrub, dead areas, or a lack of greening.

Sprouts

Unless the whole tree or shrub looks as though it's dying, just let nature do its own curing. The plant may recover.

Mycoplasma

These tiny organisms cause at least 150 plant diseases, usually arriving via a leaf-hopper insect. They multiply to interfere with the tree's or shrub's circulatory system, causing ash, elms, and palms to yellow, for example. And they cause witches' broom, dieback of branches, and a halt to flower and fruit development. The best coping mechanism is to keep the tree or shrub healthy enough to fight them off.

Insects and Mites

To insects and mites, your trees and shrubs are everything from a banquet to a maternity ward. They chew, furrow, suck, and drill through leaves, as well as lay their eggs on them. Sometimes you can see them at work, although many have evolved nocturnal habits. (In that case, look for little slimy tracks or egg cases in the morning!)

Parasitic Plants

One common example here is the well-known mistletoe and dwarf mistletoe, a large family of parasites that infects trees and shrubs across all but our northern tier of states. Some can seed explosively, emitting their seeds as far as 30 feet from the plant. These small seeds have even been found 400 miles away after a strong windstorm. Birds and small mammals also spread the seeds. When it's on the trunk of your ash tree, for example, the mistletoe begins to burrow in and can make a swollen area that looks like a swollen muscle on a human arm.

This parasite also reduces its host's vigor because it taps into—and uses up—some of the nutrients. It also makes it more vulnerable to all the other problems discussed in this chapter.

Diagnosing Nonbiological Causes

These problem-causers include moisture problems, soil compaction from equipment, and fill dirt. Usually roots suffer the most, but there are more culprits, too, as the following sections outline.

Mechanical Injury

Most common agents here are lawnmowers, weed whackers, and other destructive "tools." Almost any lawn equipment can unwittingly slice into bark or into above-ground root. This is particularly easy to do along the driveway or in tight corners. Even vandals can cause damage.

If more than a half circle of bark has been lost around the circumference of any young tree, whatever the width of that circle, you're better off destroying that tree. If your area might have a problem such as this, note that bark is the most vulnerable part of the plant because it protects the tree's or shrub's circulatory system. The most vulnerable seasons, when an injury can lead to severe problems, are spring and summer when growth is most vigorous—and necessary. The youngest plantings also suffer the worst damages. Even when it isn't evident, inner decay can take hold because some microorganisms can "smell" a plant's injury and come on over.

Storm Damage

This kind of problem goes beyond the obvious loss of a limb or uprooting of a whole tree. Heavy, wet snow is one culprit. Especially vulnerable here are the small to medium-size conifers and any young trees. You might want to rake or broom some of the snow off—and, if you do, loosen the load gently from the underside of a branch up, shoving it upward, redistributing the snow that way.

Hail and wind can be successfully challenged, too. Check for any wounds from a hail storm on the upper parts of the branches, where they will appear as elliptical depressions. You might need to make a note to do some pruning later, at the proper time.

Sprouts _____

Get out the hose and soak the soil at the dripline, especially if it's a young tree. This works against the hot, dry winds!

Chemical Injury

Herbicides and pesticides are what you need to watch out for here. Herbicides are supposed to kill plants, and they do, but sometimes the wrong ones. Combination herbicide/fertilizer products are the worst, resulting in distorted or discolored leaves and shoots. Check for this kind of problem and water well—or risk losing the plant.

The chemical 2, 4-D is particularly damaging. After it's absorbed, it moves throughout the plant. When applied to nearby weeds, it can reach your tree and shrub roots through water movement in the soil as well as by wind. Problems can show up even the next spring after a fall application in the area. Check your trees for curled-up or cup-shaped leaves, leaves drooping down, twisted shoot tips, cracked calluses on larger shoots, and leaf drop.

Pesticides injure trees and shrubs most easily when temperatures rise above the mid-70s, especially on humid days. The liquids are worse than the powders, and the sprays are the worst, especially those made of lime sulfur and sulfur. Strong trees can survive pesticides more easily than herbicides.

Salt Problems

Salts can come from fertilizers, road chemicals, ocean breezes, and even from watering and the soil itself (mineral particles, from broken-down rock that makes up soil, have salts as part of their chemical makeup). Usually salt needs to build up across a period of years to become a problem.

Look for simply slower growth (which we realize is hard to notice), earlier fall color and leaf drop, and scorching at the tips and edges of the leaves on deciduous trees. Conifers suffer from death at the needle tips, which proceeds inward more and more with increased exposures. Low rainfall only makes a salt situation worse. Regardless of weather, effects usually appear in late winter on conifers but not until spring on deciduous trees and shrubs.

Trees native to ocean areas can withstand sea spray, provided a hurricane doesn't push inland to areas where the trees are not accustomed to it. But street trees all over the country can have real trouble, especially if city trucks or passing cars hurl the salts far enough up to hit them or drift onto them.

Pollution

Trees and shrubs evolved over the millennia, when the air was cleaner. When they don't get good air, the leaves show the problem the most. Not only the tips and edges are affected but also stippling occurs on their tops and silvering on their lower sides.

The biggest problems are usually from sulfur dioxide, fluoride, and ozone, from power plants (especially coal-fired), other industries, and large concentrations of gasoline-burning vehicles. The sulfur dioxide creates bleached or brownish areas on leaves and dead tips and discolored banding on needles. Fluoride affects mainly the tips of both leaves and needles. And ozone causes flecking, stippling, banding, and mottling on the leaves and needles.

Root Rot

Road re-paving equipment that emits heat as well as asphalt chemicals is also especially damaging.

When to Call in a Pro

Even after all you've learned in these pages, you still might need to call in a pro. Call a free source of advice first, such as a top nursery's or university's help line. Also visit the staff of a local arboretum, botanical garden, environmental organization, or garden store. It's helpful to take in evidence such as a damaged leaf or a photograph of your diagnostic problem. These people might tell you that you don't need to do anything about some or all of the problems you've found. Or they might just solve the problem for free.

But you may need some more expert help …

- If the diseased area is high up in a tall tree and large branch sections need to be pruned.

- If the "patient" is a most beloved one you want to do everything possible to save.

- If the problem is affecting several trees and shrubs in your yard at once.

- If you need an expert report for insurance purposes, a dispute, or even a lawsuit.

- If you think there's a chance that a tree part falling down or toppling over might injure someone or damage property.

- If you're considering buying a new home and the trees and shrubs are a key to its appeal.

The Least You Need to Know

- You can diagnose many problems by looking at leaves.

- Many tiny creatures can invade your trees and shrubs, but most plants will recover.

- Keeping trees and shrubs healthy in general is the best defense.

- You can play CSI yourself to find info on symptoms and get free or low-cost advice before hiring a professional.

22

Bacteria, Viruses, Fungi, and More

In This Chapter

◆ All about bacteria

◆ Understanding viruses

◆ Fungi: the good, the bad, and the ugly

◆ But wait! There's more!

Most of the starring characters in this chapter are invisible. A few are visibly unattractive (some of the larger soil organisms), and two (that make only cameo appearances) are easy to spot and usually beautiful (the lichen and the mosses). What you can't—and can—see either helps *or* hurts your trees and shrubs. Let's take a look.

Meet the Microorganisms

Bacteria, viruses, and fungi—all considered *microorganisms*—are in either a mutual relationship with your yard companions, in which they help each other, or a parasite-prey relationship, in which the microorganism damages the tree or shrub. They usually gain access into the trees through minor wounds, just as we carry around small scratches that can become infected.

def•i•ni•tion

Microorganisms are tiny organisms, so small that you'd need a microscope to see them. Bacteria, viruses, and fungi are three kinds.

Bacteria Basics

Bacteria can't move around very well—and so most have evolved to have a relationship with only one species of plant. And the young tree or shrub is usually their best—and easiest—mark. This plays out differently in a natural forest versus in your yard.

In the forest, the trees and shrubs have figured out the bad bacteria (sort of) and try to spread out to get their offspring to grow up as far from home as is feasible. The "parents" do this by designing their seeds to blow away or be taken away some distance by an animal or a bird. A nice distance in nature is about a third of a mile, far enough to be a quite *in*convenient distance for the bacteria, viruses, and fungi looking to colonize them. But in our yards, we don't set up this flexibility. In fact, having a grove (or even a pair) of trees of the same species close together makes it quite likely that one of these microorganisms will begin to spread through your yard.

The Good Guys

Not every microorganism is a bad guy, though—far from it. Somewhere between 700 and 3,000 species of our trees (and unimaginably large numbers of shrubs) worldwide actually couldn't live without soil bacteria. These bacterial friends allow the trees to live in quite poor soils of various kinds—alders growing in soggy places and mangroves in water are two examples. Bacterial microorganisms, usually composed of only one cell, change the soil so it provides nutrition for the tree or shrub, essentially making fertilizer.

 The Real Dirt

Soils and their constituents are also useful in archaeology, telling us about what early people did above that area of soil. Extra phosphorous means wastes, including food remains, and even burials occurred there. Extra potassium and magnesium tend to indicate that wood was burned above that swatch of soil.

Large numbers of soil bacteria—from about 12 different huge families and represented by billions of bacteria in every tablespoon of soil—can "fix nitrogen." They break it down chemically into a form your yard companions can use, generally nitrate or ammonia. That nitrogen got there in the soil to begin with as rocks crumbled into dirt, organic matter decayed, and lightning burned it out of the atmosphere into the rain which dripped down into the soil. Trees and shrubs can't use "raw" nitrogen until it's broken down by the bacteria, whereupon it's like pure protein for the plant, used to grow every part of their bodies from the roots to the newly born leaves.

To get this benefit, trees and shrubs have to offer something in return. In addition to providing housing for some of the species in their roots, they also share a portion of the carbohydrates they produce in their own photosynthesis. They could use this extra food themselves—but there's no free lunch. The bacteria need to eat, too. It *is* a free "lunch" for us, because it means we almost never need to go out and buy nitrogen fertilizer for our trees and shrubs.

 The Real Dirt

Bacteria probably caused the invention of sex! Sex evolved as a way to shuffle genes—it leads to variety in the next generation instead of cloned sameness. This variety developed to confuse parasites (of all kinds) that wanted convenient uniformity in their "hosts" so they could spread better.

The Bad Guys

Some bacteria are nasty! You'll know if you see black, shriveled, or wilted leaves on a tree or shrub, perhaps a growth on the twigs, branch, or trunk, maybe even a substance oozing from the bark. These bad guys might have arrived in your yard on diseased firewood, in the feces or mouths of insects, or on pruning tools.

An excellent example of a bacterial disease is crown gall. The organism comes in via the soil, creates nasty nodules there and then even larger, bulbous ones on the trunk of the tree. Those forming only on individual branches may not shorten the life of your plant, but large galls of this type on the trunk mean poor growth and perhaps early death. (You can find general info on galls in Chapter 21.)

Fire blight is another common bacterial disease. It goes after some fruit trees and common shrubs such as the cotoneaster. An attacked plant looks as though it was singed by fire and the affected shoots are bent. Prune off the infected areas well below the end of the infected area. Don't fertilize the plant, though, because that fertilizes the fungus, too!

We can't really treat most bacteria-borne diseases in trees and shrubs effectively. The trees and shrubs do it themselves. Trees, especially, can surround a lot of infections, creating compartments or physical barriers out of xylem cells in the trunk. These six-sided jails for wounds usually hold up pretty well, confining decay from bacterial or other infections, pruning, wounds, and other problems.

Some ordinary galls, also called "burls," are often caused by an invading organism but can be pruned away.

Viruses

Even tinier than bacteria (and not even complete cells), viruses can only multiply inside the cells of another organism. When in, they commandeer those cells to produce themselves instead, the way cold viruses do in our noses. Tree and shrub viruses are spread mostly by sucking insects such as aphids and leafhoppers and by grafting projects.

The Real Dirt

Occasionally, viruses leave your tree with a decorative result. The mosaic virus on hackberry trees, for example, makes their foliage variegated, although that does stress the tree. The lovely stripes on some tulip trees are caused by a virus—one deliberately introduced into the tulip genome long ago.

Symptoms of viral diseases include leaves that aren't properly green (they can no longer make chlorophyll), whole trees or shrubs that don't grow as vigorously or may grow in a distorted way, or even dead areas on the plant. There's very little you can do, so just let the tree or shrub try to take care of it by compartmentalizing the problem. But don't worry. Although viral infections do weaken the tree, they're almost never fatal.

Fungi

If we had eyes that could see underground or could observe the microscopic "rainstorm" every autumn that decorates the air over our yards with fungal spores, we'd be flabbergasted at the array and extent of the *fungi*. Soil fungi are all around you. At least 85 percent of the plant species on Earth have a species of fungus evolved specifically to live with them, and many have more than one such species. And as with bacteria, some fungi are good guys and some are bad guys.

If your trees and shrubs are growing vigorously, they can enjoy the good fungi while they compartmentalize off, chemically combat, or even outgrow the bad ones. Just be sure to water, mulch, and maybe fertilize your young trees and don't injure them with improper pruning or compacting their soil with construction equipment. For older trees with fungal infections such as those described later in the chapter, watering them during dry spells can enable them to thrive better.

def•i•ni•tion

A **fungus** (plural: *fungi*) is one of a vast nonplant kingdom that are not green and that spread by microscopic filaments. Soils that are too warm or too cool, in general, are more conducive to the spread of soil fungi.

There's also no need to remove what you *can* see of the fungi such as a mushroom because that isn't the main part of their bodies anyway. And it hasn't proved effective or necessary, scientists say, to add the good fungi by inoculating the roots of your trees and shrubs. So no work is required!

Fungi spread so easily—by wind, insects, raindrop splashes, along with infected garden tools—that it would usually be pointless to interfere anyway (with some exceptions discussed later in this chapter). Their spores, which function as seeds but are more primitive in evolutionary terms, are emitted by the millions by each fungus.

What You See and What You Don't

Because fungi colonize new areas by spores, spread underground by microscopic filaments, and live hidden inside other plants, they're mostly invisible. Tiny enough to drill their way into an evergreen needle, they also inhabit leaves, stems, roots, and virtually every part of your tree or shrub, depending on the species. Whole kingdoms live on roots.

The visible evidence we most commonly encounter takes three forms: mushrooms, cankers, and conks. These are only their "fruiting bodies," much as an apple is the fruiting part of an apple tree. It's the body part that houses the seed, there to create the next generation.

Mushrooms in the natural woods usually "bloom" in autumn or the dry season. Most can be seen on or near dead vegetation (leaf litter or tree trunk, for example). These fungi are a sign that your soil is hospitable. Picking one has no effect on the below-ground plant.

Cankers are knoblike lesions, most obvious on the trunk of a tree and usually but not always caused by a fungus. The fungus has killed part of the inner bark layers in that area or on part of a branch, twig, even a root. Their shape is circular, oval, more distinct or more diffuse, and fast- or slow-growing, depending on the fungal species involved. Most trees can seal off the canker and go about their lives.

Root Rot

A canker that encircles the trunk is a major problem because it makes the tree less efficient at processing water and nutrients.

Conks are pale, shelflike protuberances from the trunk of a tree. As with other visible fungal structures, they are a sign that the fungus is already established. There's really nothing you can do.

Other fungal evidence includes small spots up and down part of a conifer's needles or splotched on the leaves, or formed into large blobs where the trunk meets the ground. And perhaps the most colorful large entry in the fungus sweepstakes is the brilliant orange and red "chicken of the woods."

Good Fungi

Many fungi species are in harmless relationships with your trees and shrubs—and even benefit them. Fungi we humans enjoy include the many that taste great. Others cause lovely colors in the grain of the wood and so beckon makers of furniture.

Other fungi provide significant benefits to your trees and shrubs, doing everything from anchoring the trunk more fully (they flesh out its roots), detoxifying soil pollutants, warding off grazing animals and predatory insects (by making the plants' leaves taste bad to these creatures), adding vigor by helping the tree absorb nutrients, and even virtually taking over as food service managers by completely encasing the roots and orchestrating both water and nutrient absorption by the trees' roots.

The stand-out good guy fungi for your trees and shrubs are the mycorrhizal (*mike-oh-rise-ell*) fungi. These underground root friends for your trees and shrubs haul in the nutrients and sometimes even keep root diseases from taking hold by sheathing entire roots with their own bodies. They look and act as the tiniest root hairs of the tree itself. All they ask in return is for some of the tree's carbohydrates, made by the plant aboveground through photosynthesis, usually between 4 and 20 percent.

Bad Fungi

If you see a blob at the base of a tree or shrub, it might be one of the decay fungi that attack living plants. Other bad guys, ones you won't see, specialize in invading the most significant part of the root system or living entirely inside the trunk. Usually either white or brown, these fungi consume different parts of the plant.

With a fungus specialized to each of thousands of trees and shrubs, we can't list all the bad guys here. But here are the common ones:

Do you have brown, spotted, or shriveled leaves falling off an oak, an ash, a dogwood, or a maple? It might be *antracnose*. Prune off lower branches, sweep up everything, and fertilize and mulch your affected plant. Then consult a professional to apply the proper fungicide. The plant will replace the lost leaves.

Root Rot _____

If you see dry, powdery stuff at the base of a tree or shrub, that probably used to be part of your plant's soft wood and is the residue of a fungal attack, excavated by carpenter ants. Everything might be okay, but you should probably consult a professional to be sure.

Wilting in summer, even when there's been enough rain, may be a sign of *verticillium wilt*, although it can be confused with the effects of pollution or herbicides. Often only one side, or one part, of your tree is affected. The best things you can do are to water, mulch, and fertilize your plant to provide it with more vigor to combat the disease.

Powdery mildew can arrive on the heels of cool, moist weather and looks like grayish or whitish powder on the tops of the leaves of a tree or shrub. Again, water, mulch, and fertilize. You could try pruning to open the plant to better air circulation or spray on an anti-desiccant from the garden store.

What Else Is There? A Lot!

Yet more creatures are interacting—up close and personally—with your trees and shrubs. Not all are unpleasant, damaging, or even creepy—but some are! Often, though, they function as a small helpful brigade of yard workers for you.

Slime Molds

No more attractive than their name, these mucuslike splotches are not fungi although they can reproduce or spread like them at times. Living in tree stumps, in old fallen logs, or under almost any kind of rotting wood, they're large (up to a yard across) and they can creep on "feet" that resemble a snail's, spreading out like warm Jell-O, seeking bacteria to eat. When they don't find any, they can harden up a bit and simply stay in place until conditions improve.

They won't hurt you, and they could even be saving you money by helping get rid of a stump, although they might be there because too much watering was done over mulch.

Mosses

Mosses are another part of the clean-up crew for the dead wood in your yard and also provide some decoration for your living tree trunks. Mosses are responsible, in huge measure, for the creation of soil itself—that's how much material they break down into the tiny particles that make up what we call dirt! They not only eat dead wood, but also consume rock and organic particles in the air that settle down onto their pleasingly variegated green surfaces.

Bacteria, fungi, and the expansion of water into ice in the cracks of wood and rocks also end up creating our yard soil, too. So our trees and shrubs can thank all of them.

> **The Real Dirt**
>
> Mosses break down materials so well, so they can also consume most roofing materials. At least that takes quite a while.

Moss is not only powerful but a quite unusual plant, the very first to colonize the land in the Devonian period of Earth's history. Working ever since, they are now 22,000 species strong worldwide and in every ecosystem. They are so primitive that they have evolved no flowers, no seeds, no roots, not even a circulatory system. Just about the opposite of your trees and shrubs!

Mosses trap heat, water vapor, rain, and their nutrients almost like inert sponges do and can hold 20 to 40 times their weight in water. Up on a tree or shrub this can be a useful reservoir, because the moss gradually releases some of the water, which then humidifies the aboveground or underground parts of your plant. Losing 98 percent of this moisture doesn't really bother them either—even 40 years straight of dryness won't kill many mosses. When the air becomes damp or it rains again, they just rehydrate themselves.

Lichen

Much dryer and forming attractive patches that can look like leathery or feathery leaves pressed against a tree trunk, or diaphanous necklaces draped over branches, lichen come in many varieties and also work to transform dead wood, rock, and other materials into enriched soil for your trees and shrubs. (Pieces of lichen are also good fertilizer.) In fact, they're even better at breaking down rock than the mosses are.

Trees may be festooned with Spanish moss (really a lichen) in the South or grandfather's beard lichen in the North, but the lichen doesn't cause any damage. Instead, these small plants add texture and color, as well as bits of soil whether orange, black, light green, or yellow.

> **The Real Dirt**
>
> Lichen cannot grow in the presence of air pollution, so wherever you see them, you know the air is clean. Scientists have even used lichen to provide a rough measure of where a power plant's plume extends.

The Least You Need to Know

- Bacteria are not all bad—many create nitrogen fertilizer for your trees and shrubs.

- Viruses aren't good for your tree or shrub, but they're rarely fatal.

- Fungi enhance root systems, but some species try to kill trees and shrubs instead.

- Smaller organisms such as mosses and lichens are quite helpful.

23

Beware: Creatures!

In This Chapter

- Protecting your plants from Bambi and Thumper
- Habits of rodents and other unsavory visitors
- What to do

Tired of creatures who consume, or at least damage, your beautiful—and valuable—trees and shrubs? In this chapter, we offer plenty of choices for your zone that are *un*popular with rabbits and deer.

The News Isn't All Bad

Rabbits (and other rodents) do transport seeds, some in their waste, some in their fur. Squirrels are an especially helpful rodent ... if you're a tree with acorns or seed cones of any kind. Some squirrels have even been known to conceive an extra litter per season just to take advantage of a bumper crop of nuts or seeds—and they never remember to eat all that they've buried. Of course, insects, birds, water flow, and, especially, wind, also pollinate and transport seeds and nuts, and they don't restrict themselves to the likes of acorns and pine nuts.

The amount of assistance animals offer plants is very small compared to the destruction they wreak. Plants, unwilling to lose all their "arms and legs" to creatures such as rabbits and deer have made considerable effort, evolving body armor in the form of thorns, spines, prickles, and matted hairs—as well as camouflage. Some trees and shrubs use these structures for other purposes simultaneously, such as attracting dew, reflecting or absorbing light, even helping in holding up the plant, but they're mainly there as protection.

So Long, Thumper

To combat rabbits, you can simply plant things rabbits don't like. If rabbits have already gone after your shrubs, the plants may well survive. New shoots coming up are the good news that you want to look for here—just prune off the damaged shoots at ground level. The ones that have been girdled (eaten all the way around, bark gone) are unlikely to live and should also be pruned off.

> **The Real Dirt**
>
> A very hungry rabbit will probably eat anything green. Chances are, though, that he'll go to your neighbor's yard for something he'd like far better than chowing down on the shrubs meant to deter his nibbling.

In wintertime, rabbits (and other rodents) have so few food choices they might go after anything edible. You might want to protect the trunks of your trees and shrubs by *loosely* wrapping mesh hardwire cloth or plastic piping around them up to about 2 feet above your best estimate of the highest snow level and down 2 or 3 inches into the ground. Do not use black cloth or plastic around your trees and shrubs, though, because that can easily overheat the trunks.

Zones 2/3 and 4

Try some of these plantings instead of—or around—your more vulnerable shrubs:

Beach plum and sand plum (*Prunus maritima*). You can eat the plums, but rabbits won't. White blooms. Zones 3 through 7.

Black currant and mountain currant (*Ribes melanocarpa* and *alipnium*). Greenish or yellowish blooms, often fragrant, are followed by fruit and then often yellow leaves for fall. Zones 2 through 8.

Bog rosemary (*Andromeda polifolia*). Tiny bell-shape flowers in either pink or white or lavender. This shrub does not require a bog, but needs moist ground. Zones 3 through 6.

Cotoneaster (*Cotoneaster*). Many varieties exist around the country. White or pink flowers and red or orange autumn color make this a pleasant anti-rabbit choice. Zone 4.

Daphne (*Daphne*). Go for its yellow-orange flowers and red-orange berries, none of which rabbits like. Zones 4 through 8.

Deutzia. White blooms and no rabbit food. Zones 4 through 8.

Dogwood (*Cornus*). Cultivars of this shrub or small tree are available in every zone. Their yellowish-white flowers and red-toned leaves make this hardy plant even nicer. Zones 2 through 7/8.

Elderberry (*Sambucus*). A large shrub with creamy-white flowers. Some, but not all, cultivars yield berries right for wine. Zones 4 through 9.

Fringetree (*Chionanthus*). Nice white flowers and dark blue berries are features. Zones 4 through 9.

Honeysuckle (*Lonicera*). Sweet-smelling, small, pale yellow or creamy-white flowers are followed by blue or red berries. Zones 2 through 6.

Hydrangea (*Hydrangea*). Although many more cultivars exist for the warmer zones, you can go with a white-bloomed one here. Zones 4 through 8.

Lilac (*Syringa*). Our least favorite rodents don't bother these. Many cultivars exist for this zonal region, but you might look for *Chinensis* and *Vulgaris*. Zones 4 through 8.

Sand cherry (*Prunus*). White flowers are followed by small, dark fruits that neither humans nor the familiar rodents enjoy. Zones 4 through 7.

Sheep laurel (*Kalmia augustfolia*). Reddish flowers look similar to stars but don't pull in the bunnies. Zones 2 through 6.

Sprouts _____

If blended with an oil, any strong-smelling substance such as hot pepper, chilies, garlic, castor oil, dog urine, and especially rotten egg can be sprayed on your shrubs for some bunny protection. Homemade ones work as well as the ones you buy. Just reapply it every couple weeks.

Spirea (*Spiraea*). Two less-typical cultivars are worth mentioning here: japonica, with its pinkish flowers, and Goldflame, which adds orange foliage in fall to its springtime pink. Most cultivars have white blooms. Zones 4 through 9.

Sumac (*Rhus*). Several cultivars work here, featuring very small yellowish or greenish fragrant flowers. Red berries are followed by scarlet leaves. Zones 2 through 9.

Snowberry (*Symphoricarpos albus*). The snowberry and white hedge cultivars are lovely anti-rabbit plants. Both feature clusters of large white berries. Zones 4 through 7.

Viburnum (*Viburnum*). This popular, exceptionally unpicky shrub has many cultivars for these zones, including *Acerifolium*, crimson-leafed in fall, the *Dentatum* (Southern arrow wood) with its blue-black berries and large size, and the *Lantana* (Wayfaring tree) dressed in creamy-white flowers followed by red berries that gradually turn black. Zones 4 through 8.

Yucca (*Yucca agavaceae*). These sun-loving, bunny-free plants have giant white, bell-shape flowers and even add the fragrance of lemon in evenings to attract moths for pollination. Look for the *Filamentosa* (Adam's needle). Zones 4 through 9.

Zones 5 Through 9

As usual for this broad part of the country, choices are wide. Say bye-bye to the bunnies with shrubs such as these:

Boxwood (*Buxus*). Several cultivars work for you here, often with yellowish blooms. Zones 6 through 9.

Butterfly bush (*Buddleia*). Any of the many cultivars will annoy rabbits while pleasing you. Zones 6 through 9.

Snowball (*Ceanothus rigidus*). Not resembling the traditional lilac, its flowers are blue or grayish white. Zones 4 through 9.

Cherry laurel (*Prunus laurocerasus*). Along with the other laurels, as well as the beach plums and sand plums (also within the cherry family), these deter those rodents. The "blackthorn" thicket cultivar is especially good. Zones 5 through 9.

Cotoneaster (*Cotoneaster*). Many cultivars work, all with pink or white flowers, plenty of berries, and autumn color. Zones 5 through 8.

Daphne (*Daphne*). Myriad choices are available, with flowers in white, orange, pink, purple, white, lilac, or mauve. Zones 5 through 9.

Dogwood, silky (*Cornus*). Often white-blooming and in profusion. Zones 6 through 8.

Fringetree (*Chionanthus*). A very popular shrub, it features white, foamy-looking flowers. Zones 4 through 9.

Gooseberries (*Ribes*). Many choices are available, including raspberries, blackberries, currants, and elderberries. Zones 5 through 9.

Honeysuckle (*Lonicera*). The *Chaetocarpa* cultivar might be our favorite here with its bright-yellow flowers and red berries, but there are certainly many others. Zones 5 through 8.

Hydrangea (*Hydrangea*). Although the *Macrophylla* cultivar may be the most popular, other sizes and flower colors are available. Zones 6 through 9.

Lilac (*Syringa*). Many cultivars are up for choice here, in the eponymous color as well as in white, even pink, with blooms large and small. The *Tigerstedii* is one possibility. Zones 6 and 7.

Mockorange (*Philadelphus*). White or creamy blooms decorate these cultivars available in a great variety of sizes. Zones 5 through 9.

Potentilla (*Potentilla*). Long-blooming flowers in white or yellow. Zones 5 through 8.

Rhododendrons and azaleas (*Rhododendron*). Lots of them will work for you here. Zones 3 through 7.

Snowberry (*Symphoricarpos doorenbosii*). This group of hybrids makes nice hedges that rabbits won't be tempted to. Most have rosy or pinkish berries. Zones 6 and 7.

The Real Dirt _____

Plants have had many millions of years to develop nasty tastes or physical deterrents such as thorns to keep away various kinds of predators.

Spirea (*Spiraea*). Many of these nice cultivars deter bunnies. Don't forget the *Arguta*, with its profusion of tiny white flowers, the *Prunifolia*, which adds red-crimson foliage to fall, and the *Thunbergii*, with its orange leaves in autumn. Zones 5 through 8.

St. John's wort (*Hypericum*). Yellow flowers are followed by nice autumn foliage. Zones 5 through 8.

Sumac (*Rhus*). Cultivars come with yellowish flowers and greenish ones. Zones 5 through 9.

Tree peony (*Paeonia suffruticosa*). Yes, they are shrubs, not garden flowers. Blooms usually in yellow or red, large or small. Zones 4 through 8.

Viburnum (*Viburnum*). Among the many cultivars of this popular shrub are the *Rhytidophyllum*, with very large, creamy-white flowers and scarlet berries that turn to black; the *Burkwoodii*, whose large, fragrant flowers are particularly long-lasting; the *Carlesii*, also fragrant; and *Dilatatum*, with its scarlet berries. Zones 5 through 8.

Yucca (*Yucca*). From the small *Smalliana* to the very dramatic *Recurvifolia*, these white flowers won't attract rabbits. Zones 7 through 9.

Zones 8 Through 11

There are rabbits to watch out for everywhere. Try these:

Boxwood (*Buxus*). Great in the cooler parts of this region. Yellowish flowers. Zone 8.

Butterfly bush (*Buddleia*). Any cultivar available in your area will work. Zones 8 through 10.

California lilac (*Ceanothus rigidus*). Cultivars here have the blue or grayish-white flowers that resemble lilacs, but aren't. Zones 8 through 10.

Cotoneaster (*Cotoneaster*). Many cultivars, from dwarf to large, block bunnies. Often white or pink flowers. Zones 7 and 8.

Currants, gooseberries, and other berry bushes (*Ribes*). These are all generally great choices. Zones 8 through 11.

Daisy bush (*Olearia*). You can choose from many cultivars, with large clusters of white flowers, often fragrant. Zones 9 and 10.

Daphne (*Daphne*). Sweet-smelling with flowers in mauve, white, pink, creamy-white, or orange-yellow. Usually scarlet berries. Zones 8 and 9.

Dogwood (*Cornus*). Various cultivars with yellow or white flowers decorate this small tree. Zones 8 and 9.

Fatsia (*Fatsia*). This nice evergreen shrub has creamy or crimson flowers. Zones 7 through 10.

Fringetree (*Chionanthus*). This features blossom-y white blooms that rabbits don't like. Zones 8 and 9.

Gaultheria (*Gaultheria*). From tiny to large cultivars, with often white but also greenish or pinkish flowers, in various sizes from groundcover to large; however, most are small. Fruits are often blue, sometimes white. Zones 8 and 9.

Mexican orange blossom (*Choisya ternata*). Large clusters of white flowers are anti-rabbit. Zones 8 through 10.

Skimmia. Cultivars such as the *japonica*, with its fragrant white flowers followed by scarlet berries, and the *Laureola*, with similar flowers but black berries, are good bets. Both are evergreen shrubs with a small-medium, rounded shape. Zones 7 through 9.

St. John's wort (*Hypericum*). Many choices here, including the popular Rose of Sharon. Yellow blooms. Zones 7 through 9.

Strawberry tree (*Arbutus unedo*). This small or large evergreen shrub or small tree offers orange-red berries that are not strawberries and are not admired by rabbits. Cream, pink, or red flowers. Zones 8 and 9.

Viburnum (*Viburnum*). Most of the cultivars here are large shrubs, including the *Cinnamomifolium*, with its white flowers and bluish-black berries; the *Tinus*, which features pink flowers; and the *Davidii*, which boasts white flowers and bright blue berries. Zones 8 and 9.

Yucca (*Yucca*). Several choices are available in the anti-rabbit department. Take a look at the *Aloifolia*, very large and creamy flowers, and the even more tropic-friendly *Whipplei*, which is drenched in creamy bell-like blooms and adds a lovely lemon fragrance. Zones 4 through 9.

Good ... Well, *Bad* ... for Rabbits and Deer

Deer are often as equally present, annoying, and damaging to your plantings as bunnies, although this depends on where you live, of course. Many, although not all, of the plants that deter rabbits also deter deer, so plant these for the double benefit! Just be sure you have cultivar(s) for your zone:

- Butterfly bush, zones 6 through 10
- Boxwood, zones 6 through 9
- Currants, zones 2 through 8
- Daphne, zones 4 through 9
- Dogwood, zones 2 through 8
- Gaultheria, zones 8 and 9
- Honeysuckle, zones 2 through 6
- Hydrangea (some of them), zones 4 through 8
- Mexican orange blossom, zones 8 through 10
- Mockorange, zones 5 through 9
- Rhododendron, zones 3 through 7
- Spirea, zones 2 through 8

Sprouts

If your neighborhood has more unusual critters such as moose, elk, or caribou, there's a good chance you can use this anti-deer list to deter them, too. But check with your local garden store.

- St. John's wort, zones 4 through 9

- Viburnum, zones 5 through 8

- Yucca, zones 4 through 9

Bye, Bye Bambi

You might have noticed that the anti-rabbit suggestions earlier in this chapter are mostly shrubs, not trees. Trees are hard for bunnies to reach and, therefore, ruin (except for the bark girdling issue mentioned earlier in this chapter). This certainly isn't the case with deer. If you've ever seen a natural forest at the end of a long, hungry-critter winter, you've seen their "browse line," the ultimate height they can reach to shear off *all* the foliage. The deeper the snow, if you have snow, the higher they can reach.

Can trees and shrubs fight back against deer? Their adaptations to insects might be more complex, but some of our green yard companions don't have those spikes, thorns, and such for nothing—these can make a nasty mouthful for a deer. Some have even evolved to sport this armor on only their lower branches to avoid using precious energy for a non-necessity higher up. Some trees and shrubs have also developed bitter or even toxic foliage to keep browsing critters away; eucalyptus and cherry trees are known for this.

What You *Can* Do

Hanging small bars of soap from branches helps deter deer, although it might be good if you could keep the rain away because soapy soil isn't healthful for plants. And strong-smelling sprays such as hot pepper oil, garlic, chili powder, dog urine, and especially rotten eggs mixed with water or oil work for deer as they do for rabbits. Reapply after rain.

Sprouts

Catnip extract works pretty well to deter deer, and you can probably go a month before you spray this potion on again.

Wire cages are another barrier. Look for chicken wire at the big box or garden store and buy enough to make a circle around every vulnerable tree or shrub. Dig a little trench about 6 inches out from the plant, bury the wire a few inches down—*and* be sure the structure is high enough that a deer can't stand on the ground or snow and just reach over for dinner.

Anti-Deer Shrubs

Nothing is foolproof in a deer's hungry season, but the following shrubs should be low on a deer's "to sample" list:

Barberry (*Berberis*). Plenty of sharp thorns deter deer. They're fragrant and usually have yellow-toned blooms followed by dark berries and, in the case of the deciduous ones, nice autumn color. Many dozens of cultivars are available, quite a few in zones 6 through 9 with several in both the warmer and the colder zones.

Cotinus (*Cotinus*). These prefer full sun but aren't picky as to soil, and most provide a hazy effect with their fluffy flowers. Most cultivars are in zones 4 through 8.

Dogwood (*Cornus*). Cultivars of this shrub or small tree are available in every zone. Here, yellowish-white flowers and red-toned leaves make this hardy plant even nicer. Zones 2 through 7/8.

Japanese rose (*Kerria japonica*). Not at all picky as to conditions and featuring its bright-green twigs all winter, it has large, long-lasting, yellow-toned flowers. Most in zones 5 through 9.

Laurel, bay (*Laurus nobilis*). A large shrub or small tree that's the origin of the expression "resting on your laurels." And you can, without sharing them with the deer. Large, yellow-flowered. Zones 8 through 10.

Potentilla (*Potentilla fruticosa*). Only this cultivar of the popular potentilla shrub is disliked by deer.

Rock rose (*Cistus*). These love the sun and are both fast-growers and fragrant. Pink and white flowers are the most common. Many dozens of cultivars are available, most in zones 8 through 10.

Tree poppy (*Romneya*). Classic California, these deer-enemies aren't picky as to soil but need lots of sun. White flowers. The cultivars White Cloud and Butterfly are especially nice. Zones 8 through 10.

The Real Dirt

Don't give up on a tree or shrub that's been deer chow. It might take 2 years, but, if there is any new growth, the plant could recover.

Anti-Deer Trees

Deer like trees, but they like those in the following list less than others, so they're probably good planting for your yard, depending on your zone:

Root Rot _____

Keep dogs from toileting too near a young or delicate plant (especially an evergreen), even on its bark. Their urine is salty enough to burn. Immediately pour water on the "pee place" to dilute the salt. And consider adding loose white plastic piping until you can train the dog to go elsewhere.

- Ash, zones 2 through 9.

- Baldcypress, zones 5 through 9.

- Beech, zones 3 through 10.

- Blue spruce, zones 2 through 8.

- Gingko, zones 5 through 9.

- Golden raintree, zones 5 through 9.

- Juniper, zones 3 through 7.

- Magnolia, zones 5 through 10.

- Sassafras, zones 2 through 6.

The Least You Need to Know

- It's possible to fill in your whole yard with trees and shrubs disliked by rabbits.

- Cut into the deer population with a few strategic plantings.

- Rodents may randomly appear, but you can limit their visits.

Chapter **24**

Insect Alert!

In This Chapter

- ◆ Insects 101
- ◆ Insect-proof trees and shrubs
- ◆ Tips for combating an insect invasion
- ◆ Common plant-versus-insect battles

There are billions and billions more insects on this planet than there are people—and scientists haven't even been able yet to count the number of *species* of them. Some of those insects may have their eyes on your yard.

You want to have healthy trees and shrubs, not ones chewed up, sawed off, spit on, swollen up, dug into, or dried out. Insects can get in the way of that plan. In this chapter, we show you how to get back at the bugs.

Understand Your Enemy

Insects love warmth and dampness. Most actually move faster when it's hotter, and many die when it's too dry outside (although their eggs probably survive). The larval form of the insect is usually its most destructive stage. The population of an insect species in your yard can be huge one year and moderate the next, whether you do anything to affect them or not.

Bad guy insects tend to focus on one tree or shrub species, or at least one broad family of them, having evolved to use that plant's body to eat, lay eggs, or conduct some other specific life task. Some trees and shrubs are the focus of more than one species of insect, but many only attract one species. Plantings of the same species are safest if they're as far apart as you're able to have them. Although some insects fly or travel by wind for long distances, most prefer not to—and many also can't fly at all. So they can't always go far fast. With global warming, insects you and your trees and shrubs aren't familiar with are gradually moving north. Your plantings, especially the native ones, have natural defenses, although they evolved long ago under different conditions. But so do insects.

Insects can also bring viral and fungal infections to your trees. Picnic beetles transport the spores of the fungus that causes the common tree disease called oak wilt, for example. (More on that later.) Proper pruning and enough watering give your plantings a good fighting chance against anything, even these creeps.

> **The Real Dirt** _____
>
> Remember that damage to your tree or shrub can be caused directly by viruses, bacteria, deer, and even drought, so the problem isn't always an insect. And an insect that is fatal to a tree or shrub in one region of the country can be only a minor issue in another region. Although insects don't usually kill a tree or shrub, they do very often weaken it, allowing other stresses ranging from drought to viruses to build up, which can eventually lead to tree failure.

The Types of Insects and What They Do

The creepies most relevant to our trees and shrubs can be thought of according to *how* they attack, either by chewing or by sucking the plant for food or by laying eggs on it in a way that interferes with the plant. Whatever the process, either the leaves or the bark and trunk are damaged, but not usually both.

The Chewers

In the "chewing insect" category, we find mostly leaf miners, saw flies, beetles, and caterpillars.

Leaf miners actually "mine," not for gold but for green. You can see their mining tunnels between the top and bottom layer of the leaf, where the inner tissue is dinner for the tiny larval form of the insect. If enough is removed, the leaf develops brown blotches. If you see tiny black dots in the tunnels, those are their feces (called *frass*).

Unless they've conducted a huge invasion, you'll only find a few leaves mined. The trees most often affected are birches, hawthorns, oaks, and elms.

Leaf miners tunnel in between the top and bottom of the leaf.

With rear ends that resemble tiny saws, hence their name, *sawflies* also make tiny holes in a leaf or needle, depositing their eggs there. You can see their activity as thin, yellowed lines. When the young are born, they feast on the needle. Sometimes an army of them eats so much that the leaf or needle dies.

Some *beetles* chow down on leaves, as do quite a few *caterpillars*. The latter, a life stage of an insect-to-come (sometimes a butterfly), can be a quarter-inch long up to about 4 inches. Evidence of them on leaves is varied. Some make what are called "shotgun holes." Others do "window feeding," eating only the leaf's surface, while still others make the leaf look like a skeleton of its former self.

Sprouts

Camouflage evolved in insects about 47 million years ago. A few thousand species have bodies or legs that resemble a stick, twig, or even the leaf of the plant they prefer to hang out on.

Ever wonder why you don't always see these insects even while serious damage is being done to your tree or shrub? It's because many feed only at night and hide during the day. This helps keep them safe from birds, who need daylight to see well.

The Suckers

This group sucks the juices out of leaves and the sap out of twigs. The result is often dried-out, bleached-out, yellowed leaves or those patterned in a kind of stippling.

(Remember, though, that fungi and other invaders can leave this same kind of calling card.) The largest groups here are the aphids, the mites (not literally insects), and the scale insects, but other suckers include the lace bugs, plant bugs, and leafhoppers.

In addition to the yellowing, *aphids* can leave curled-up or crinkled leaves. And their waste, called honeydew, forms sticky, sugary blobs that attract ants, even some birds, and can also build up by collecting wind-blown fungal spores. Linden trees are known for this honeydew.

Mites are everywhere in your yard, and droughts and heat boost their numbers hugely. So does using too much pesticide. Tiny mites feed on the underside of the leaf and rarely kill it. Some species of mites cause a swelling or twisting of the leaf, too.

Scale insects got their name because their adult form is a hard bump on a twig that looks like a scale. When younger, they crawl. Scalers are most often found on maples, ash, and oak and usually aren't too serious.

The Trunk Attackers

Some scale insect species go after the bark and penetrate into the trunk. These *bark borers* tunnel right in to eat or to lay their eggs, which can interfere with the tree's or shrub's circulatory system. The result, quickly or over several years, wilts leaves, kills branches, or causes too-early fall color.

The Real Dirt

Do you have borers on your trees and shrubs? Look for small openings on the trunk shaped like a D.

Other tree attackers, from carpenter ants to beetles to maggots, either go after dead areas of the plant or entirely dead trees and shrubs—or do not harm the plant at all.

Trees' and Shrubs' Natural Defenses

Some good news: trees and shrubs haven't been growing on the planet for hundreds of millions of years without structurally and chemically evolving in some amazing ways. Among these are adaptations to insects. The battle continues, of course, because insects continue to evolve (faster!) to use the trees and shrubs for their own purposes.

But the longer a tree or shrub has been at this evolution work—in your region against "your" insects—the better the result. This is a key reason why native plantings are often an excellent choice.

Structural Defenses

These include features such as spines, thorns, and prickles (to protect leaves, seeds, trunks, whatever), but they go beyond the obvious. Some trees and shrubs grow in places more difficult for insects to colonize in large numbers, such as very windy or very cold areas, or those very high in elevation. Other plants have developed "housing" for some nondamaging insects in their bark, even inside their leaves and needles. Still others have evolved fraying bark, which they shed to carry bad guys away. And others have very flat, light bark that makes it harder for the insects to hide from birds, for example.

Chemical Defenses

Trees and shrubs make and circulate a lot of natural chemicals in the course of conducting their lives, just as we do. These include a group of specific chemicals called *secondary metabolites* manufactured as part of their metabolism. Some remain an interior part of the tree or shrub, while others are released and carried out on the wind.

Two of the defenses incorporated into the tissue of the tree are the *tannins* and the *terpenes*. Tannins are a specialty of oak trees, although they're found in many trees, and they taste so bad that a lot of insects won't chow down on the tree. The terpenes are actually toxic to insects that decide to take a bite—and then don't seek another one. Pines and firs have one type; citrus trees have another. Some commercial pesticides are based on these chemicals. The system has become elaborated enough that some natural terpenes are able to attract the predators of the bad insects to enlist their help.

Wind-borne metabolites are actually essential oils, released into the air to discourage the insects from even coming near the tree or shrub. The eucalyptus tree is known for this.

Some trees are a lot better at protecting themselves from insects than others, but remember that no protection is perfect—and no plant has evolved natural defenses against creepies that weren't even there until our recent warming trend.

Insect-Resistant Trees and Shrubs

Choices of tough trees and shrubs such as these can save you time and money because you won't have to help them as much—probably not at all—defend against insects. Remember that just a few insects can't kill a planting—an oak can lose half its leaves during one year and you might not even notice.

The resistance comes not only as a natural product of evolution, but also hundreds and hundreds of cultivars of trees and shrubs developed by scientists to enhance and extend this resistance. Ask about them at your garden store as you're selecting cultivars for size, color, and so on.

The following are good bets:

- Arborvitae, zones 2 through 9
- Basswood, zones 2 through 5
- Black gum, zones 3 through 10
- Black locust, zones 3 through 5
- California redwood, zone 9
- Gingko, zones 5 through 9
- Golden raintree, zones 5 through 9
- Hickory, zones 3 through 10
- Juniper, zones 3 through 7
- Linden, zones 3 through 8
- Oaks (white, bur, pin, red), zones 3 through 11
- Sugar maple, zones 3 through 9
- Tulip poplar, zones 4 through 9
- White spruce, zones 3 through 8

What You Can Do

To avoid an insect infestation in the first place, maintain your trees and shrubs in good general health and never transport any firewood into your yard. Also, regularly pick up all organic debris such as sticks that have blown or been raked in near your trees and shrubs. These can conceal bad guy insects.

If one or more of your trees or shrubs develops an insect issue at some point, there are quite a few things you can try before investing in mega-poisons.

One of these simple solutions is highly likely to work:

- Using a garden hose, wash the creepies right off the plant, soaking them into oblivion. Of course, this is easier with shrubs and smaller trees!

♦ Pick them off, one by one, and squish them. Again, not suitable for that Giant Sequoia.

Some of the following home remedies might work, and they're pretty simple, too. Try your potion on one small part of your tree or shrub before treating the whole thing. Soaps, in particular, can be bad for the plant if too concentrated.

♦ Grate the peel off two oranges. Boil 1 cup water and soak the peel in it for 24 hours. Add 1 teaspoon liquid soap and mix thoroughly. Spray on the leaves.

♦ Mix 4 ounces garlic oil or hot pepper oil with 1 teaspoon liquid soap into 1 quart water. Spray on.

♦ Use the finest-ground chewing tobacco you can find, going with somewhere between a half tin and a tin per quart of water. Spray on.

♦ This last tip is practical for small fruit trees only because the fruit remains *on* the tree: place a small plastic bag over every piece of fruit you want to protect, affixing the "neck" of the bag with a twist tie. Insects will throw up their feelers in frustration.

The Real Dirt

These "recipes" work best for shrubs or very small trees because you need to do every leaf. And remember that you must be able to actually see the insects and spray onto them for this to work.

Although organic insecticides aren't hugely better than synthetic ones, here are some ideas (not all of them insecticides):

♦ Purchase nematodes in a bag at the garden store mixed in with dry clay. Follow the directions for adding water and spraying. This works well for—and only for—insects that live in the soil.

♦ You can find insecticidal soap at the store with directions for proper use.

♦ Available in different types, "superior oil" or "horticultural oil" suffocates insects but doesn't hurt the tree or shrub (provided that the temperature doesn't go below freezing in the next day, an unlikely scenario, because you wouldn't be encountering too many insects at that time of year).

♦ Diatomaceous earth is a natural mineral, in powder form, often used to combat crawling insects.

♦ Bt. Bacillus thuringiensis (Bt) is the name for a natural bacterium carried around by a nematode. It gets into the bodies of many insects where it destroys their internal organs. It's safe for noninsects and doesn't persist in the soil.

Root Rot _____

Importing predator insects to kill invading insects, as well as using insects' own pheromones, is beyond the scope of this book. Beware of repercussions, even if you hire a professional to do these things, because you're altering the ecology of your yard.

A Word About Pesticides

The overuse of pesticides has allowed insects to become resistant to them, to say nothing of the health effects on families and our ecosystems. Most of the time, you're better off with simpler measures—or even letting the plant cope.

If you have a major infestation, you might need the kind of plan called *integrated pest management*, available from professionals. This involves careful professional analysis and planning, for as many noninsecticides and nontoxic insecticides as possible. It also takes into account as many of the milder remedies as possible. And it adds in elements of proper pruning and fertilizing as necessary, followed perhaps by a major insecticide dose.

When You Need to Call the Pros

There are some biggies, the most destructive diseases and damages that can damage—or kill—your prized yard companions. Do you suspect Dutch elm disease, oak wilt, emerald ash borer, spider mites outside, or sawflies? If so, call a professional.

The Least You Need to Know

- Most of the millions of insect species are not damaging to trees and shrubs.
- The main kinds of bad guys are the chewing insects, sucking insects, and boring insects.
- Trees and shrubs have natural defenses against insects, which sometimes work quite well.
- Some diseases such as Dutch elm disease, oak wilt, and emerald ash borer disease require professional help.

Glossary

allelopathy   The process in which plants release their own chemicals onto or into the ground to prevent the seeds and seedlings of other plants from growing too near to them. It comes from the Greek word for "mutual suffering."

bark   The outermost layer of a tree or shrub.

branch collar   The slightly raised area where the branch meets either the trunk or a larger branch than itself.

cambium   The corklike layer where the main growth of the tree or shrub occurs.

candles   On an evergreen, these are the lightly colored new growths of a conifer in spring. They point upward similar to tiny candles.

cellulose   The fibrous woody part of a plant's trunk or stem.

chlorophyll   A pigment that makes trees and shrubs green. It's created by the plant via a chemical reaction with sunlight.

chloroplasts   The part of a green plant of any kind that contains the chlorophyll.

compost tea   A highly nutritious—not for you but for your trees and shrubs—fertilizer brew of biological organisms from compost plus water.

conifers   The evergreen family of trees that set their seeds in cones; also known as gymnosperms.

crabapple   Any apple tree with fruit less than 2 inches across.

crown   The size and shape of a tree's or a shrub's canopy of leaves, from the lowest branches to the arching top.

cultivar   A variant of a tree species, developed by scientists or arborists to more perfectly suit different areas. Some are tried and true; others are newer and still a bit experimental.

cuticle   The waxy surface of the leaves or shoots of a tree or shrub.

deciduous   Trees that drop their leaves and set their seeds in flowers; part of the angiosperm family.

dendrochronology   The word for the study of tree rings. Analysis of the rings tells the age of the tree but can also be used to study ancient climate.

dioecious   Trees whose flowers are either male or female on separate plants.

dormant season   When the tree is not growing. This is usually late fall, winter, and very early spring in the North and the dry season in the South.

dripline   The circle around the tree where the outermost leaves would drip if it were raining.

epidermis   The "skin" or surface layer of roots, stems, and leaves.

ethylene   An organic gas that serves as an active hormone within a plant and in its reaction with the environment.

fungus   A microorganism that can damage trees and shrubs or be beneficial to them.

girdling roots   The root or roots that circle the root ball at the surface or just underground, a bit like a necklace (or girdle top) all the way around horizontally. If roots look like this, they probably will never truly straighten out and can limit the health and longevity of the tree.

guy wires   Metal wires extending out from a tree trunk like spokes that are then anchored by winding them around short stakes buried in the ground.

hammock   Ecologically speaking, this is a raised, moundlike area where drainage provides slightly dryer soils.

hardscaping   All landscape features that are not biological such as decks, fountains, etc.

heart root   Roots that thicken as they grow down.

heartwood   The central part of the trunk of a mature tree or shrub.

lignin   The substance that binds together the cellulose fibers in a woody plant, giving its trunk stiffness and strength.

macroclimate   The pattern of temperature, light, and other such factors over large areas such as your region of the country.

mesoclimate   The pattern of temperature, light, and other such factors at the level of medium-size areas such as your neighborhood, city, or county.

microclimate   The pattern of temperature, light, topography, wind, and other such factors over a smaller area such as your yard.

microorganisms   Tiny organisms, so small that you'd need a microscope to see one of them. Bacteria, viruses, and fungi are three kinds.

monoecious   Trees that have both male and female flowers on the same tree, but each flower is either male or female.

mulch   Any material that covers and protects the soil.

petiole   The leaf's stalk or base, where it connects to the branch.

phloem   Conductive tissues between the xylem and the bark on a tree.

photoperiod   The length of the daylight hours versus nighttime darkness. This varies throughout the seasons and also changes more during the year at higher latitudes; daylight hours change very little near the equator. The main reason trees and shrubs grow more in spring and summer, no matter where they are, is because of the photoperiod.

photosynthesis   The process by which trees and shrubs use sunlight to turn carbon dioxide and water into the food they need to grow.

pollination   The process in which pollen is transferred between the reproductive parts of the plant.

pot- or **root-bound**   Refers to a tree or shrub whose roots are mashed like a clump of white threads. They may straighten out fine, but the tree or shrub has been stressed.

pruning   The removal of part of a plant—not only a shoot or branch, but also, occasionally, its buds, roots, flowers, or fruit.

respiration   The process by which plants take the "food" energy they've made and use it for their life processes. The carbohydrates, in the presence of oxygen, become energy, along with some water and carbon dioxide.

rhizomes   The underground propagation engines that some species, such as the quaking aspen, use for reproduction. Each tree is like a stem off the same root.

root flare   Part of the process of planting a tree or shrub in which you spread the roots out to make a kind of skirt. This gives a new plant the ability to collect more moisture more quickly.

saplings   Young trees.

seedlings   "Baby" trees.

senescence   The process of shedding leaves and limbs.

sinker root   Vertical roots that help make the tree more stable and enable it access to deeper soil levels. (Most roots are horizontal.)

stomata   The pores within the leaves of a plant.

sucker   A smaller offshoot of a tree growing close to its trunk. They can be removed.

taproot   The root sent down by a seedling. It usually atrophies as the plant grows.

transpiration   The process by which trees and shrubs shed water. Most of it "sweats" out of the stomata of the leaves, although a little is released through tiny openings in the bark.

understory   The level of plant life that thrives (although on less sunlight) under the taller trees and shrubs.

waterdrip   A hose that simply drips water from the mouth or from more than one opening, at the rate of about 1 or 2 cups per hour.

winterburn   Also called "sunscald," it can turn some of tree boughs brown, permanently dead.

xylem   The tissue inside the trunk of a tree or shrub that moves water and dissolved substances.

Appendix B

Further Resources

We're offering here a list of the books we used, and loved, while writing this one, along with some top online resources, advocacy and advice sources, and other organizations.

Print Publications

American Horticultural Society. *Plant Propagation*. New York: DK Publishing, 1999.

Barth, Steve, and Kim Heacox. *The Smithsonian Guides to Natural America: The Pacific*. Washington, D.C.: Smithsonian Books, 1995.

Capon, Brian. *Botany for Gardeners*. Portland, Oregon: Timber Press, 2003.

Chasan, Daniel Jack. *The Smithsonian Guides to Natural America: The Pacific Northwest*. Washington, D.C.: Smithsonian Books, 1995.

Finch, Robert. *The Smithsonian Guides to Natural America: Southern New England*. Washington, D.C.: Smithsonian Books, 1996.

Gillman, Jeff. *The Truth About Garden Remedies*. Portland, Oregon: Timber Press, 2006.

Hanson, Jeanne K., and Deane Morrison. *Of Kinkajous, Capybaras, Horned Beetles, Seladangs, and the Oddest and Most Wonderful Mammals, Insects, Birds, and Plants of Our World*. New York: HarperCollins, 1991.

Harris, Richard W., James R. Clark, and Nelda P. Matheny. *Arboriculture*. Upper Saddle River, New Jersey: Pearson Education, 2004.

Holing, Dwight. *The Smithsonian Guides to Natural America: The Far West*. Washington, D.C.: Smithsonian Books, 1996.

Hopkins, Bruce. *The Smithsonian Guides to Natural America: Central Appalachia*. Washington, D.C.: Smithsonian Books, 1996.

Lamb, Susan. *The Smithsonian Guides to Natural America: The Southern Rockies*. Washington, D.C.: Smithsonian Books, 1995.

Little, Elbert L. *National Audubon Society Field Guide to North American Trees*. New York: Alfred A. Knopf, 1980.

Logan, William Bryant. *Dirt: The Ecstatic Skin of the Earth*. New York: Riverhead Books, 1995.

Maloof, Joan. *Teaching the Trees, Lessons from the Forest*. Athens and London: The University of Georgia Press, 2005.

Page, Jake. *The Smithsonian Guides to Natural America: The Southwest*. Washington, D.C.: Smithsonian Books, 1995.

Pakenham, Thomas. *Remarkable Trees of the World*. New York, London: W.W. Norton & Company, 2003.

Preston, Richard. *The Wild Trees*. New York: Random House, 2007.

Ross, John. *The Smithsonian Guides to Natural America: The Atlantic Coast and Blue Ridge*. Washington, D.C.: Smithsonian Books, 1995.

Schmidt, Jeremy, and Thomas Schmidt. *The Smithsonian Guides to Natural America: The Northern Rockies*. Washington, D.C.: Smithsonian Books, 1995.

Schrock, Denny, ed. *Better Homes and Gardens, Garden Doctor*. Des Moines, Iowa: Meredith Books, 2005.

Science News, issues 2002–2007, passim.

Shepard, Lansing. *The Smithsonian Guides to Natural America: The Northern Plains*. Washington, D.C.: Smithsonian Books, 1996.

Silvertown, Jonathan. *Demons in Eden: The Paradox of Plant Diversity*. Chicago and London: The University of Chicago Press, 2005.

Sternberg, Guy, with Jim Wilson. *Native Trees for North American Landscapes*. Portland and Cambridge: Timber Press, 2004.

Strutin, Michele. *The Smithsonian Guides to Natural America: The Great Lakes.* Washington, D.C.: Smithsonian Books, 1996.

———. *The Smithsonian Guides to Natural America: The Southeast.* Washington, D.C.: Smithsonian Books, 1997.

Tekulsky, Matthew. *The Butterfly Garden.* Harvard and Boston, Massachusetts: Harvard Common Press, 1985.

Walter, Eugene. *The Smithsonian Guides to Natural America: The Mid-Atlantic States.* Washington, D.C.: Smithsonian Books, 1996.

Wetherell, W. D. *The Smithsonian Guides to Natural America: Northern New England.* Washington, D.C.: Smithsonian Books, 1995.

White, Mel. *The Smithsonian Guides to Natural America: The South-Central States.* Washington, D.C.: Smithsonian Books, 1996.

Winckler, Suzanne. *The Smithsonian Guides to Natural America: The Heartland.* Washington, D.C.: Smithsonian Books, 1997.

Online Resources

Every state has some sort of agricultural extension service—and they're not just for farmers! They offer lots of resources to homeowners, too.

Extension service of any state.

U of M Extension Service, *Woodland Advisor,* various issues.

Ibid *Master Gardener,* various issues. An excellent source.

Advocacy Groups, Advice Sources

Many organizations are pro-tree, from the Sierra Club to the U.S. Forest Service. But several focus on them most fully:

American Forests
www.americanforests.org

Embrapa
www.embrapa.br/English/index_html/mostra_documento

Forest Stewardship Council
www.fscus.org

Green Belt Movement
www.greenbeltmovement.org

The National Arbor Day Foundation
www.arborday.org

The Orion Society
www.orionsociety.org

Tree Trust
www.treetrust.com

The Trust for Public Land
www.tpl.org

Organizations

By supporting organizations such as the following with your membership, you'll receive mailings well worth the paper (from trees) they're printed on. Read, and then recycle.

Bailey Nurseries
www.baileynurseries.com

Gardens Online
www.gardensonline.com.au/PlantSearch/PlantSearch.asp

Monrovia
monrovia.com

My Garden Guide
www.mygardenguide.com/plant_search.html

The National Arbor Day Foundation
www.arborday.org/treeguide

Nursery Guide
nurseryguide.com

PLANTS National Database
plants.nrcs.usda.gov/cgi_bin/topics.cgi?earl=advquery/adv_query.html

White Flower Farm
www.whiteflowerfarm.com

The Top Native Trees

These are the trees featured in wonderful detail in the excellent book *Native Trees for North American Landscapes* (see Appendix B). They're our classic trees, the ones that may already be in your yard or park or a woods nearby. They are long adapted to our North American settings and so tend to grow well, avoid problems, and are good choices for new plantings. You'll see them featured throughout the book, but you might find it useful to see them all in one place.

American chestnut	black locust
American elm	black oak
American holly	black walnut
aralia	black willow
arborvitae	blackhaw
baldcypress	blackjack oak
balsam fir	blue ash
basswood	bur oak
beech	cabbage palm
bitternut hickory	Canada hemlock
black gum	chinkapin oak

common hackberry

corkwood

cucumbertree

downy serviceberry

dwarf hackberry

eastern cottonwood

flowering dogwood

fringe tree

Gambel oak

green ash

honey mesquite

honeylocust

hornbeam

ironwood

jack pine

Kentucky coffeetree

live oak

loblolly-bay

Manitoba maple

mockernut hickory

mountain ash

native buckthorn

northern catalpa

Ohio buckeye

Osage-orange

paper birch

pawpaw

pecan

persimmon

pin oak

pinckneya

post oak

prairie crab

quaking aspen

red buckeye

red hawthorn

red maple

red mulberry

red oak

red pine

redbud

redcedar

river birch

roughleaf dogwood

sassafras

shagbark hickory

shining willow

shortleaf pine

Shumard oak

silverbell

smoketree

soapberry

sourwood

southern magnolia

staghorn sumac

sugar maple

swamp privet

swamp white oak

sweetgum

sycamore

tamarack

tuliptree

wahoo

water oak

white ash

white oak

white pine

white spruce

wild cherry

wild plum

willow oak

witch hazel

yellow birch

yellowwood

Trees and Shrubs for Butterflies, Bees, and Fragrance

The trees and shrubs featured in this appendix attract the good insects—butterflies and bees—to your yard with their flowers as well as their fragrance.

Shrubs That Attract Butterflies

Blackberries draw in the Satyr Anglewing (western states), Spring Azure (all over), and Western Tiger Swallowtail (most of the western United States).

Butterfly bush (*Buddleia*) as you might guess, is popular with butterflies! Plant them to attract the Painted Lady (all over the country), the Comma (everywhere east of the Great Plains), Milbert's Tortoiseshell (northern states), Western Tiger Swallowtail (most western states), West Coast Lady (Great Plains to the Pacific), and Monarch (all over except for the extreme Northwest).

The *buttonbush* (*Cephalanthus*) shrub attracts the Tiger Swallowtail (everywhere east of the Rockies), Silver-Spotted Skipper (all over), Painted Lady (all over), and Monarch (all over except for the extreme Northwest).

The *hibiscus* (*Hibiscus*) shrub appeals to the Cloudless Giant Sulphur (most southern and eastern states, except for the extreme North), Common Checkered Skipper (all over the United States except for northern New England and the northwest coast), and the Grey Hair Streaker.

Lilac (*Syringa*) is popular with the Tiger Swallowtail (everywhere east of the Rockies), Giant Swallowtail (most areas except for the extreme North), Pipevine Swallowtail (most of the United States), and Western Tiger Swallowtail (most of the western United States).

Privet (*Ligustrum*) attracts the Silver-Spotted Skipper (all over), Painted Lady (all over), and Spring Azure (all over).

The *spice bush* (*Lindera benzoin*) is beloved by the Spicebush Swallowtail (most of the United States east of the Rockies).

Sumac (*Rhus*) shrub attracts the Spring Azure (all over).

Trees and Shrubs That Attract Bees

These are some trees and shrubs that are the bees' knees:

Acacia, false and rose acacia (*Robinia*). Large, fast-growing in full sun and well-drained soil, its pink flowers bring in the bees. Zones 5 through 9.

Amelanchier (*Amelanchier*). Often called serviceberry or Juneberry, many choices exist for this white-flowered and nice-foliaged deciduous shrub. Zones 4 through 9.

Aralia (*Aralia elata*). This large shrub is loved by the "buzzers" and has black berries followed by yellow leaves in fall. Zones 4 through 9.

Arbutus (*Arbutus*). The evergreen Strawberry tree has creamy blooms and orange-red or red berries. Various cultivars in zones 8 and 9.

Barberry (*Berberis*). Probably hundreds of choices are available, some evergreen and some deciduous. Most in zones 6 through 9, a few in 4, 5, and 10.

Bay laurel (*Laurel nobilis*). Very large shrub or small tree with yellow flowers. Zones 8 through 10.

Beauty bush (*Kolkwitzia*). This graceful, medium-size shrub with its eye on the bees boasts pink blooms. Zones 5 through 8.

Blueberry (*Vaccinium*). Zillions of choices of cultivars related to the blueberry grow best in moist soil. They come in all sizes, with white or pink flowers, edible berries, and autumn color. Zones 2 through 10.

Boxwood (*Buxus*). Sun or shade, bring on the bees. A very nonpicky fragrant shrub, many choices in zones 6 through 8, also in zones 8 through 11.

Broom (*Cystisus*). Sun-loving and fragrant, its many cultivars are mostly in zones 6 through 9.

Broom (*Genista*). Another family of "brooms," these shrubs stay green whether they're deciduous or evergreen. Zones 6 through 10, most choices in 8 through 10.

Butterfly bush (*Buddleia davidii*). Fast-growing, the small flowers are gathered into large, fragrant heads. Mostly in zones 8 and 9, a few in 6 and 7.

California lilac (*Ceanothus rigidus*). Most varieties are a true blue, some white, none lavender, all fragrant. Comes in all sizes. Zones 8 through 10.

Cotoneaster (*Cotoneaster*). Not picky and bringing nice berries, autumn color, and bees. Myriad cultivars in zones 5 through 8, a few in 3 and 9.

Crabapple (*Malus*). This shrub blooms cream or crimson, and it's not picky as to soil. Zones 5 through 8.

Daisy bush (*Olearia*). Many, many choices are available in zones 8 through 10, in white or purple-toned flowers.

Daphne (*Daphne*). Mostly small flowers and fragrant for the bees. Most in zones 5 through 9.

Dogwood (*Cornus*). Out of many cultivars, only a few will pull in the bees: the *alba*, with white flowers and blue-white berries (zones 2 through 8); the *sericea*, similar with red branches and twigs (zones 2 through 8); and the *mas*, very large, bright-yellow blooms and edible fruit (zones 5 through 8).

Enkianthus (*Enkianthus*). Great fall color. Zones 5 through 8.

Escallonia (*Escallonia rubra*). For sun and a salty wind. Zones 8 through 10.

Firethorn (*Pyracantha*). A spiny cousin to the cotoneaster that blooms in spring in any soil and features white-toned berries. Zones 6 through 9.

Holly (*Ilex*). Medium shrubs or small trees, these are adaptable bee fans with glossy berries. A couple cultivars work in zones 7 through 9, a few in 5 and 6, one in 4, and one in 10.

Horsechestnut (*Aesculus hippocastanum*). The *parviflora* cultivar is a great bee attractor in zones 5 through 9.

Mahonia (*Mahonia*). Flowers from autumn to spring, an extended season for bees. Many choices in zones 8 through 10, a few in 5, 6, 7, and 11.

Maple (*Acer*). Large shrubs with nice autumn color in zones 3 through 7, the *ginnala* or *spicatum* cultivar, or the *japonicum*, *palmatum*, and many others in every leaf color in every season. Zones 6 through 8.

Mountain ash/white beams (*Sorbus*). These small trees have small flowers and smell strong. They're not soil-picky. Most in zones 5 through 7, although also a choice in 4 and one in 8.

Ninebark (*Physocarpus*). They look like spiraea with lovely white flowers. Almost all pull in the bees in zones 5 through 7.

Photinia (*Photinia*). Large shrubs or small trees, usually with white flowers. Most in zones 6 through 8, but look for them elsewhere, too.

Potentilla (*Potentilla*). All dwarf, very hardy, they flower in yellow or white for months on end to haul in the bees. Any soil is fine. Most in zones 3 through 7.

Privet (*Ligustrum*). Great for hedging, medium to very large. Has a strong smell. Many choices in zones 7 through 10 with a couple in 3, 5, and 6.

Prunus. A huge family of fruit and nut trees, all large shrubs or small trees that are hardy and not picky as to soil. Zones 3 through 9.

Raspberries, also many blackberries, salmon berries, wineberries, and many others—all the flowers of this *Rubus* family of berries seem to be beloved by bees! Most zones 5 through 9, one in 4, and a couple in 10.

Ribes. The family of currants and gooseberries is popular with bees when in flower. Many, many choices in zones 3 through 10, with one in 2 and one in 11.

Rock rose (*Cistus*). Fast-growing, this fragrant sun-lover is a bee favorite. White flowers. Zones 8 through 10.

Siberian peashrub (*Caragana arborescens*). Hardy and spiny, it tolerates a dry, hot sun well. Plenty of bee-magnet cultivars in zones 3 through 8.

Skimmia (*Skimmia*). This small evergreen shrub is happy in the sun or shade and any soil. The males are the most fragrant while the females have lovely red berries. Zones 7 through 9.

Snowberry (*Symphoricarpos*). The snowberry and other such shrubs love the shade, where they bear tiny pinkish flowers bees appreciate. Zones 4 through 10.

Spirea (*Spiraea*). Cascades of bloom in white or pink. Many choices of bee-happy cultivars in zones 4 through 9.

Stephanandra (*Stephanandra*). Creamy flowers on arching branches decorate this small to medium shrub. It likes moist soil but is flexible as to sun. Zones 4 through 8.

Stranvaesia (*Stranvaesia*). An evergreen shrub that grows vigorously and very large, it's not picky to soil, has nice berries, and boasts scarlet autumn color. Zones 6 through 10.

Sweetbox (*Sarcococca*). This small evergreen shrub likes well-drained soil but isn't terribly picky. Glossy leaves and a late winter flowering and fragrance arrive to attract the bees in sun or shade. Most in zones 6 through 8.

Weigela (*Weigela*). A popular deciduous small shrub that bears lots of pink-toned flowers and is hardy in sun or shade. Its leaves are a purplish gray-green. Zones 5 through 7.

Willow (*Salix*). The shrub form of the *Salix* family has tons of choices for fragrant shrubs in all sizes. They like full sun, any soil, and any level of wind. Zones 2 through 9.

Fragrant Shrubs

The smell of lilac blooms in the spring. The lemony scent of weigelia in the evening. The unmistakable white fragrant flowers of the magnolia. These are just a few of the wonderful fragrant shrubs available to you and your yard.

Zones 2/3 and 4

Arctic willow (*Salix arctica*). Low to the ground, the fragrance from this shrub comes from the leaves as in most willows of any kind. Zones 2/3 and 4.

Barberry (*Berberis vulgaris*). Its second name means "common" (not "vulgar"!). Large, with fragrant yellow flowers followed by real berries. Virtually all barberries across all zones are fragrant. Zones 3 and 4.

Carol Mackie (*Daphne burkwoodii Carol Mackie*). The month of May brings pale pink to white blooms with a lovely scent. The berries, though, are poison. Likes the sun and a cool, well-drained soil. Zone 4.

Fringetree (*Chionanthus virginicus*). Very large, with lacey white, fragrant flowers in early summer. Zone 4.

Lilac (*Syringa vulgaris* and *chinensis*). Classic lilac color. Likes full sun, and is not picky as to soil, as long as it's well drained. Zones 4 through 7.

Mockorange (*Philadelphus*). Not all varieties are fragrant (so check at the store). Small but numerous white blooms. Zones 2/3 and 4.

Summersweet (also called hummingbird shrub) (*Clethra acuminata*). White and pink, blooming scentfully in mid-summer. Tolerates a lot of moisture. Zone 4.

Sweet pepper bush (*Clethra alnifolia*). Creamy, fragrant, and feathery blooms in late summer. Not picky as to soil although prefers moistness. Medium-size with dwarf varieties available. Zone 4.

Weigela (*Weigela filamentosa*) (also called Adam's Needle). Releases its lemony scent in the evening from creamy flowers with a greenish tint. Zone 4.

Zones 5 Through 8

Abelia (*Abelia triflora*). Large shrub with wooly white, fragrant blooms in early summer. Zones 7 through 9.

Allspice (*Carolina*). Medium-size summer bloomer with fragrant red-brown flowers. Zones 5 through 9.

Barberry (*Berberis*). Among the many fragrant varieties are the Calliantha, Candidula, and Frikart, all yellow. All spring bloomers, all rather small, and all zones 3 through 9.

Boxwood (*Buxus sempervirens*). Yellowish blooms appear in spring on this good-bet, large shrub. Comes in many varieties. Zones 4 through 8.

Buttercup or buttercup winter hazel (*Corylopsis pauciflora*). Blooming in early spring, its yellow flowers hang from the branches and smell nice. Rather large. Several other varieties are fragrant, too. Zones 6 through 8.

Butterfly bush (*Buddleia alternafolia* and *davidii*). These both grow fast and need full sun. Flowers are tiny but occur in large fragrant heads. Large. The first variety blooms with heliotrope flowers in early summer, the second in late summer with orange-throated blooms. Zones 6 through 9.

Daphne (*Daphne burkwoodii* and *cneorum*). The first blooms a blush color, the second more of a pink, both fragrant in early summer. The second is much smaller. Pretty much any Daphne you buy will smell wonderful, too. Zones 5 through 8 and 5 through 7, respectively.

Fragrant wintersweet (*Chimonanthus praecox* and *luteus*). Fragrant blooms are light yellow and come out in mid to late *winter*. Zones 6 through 9.

Horsechestnut (*Parviflora*). This wide shrub needs full sun. Late summer brings sweet-smelling, white spikey blooms. Zones 5 through 9.

Kew broom (*Cytisus kewensis*). A low shrub blooming with creamy flowers in late spring to early summer. Popular for its scent and especially cascading down a slope. A larger variety, *Nigracans*, flowers yellow in late summer to early autumn, smelling just as pleasant. Both zones 6 through 8.

Mockorange (*Philadelphus delavayi* and *magdalenae*). Both are white-flowering in early summer, the first variety a significantly larger shrub and the second flowering a bit earlier. Fountainlike in shape and sweet-smelling. Zones 6 through 9 and 6 through 8, respectively.

Sweet pepper bush (*Clethra acuminata*). Creamy blooms in late summer create fragrance from this large bush. For smaller gardens, choose the *Tomentosa* variety, which blooms a bit later but is also creamy and sweet-smelling. Zones 6 through 8 and 6 and 7, respectively.

Zones 8 Through 11

Some of the same shrubs appear here, although in more southerly variants:

Adenocarpus (*Adenocarpus anagyrifolius*, *decorticans*, and *Valdiviana*). The first two are early summer bloomers with fragrant yellow flowers, the first variety medium-size and the second one larger. The third, very large, blooms in spring with fragrant, light-yellow flowers. Zones 9 and 10, 9 and 10, and 8 and 9, respectively.

Barberry (*Berberis hookeri* and *insignis*). Among the many varieties, all yellow and fragrant are these, both pale yellow blooms on medium-size shrubs appearing in spring. Zones 7 through 9 and 8 and 9, respectively.

Boxwood (*Buxus*). Blooms over a long period in white, pink, or crimson with various varieties beginning in winter and ending in autumn. Most but not all are fragrant. Zones 8 and 9.

Broom, sweet (*Cytisus spachianus*). Large, it struts its stuff in early spring to summer, beginning its blooming early in life. And the *Supranubius* variety, flowering in early summer, shows white with a tint of pink. The *Monspessulanus* variety, also large, blooms in early summer with fragrant yellow flowers. Zones 9 and 10 and 9, respectively.

Butterfly bush (*Buddleia asiatica*, *auriculata*, *colviteii*, and many more). Fast growing in full sun and well-drained soil, they appeal to you-know-whats. The first is a large spring bloomer in white. The second, also large, has a creamier color, specializes even more in fragrance and blooms in autumn and winter. The third variety is very large, with large pink blooms in early summer. All are zones 8 and 9.

Colletia (*Colletia armata, cruciata,* and *infausta*). These sun-loving shrubs have spines instead of leaves but are rich in flowers and scent. All are large, the first two bear white flowers, and the last—which blooms first—has reddish-white blooms. Zones 7 through 10.

Magnolia (*Magnolia charles coates, grandiflora, lilliflora,* and *sieboldii*). The first is large and blooms creamy in early summer. The second, even larger (and arguably a tree), blooms in summer and autumn. The third, also very large, has lavender blooms with white inside in early summer. And the fourth chooses early to late summer with white fragrant flowers. Zones 6 through 9, 7 through 9, 6 through 8, and 7 and 8, respectively.

Mexican orange blossom (*Choisya ternata*). Middle-size with a profusion of fragrant white flowers. Blooms in spring, perhaps adding a later stage also. Zones 8 through 10.

Mockorange (*Philadelphus microphyllus* and *insignis*). Both with small white flowers and delightful smelling, the first is smaller and has the fragrance of pineapple. The second blooms a bit later with a mild scent. Zones 7 through 9.

Trees and Your Carbon Footprint

Your *carbon footprint* is a measure of the carbon dioxide you and your family emit as part of your lifestyle. It can be "translated" into trees and then you can plant that number of trees every year—in your yard, neighborhood park, or boulevard area (with permission)—to vastly improve the environment. It is a grand green gesture.

To determine your carbon footprint, you need to consult a couple websites and fill in a few numbers. (Only fifth-grade arithmetic will be required here, though—whew!) If the next page or two looks daunting, we give you a shortcut after the next two sections.

Now assemble these lifestyle numbers:

◆ What is the—*realistic*—mileage you get on your car(s)?

◆ How many miles do you drive each year?

◆ About how many miles do you travel by bus, train, and airplane?

◆ Do you have an ATV, jet ski, motorcycle, lawnmower, or leaf blower? These add much more carbon than you'd think, unless they are all-electric.

◆ How many kilowatt hours of electricity do you use each year?

Then consult some websites to plug in your numbers. Here are some of our favorites:

◆ www.carbonfund.org

◆ www.conservationfund.org

◆ www.stopglobalwarming.org

◆ americanforests.org/resources/ccc/

Don't forget to translate your footprint into the trees you need to plant!

A Simple Shortcut

If all that makes your head spin, here's a shortcut: the average American household needs to plant 8 to 15 trees—*per year*—to compensate for its annual carbon footprint. If you have a small house and family and drive a hybrid car, aim for the 8 end of the range; if you take international airplane flights and drive SUVs, aim for the 15 end.

Need a school project for your kid's classroom, a Scout troop, or a faith-based group? You might consider a large tree-planting event. It's good exercise for the body—and for the mind—as the kids figure out these carbon footprints! Anywhere you plant trees is fine. The wind blends and moves air around the planet all the time, so it doesn't matter where you plant trees. You could lug them thousands of miles away if you like. But why not plant the trees where you can enjoy them and benefit from them in all the ways mentioned in this chapter? Your yard, neighborhood park, school grounds, business property—all are great places to plant trees and shrubs to reduce global warming.

There are no bad trees for a project like this. Our only advice: choose trees that will grow large and for a long time. Here's an example for each zone:

> **The Real Dirt**
>
> We've started a carbon footprint woods in one of our city parks. We figured that our own footprints are 10 to 12 trees per year and have planted those for this year. Other people in our community are doing the same thing. Gradually, this park is becoming a beautiful place. Come see our work in progress, at Pamela Park, Edina, Minnesota.

◆ Zones 2/3: white pine

◆ Zone 4: bur oak

◆ Zone 5: hickory

- ◆ Zone 6: American elm

- ◆ Zone 7: sycamore

- ◆ Zone 8: black tupelo

- ◆ Zone 9: Monterey pine

- ◆ Zones 10/11: live oak

But there are many more good choices.

Why Should You Do This?

First, trees are easy to "install." And each tree soaks up more than 1 ton of carbon dioxide during its lifetime. In the meantime, you can have a picnic under it and listen to a few birds. Trees also filter water run-off, improving the water quality of neighboring creeks and ponds.

The only downside is that trees release carbon when they rot, and, if crowded together, can trap heat. Getting around this is simple: keep planting trees (which is what nature has been doing for millennia to absorb carbon dioxide), and don't plant them in crowds.

Plenty of evidence already indicates global warming is a problem. *The Weather Makers* by Australian scientist Tim Flannery describes clearly and intelligently how sea temperatures have risen, sea saltness has diminished (from glacial melting), and climate features from droughts to floods have become more extreme. Not one to overstate the case, Flannery also describes what has not yet been proved: whether the number and severity of recent storms can be tied to global warming and how different types of clouds affect the earth's heat balance. The richness of our data collection is still not enough on these issues.

But the computer models of atmospheric circulation have firmly established the temperature trends during the past 70 years: up. The data for these complex and effective models comes from 85 countries, 10,000 land stations, 7,000 ship-based stations, and 10 satellites, with more being added.

The jet stream of our planet has definitely shifted its patterns. More than anything, this is why we all *notice* the warming trend here in Edina, Minnesota.

Global warming is especially dangerous because it can accelerate suddenly and become unstoppable. *The Weather Makers* details the three most serious such tipping points: the death of the Amazonian rain forest (the hotter soils that would result would release its carbon), the destabilization of the Gulf Stream (melting glaciers would dilute its salinity, a drastic event that has helped swing the planet from Ice Age to hot house and back again before, in as little as 8 to 80 years), and a sudden release of greenhouse gases could form on either the sea floor or the permafrost in the Arctic.

Trees and Shrubs Grid

Here it is—the tree and shrub grid we've talked so much about in the previous chapters. And we think we have plenty of room to brag, because the information you'll find in the following pages is a culmination of many hours and resources. We hope you find it as helpful as we do!

Some of the trees and shrubs in the following grid are native plants. Some are non-native but well established. Some are the most important cultivars—with many other cultivars mentioned in the chapters where the tree or shrub was originally described (these chapter references are also in the grid). Some have their Latin name first (when there is no widely used common name), but most have their common names first. And all the large groupings (e.g., all the oak trees) are placed together because we thought that would be easiest to access the information.

Here's a key for what you'll find in the table, after the tree or shrub name, its Latin name, and its preferred zone:

Type:

DT deciduous tree

DS deciduous shrub

DE deciduous evergreen

ET evergreen tree

ES evergreen shrub

P palm

Size:

>   **S**   small for a tree or for a shrub
>
>   **M**   medium for a tree or for a shrub
>
>   **L**   large for a tree or for a shrub
>
>   **D**   dwarf for a tree or for a shrub

Light:

>   **Su**   prefers sun
>
>   **Sh**   prefers shade
>
>   **Su/Sh**   grows in either sun or shade fine *or* partial shade/partial sun fine
>
>   **NP**   not picky

Soil and moisture:

>   **WD**   well drained
>
>   **WD/M**   well drained and moist
>
>   **W**   wet
>
>   **D**   dry
>
>   **NP**   not picky/average

Wind:

>   **Y**   yes, accepts it well
>
>   **N**   no, doesn't do well

Flowers:

>   **Y**   yes, conspicuous
>
>   **N**   no, not conspicuous

Foliage:

>   **Y**   yes, in fall, all-year, or as evergreen in winter
>
>   **N**   no, not special

Fruits:

> **Y**   yes, but inedible to humans
>
> **YE**   yes and edible for humans
>
> **N**   no, because unpleasant, poisonous, or too small

Predator hardy:

> **Y**   yes
>
> **N**   no
>
> **A**   average

Street tolerant:

> **Y**   yes
>
> **N**   no, because of intolerance to salts and air pollution, because a hazard to motorists or pedestrians, because of root and bark needs, or because of messy nuts or fruits

Growth:

> **F**   fast
>
> **S**   slow
>
> **A**   average

Length of life:

> **L**   long
>
> **S**   short
>
> **A**   average

In the last column, we list where in the book—what chapter or appendix—you can find our discussions of that particular tree or shrub.

Name	Latin Name	Zone(s)	Type	Size	Light	Soil, Moisture	Wind	Flowers	Foliage	Fruits	Predator Hardy	Street Tolerant	Growth	Length of Life	Where in Book
Abelia	*Abelia triflora*	7–9	DS	L	S	NP	Y	Y	Y	N	Y	Y	A	A	10, D
Abelia, glossy	*Abelia grandiflora*	6–9	DS	M	Su	NP	Y	Y	N	N	N	N	A	A	10, D
Adenocarpus	*Adenocarpus*	9–10	ES	M	Su	NP	Y	Y	Y	N	Y	Y	A	A	D
Alaska yellow cedar	*Cupressus nootkatensis*	2	ET	L	Su	W	Y	N	Y	N	N	N	S	L	6
Alaskan mountain heather	*Phyllodoce aleutica*	2–5	ES	S	Su/Sh	M	Y	Y	N	N	N	N	S	A	10
Alder, Arizona	*Alnus oblongifolia*	8	DT	L	Su	W	Y	N	N	N	N	N	F	S	6
Alder, common	*Alnus*	2–8	DT/DS	S	Su	W	Y	N	N	N	N	Y	F	S	9
Alder, red	*Alnus rubra*	2–10	DT	M	Su	NP	Y	N	Y	N	Y	Y	A	A	6
Allspice	*Calycanthus*	5–9	DS	M	Su	NP	Y	Y	Y	N	Y	Y	A	A	D
American chestnut	*Castanea dentata*	4–10	DT	L	Su	WD	Y	N	Y	Y	N	A	F	L	19
American hornbeam	*Carpinus caroliniana*	3–11	DT	M	NP	WD	Y	N	Y	Y	A	Y	S	L	7
American smoketree	*Cotinus obovatus*	4–8	DT	S	Su	WD	Y	Y	Y	Y	A	Y	F	A/S	9, 11
Arborvitae	*Thuja occidentalis*	2–9	ET	M	Su/Sh	NP/W	Y	N	Y	N	Y	Y	F	S	7, 9, 17, 24
Ash, blue	*Fraxinus quadrangulara*	4–8	DT	L	Su	W	Y	N	Y	N	Y	Y	F	L	7
Ash, green	*Fraxinus pennsylvanica*	2–4	DT	L/M	NP	NP	N/Y	N	N	N	N	N	F	A	4, 7, 11
Ash, mountain	*Sorbus Americana*	2–7	DT	S	Su	NP	Y	Y	Y	Y	Y	N	A	A	6, 11, D
Ash, white	*Fraxinus Americana*	3–9	DT	L	Su/Sh	NP	Y	N	Y	Y	N	Y	F	L	7
Aspen, quaking	*Populus tremuloides*	2–5	DT	M	Su	W/NP	Y	N	Y	N	Y	Y	F	A	3–4, 9, 13
Aucuba	*Aucuba*	7–9	ES	L	Su/Sh	NP	Y	Y	Y	Y	Y	N	A	L	n/a

Common name	Scientific name	Zone	DE	M/L	NP	W						A	L	Notes
Baldcypress	*Taxodium distichum*	5–9	DT	M/L	NP	NP	N	Y	Y	Y	N	A	L	4, 6–7, 9, 23
Barberry	*Berberis*	6–9	DS/ES	S	NP	NP	Y	Y	Y	Y	N	A	A	6–7, 10–11, 23, D
Basswood	*Tilia Americana*	2–5	DT	L	Su/Sh	M/NP	Y	Y	Y	N	Y	A	L	7, 24
Beauty bush	*Kolkwitzia*	5–8	S	M	Su	NP	Y	Y	Y	Y	Y	F	A	D
Beech	*Fagus grandifolia*	3–10	DT	S/M	Su/Sh	NP	N	Y	N	N	N	S	L	5, 9, 11, 16, 19, 21, 23
Bilberry	*Vaccinium myrtillus*	2–6	DS	S	NP	W/WD	Y	Y	Y	YE	N	A	A	11, 19
Bilberry, kamchatka	*Vaccinium praestens*	4–8	DS	S	Sh	M	Y	Y	Y	Y	Y	A	A	11
Birch, paper	*Betula papyrifera*	2–9	DT	M	Su	WD/M	N	Y	A	N	N	F	S	3, 9, 21
Birch, river	*Betula nigra*	4–9	DT	M	Su	NP	N	Y	Y	N	Y	F	S	4, 7, 12, 21
Birch, yellow	*Betula alleghaniensis*	4–9	DT	M/L	NP	WD	N	Y	Y	N	Y	F	A	9, 11, 19
Black cherry	*Prunus serotina*	3–9	DT	M	Su	WD	Y	N	N	Y	N	A/F	A	6
Black gum (or sourgum)	*Nyssa sylvatica*	3–10	DT	L	NP	NP	N	Y	Y	N	N	S	A	3, 24
Black locust	*Robinia pseudoacacia*	3–5	DT	L	Su	WD	Y	Y	A	N	N	F	S	5, 9, 12–13, 21, 24
Black walnut	*Juglans nigra*	4–9	DT	L	Su	WD/NP	N	Y	N	Y	N	F	A	6–7, 9, 11, 19, 21
Blackberry	*Rubus allegheniensis* and *amabilis*	4–10	DS	M	Su/Sh	NP	Y	Y	Y	Y	N	F	A	n/a
Blackhaw	*Viburnum prunifolium*	4–6	DT	S	Sh	NP	Y	Y	Y	YE	N	S	L	5
Bluebeard shrub	*Caryopteris clandonensis*	6–9	DS	S	Su	D	Y	Y	Y	N	N	F	A	n/a

Name	Latin Name	Zone(s)	Type	Size	Light	Soil, Moisture	Wind	Flowers	Foliage	Fruits	Predator Hardy	Street Tolerant	Growth	Length of Life	Where in Book
Blueberry	*Vaccinium corymbosum and augustifolium*	2–8	S	DS	Su/Sh	W	Y	Y	Y	YE	N	N	A	A	11, D
Bog rosemary	*Andromeda polifolia*	3–6	DS	S	Su/Sh	W	Y	Y	N	N	Y	Y	F	A	10, 23
Boxelder	*Acer negundo*	2–8	DT	M/L	NP	W/NP	Y	Y	N	Y	Y	N	F	A	6
Boxwood	*Buxus microphylla and sempervirens*	6–10	ES	M	Su/Sh	NP	Y	Y	N	N	N	N	S	L	6–7, 9–, 23, D
Bridal wreath (or spirea)	*Spiraea prunifolia*	5–8	DS	M	Su	WD	Y	Y	N	N	Y	N	F	A	4, 9–12, 17, 23, D
Broom	*Cytisus multiflorus and spachianus*	5–11	DS	L	Su	WD	N	Y	N	N	Y	Y	F	A	3, 6, 10–11, 16, 21, D
Broom, sweet	*Cytisus spachianus*	5–11	DS	L	Su	WD	N	Y	N	N	N	Y	F	A	D
Buckeye, Ohio	*Aesculus glabra*	3–10	DT	M	Sh	WD	Y	Y	N	Y	Y	N	A	L	4–5, 7
Buckeye, red	*Aesculus pavia*	4–10	DT	S	NP	W	Y	Y	N	Y	A	N	A	L	5
Burning bush	*Euonymus alatus*	2–9	DS	M	Su/Sh	NP	Y	Y	N	Y	Y	Y	A	A	11
Bush honeysuckle	*Diervilla lonicera*	4–8	DS	S	S	NP	N	Y	Y	Y	Y	N	A	A	11
Butterfly bush	*Buddleia*	5–10	S	M	Su	WD/D	Y	Y	Y	N	Y	N	F	A	7, 10–11, 23, D
Buttonbush	*Cephalanthus occidentalis*	5–10	S	L	Su	W	N	Y	Y	Y	Y	N	F	A	7, 9, D
Cabbage palm	*Sabal palmetto*	8–10	P	L	NP	NP	Y	Y	Y	YE	Y	Y	S	A	5–6, 9

Common name	Scientific name														
California lilac	*Ceanothus*	8–10	ES	M	Su	WD	Y	Y	N	N	N	N	A	A	10, 23, D
California redwood	*Sequoia sempervirens*	9	DT	L	Su	WD	Y	N	Y	Y	Y	N	S	L	2, 4, 9, 24
Camellia	*Camellia japonica*	7–11	ES	L	Sh	M	N	Y	Y	N	Y	N	A	A	5, 10
Camellia, mountain	*Stewartia ovata*	7–11	ES	M	Sh	M	Y	Y	Y	Y	Y	N	A	A	n/a
Camellia, silk	*Stewartia UMaine*	7–11	ES	M	Sh	M	Y	Y	Y	N	Y	N	A	A	n/a
Canada hemlock	*Tsuga canadensis*	3–7	ET	L	Su/Sh	WD/M	N	Y	Y	Y	Y	N	S	L	5
Candlenut	*Aleurites moluccana*	8–11	DT	M	Su	NP	N	N	N	Y	N	Y	A	A	11
Cat's claw	*Caesalpina decapetala*	9–11	DS	M	Su	WD	Y	Y	N	N	N	N	A	A	n/a
Catalpa, northern	*Catalpa speciosa*	4–8	DT	L	NP	NP	Y	Y	Y	Y	A	N	F	A	5, 7, 9
Ceanothus, Santa Barbara	*Ceanothus impressus*	8–10	DS	M	Su	NP	Y	Y	Y	N	Y	Y	A	A	10
Ceanothus, wavyleafed	*Ceanothus foliosus*	9–10	ES	S	Su	WD	Y	Y	Y	N	Y	Y	S	A	10
Cherry, wild	*Prunus serotina*	3–11	DT	M/L	Su	NP	Y	Y	Y	Y	N	N	A	S	n/a
Cherry laurel	*Prunus laurocerasus*	7–8	DT	L	Su/Sh	NP	Y	Y	Y	Y	Y	N	A	S	9, 23
Chinaberry	*Melia azedarach*	7–11	DT	M	Su/Sh	NP	N	N	Y	Y	Y	N	F	A	8
Chokeberry, black	*Aronia melanocarpa*	2–7	DS	S	NP	W/D	Y	Y	Y	N	N	Y	A	S	9–11
Colletia	*Colletia infausta*	7–10	DS	L	Su	NP	Y	Y	N	N	N	Y	A	A	D
Common lilac	*Syringa vulgaris*	3–7	DS	M	Su	WD	Y	Y	N	N	N	Y	F	L	1, 5, 7, 10, 23, D
Corkwood	*Leitneria floridana*	5–6	DT	S	Su	NE/W	Y	N	N	Y	Y	N	S	A	n/a

Name	Latin Name	Zone(s)	Type	Size	Light	Soil, Moisture	Wind	Flowers	Foliage	Fruits	Predator Hardy	Street Tolerant	Growth	Length of Life	Where in Book
Cornelian cherry dogwood	*Cornus mas*	4–9	DT	S	NP	NP	Y	Y	Y	Y	Y	Y	A	S	3
Cottonwood	*Populus deltoides*	3–9	DT	L	Su	W	Y	N	Y	N	N	N	F	S	3, 6–10, 15, 22
Cowberry (or lingonberry)	*Vacciniu vitisidaea*	5–7	ES	S	S	WD	Y	Y	Y	YE	N	N	S	A	11
Crabapple	*Malus*	3–9	DT	S	Su	WD	Y	Y	N	Y	A	N	A	A	6–7, 9, 17, 21, D
Cranberry cotoneaster	*Cotoneaster apiculatus*	4–8	DS	S	NP	NP	Y	Y	Y	Y	Y	N	A	A	7, 11, 17, 20
Cranberry	*Oxycoccus palustris*	3–7	S	S	NP	W	Y	Y	N	Y	Y	N	S	A	3, 7
Cucumber tree	*Magnolia acuminata*	4–7	DT	S/M	NP	WD	N	Y	Y	Y	Y	N	F	L	n/a
Currant	*Ribes*	2–8	S	S	Su	NP	Y	Y	Y	Y	Y	N	F	A	10–11, 23, D
Daisy bush	*Olearia*	9–10	ES	L	Su	WD	Y	Y	Y	N	Y	N	A	A	23, D
Daphne	*Daphne*	4–9	DS	S	Su	WD	Y	Y	Y	Y	N	Y	A	A	23, D
Daphne, Carol Mackie	*Daphne burkwoodii Carol Mackie*	5–8	DS	S	Su	WD	Y	Y	Y	Y	N	Y	A	A	D
Deutzia	*Deutzia*	4–8	DS	S	Su/Sh	WD	Y	Y	N	N	Y	Y	A	A	23
Devil's walkingstick	*Aralia spinosa*	4–9	DT	S	NP	NP	Y	Y	Y	Y	A	Y	F	A	n/a
Dogwood, flowering	*Cornus florida*	3–9	DT	S	NP	NP	Y	Y	Y	Y	Y	Y	S	A	3, 10–11, 23
Dogwood, grey	*Cornus racemosa*	3–9	DT	S	NP	NP	Y	Y	Y	Y	Y	Y	S	A	10–11
Dogwood, kousa	*Cornus kousa*	3–9	DT	S	NP	NP	Y	Y	Y	Y	Y	Y	S	A	10–11
Dogwood, roughleaf	*Cornus drummondii*	4–10	DT	S	Su/Sh	NP	Y	Y	Y	Y	A	Y	F	S	3, 10–11, 23
Dogwood, silky	*Cornus*	6–8	DT	S	NP	NP	Y	Y	Y	Y	Y	F	S	A	23

Downy Hawthorn	*Crataegus*	3–8	DT	M	NP	NP	Y	Y	Y	N	Y	Y	A/S	L	6
Elder, golden	*Sambucus nigra and aurea*	5–8	DS	M/L	Su/Sh	NP,M	Y	Y	Y	A	Y	Y	F	A	11
Elderberry	*Sambucus cerulean and nigra*	4–9	DS	L	NP	NP	Y	Y	YE	Y	N	N	A	S	9–10, 17, 23
Elm, American	*Ulmus Americana*	6	DT	L	Su/Sh	NF	Y	N	N	N	Y	Y	F	L	3
Enkianthus	*Enkianthus perculatus*	5–9	S	S	NP	CW	N	Y	N	Y	N	N	S	A	10, D
Escallonia	*Escallonia*	8–10	DS	M/L	Su	NP	Y	Y	N	Y	Y	Y	A	A	D
Fir, balsam	*Abies balsamea*	2–5	ET	L	Sh	M	Y	N	Y	N	N	N	A	A	3, 5–6
Fir, Douglas	*Pseudotsuga mensiesii*	5	ET	L	Su	WD	Y	N	Y	N	N	N	A	L	2, 4
Fir, European silver	*Abies alba*	5–8	ET	M	Su/Sh	NP	Y	Y	Y	Y	N	N	A	L	9
Fir, silver	*Abies amabilis*	5–8	ET	L	Su/Sh	M	Y	N	Y	Y	N	N	S	L	9
Fir, white	*Abies concolor*	3–7	ET	L	Su	NP	Y	Y	Y	Y	N	N	A	A	6
Firethorn	*Pyracantha atlantiodes and rogersiana*	6–9	DS	M	Su	NP	Y	Y	Y	Y	N	N	A	S	10, D
Flowering currant	*Ribes sanguineum*	6–8	DS	S	Su	NP	Y	Y	N	N	Y	N	A	S	10
Foothill paloverde	*Parkinsonia*	10	DT	S	Su	D	Y	N	Y	N	Y	A	A	A	6
Forsythia	*Forsythia*	3–9	DS	M	Su/Sh	NP	Y	N	Y	Y	N	Y	F	A	7, 23
Fragrant wintersweet	*Chimonanthus*	7–9	DS	M	Su/Sh	NP	Y	Y	N	N	Y	Y	A	A	D
Fremontodendron	*Fremontodendron mexicanum*	10–11	DS	L	Su	NP	Y	Y	Y	N	N	N	A	S	10
Fringetree	*Chionanthus virginicus*	4–9	DT	S	NP	NP	Y	Y	Y	A	Y	Y	A	A	5, 23, D

Name	Latin Name	Zone(s)	Type	Size	Light	Soil, Moisture	Wind	Flowers	Foliage	Fruits	Predator Hardy	Street Tolerant	Growth	Length of Life	Where in Book
Fuchsia	*Fuchsia*	8–10	S	M	NP	NP	Y	Y	Y	Y	A	N	F	A	10–11
Gaultheria	*Gaultheria myrsinoides*	9–11	DS	S	Su	W	Y	Y	Y	Y	Y	Y	F	A	23, D
Gaultheria	*Gaultheria*	4–10	DS	S	Sh	M	Y	Y	Y	Y	Y	Y	A	A	23
Gingko	*Gingko*	5–9	DT	M	Su/Sh	NP	Y	N	Y	N	Y	Y	S	L	7–8, 23–24
Glory pea	*Clianthus puniceus*	7–11	ES	M	Su	WD	Y	Y	Y	N	A	N	A	S	10
Golden chain tree	*Laburnum anagyroides*	5–11	DT	S	NP	WD	Y	Y	Y	N	Y	N	A	S	7
Golden rain tree	*Koelreuteria paniculata*	5–9	DS	M/L	Su	NP/WD	Y	Y	Y	Y	N	N	A	A	7, 23–24
Gooseberry	*Ribes*	5–9	DS	S/M	Su/Sh	NP	Y	Y	Y	Y	Y	Y	A	A	n/a
Hackberry, common	*Celtis occidentalis*	3–8	DT	M/L	Su/Sh	WD/NP	Y	N	Y	N	Y	Y	F	L	6
Hackberry, dwarf	*Celtis tenuifolia*	4–10	DT	D	S	WD	Y	N	Y	Y	A	A	S	L	6
Hawthorn, western black	*Crataegus douglasii*	4–8	DT	M	NP	W	Y	Y	Y	Y	N	Y	A/S	L	7
Heather (or heath, yellow mountain)	*Phyllodoce glanduliflora*	3–7	ES	S	Su/Sh	M	Y	Y	Y	N	Y	N	S	A	10, 19
Heather	*Phyllodoce nipponica*	3–5	ES	S	Su/Sh	M	Y	Y	Y	N	Y	N	S	A	10
Heavenly bamboo	*Nandina domestico purpurea*	9–11	DS	S/L	Sh	WD	Y	Y	Y	Y	Y	Y	F	A	11
Hebe	*Hebe*	9–11	ES	S	Su	NP	Y	Y	Y	N	Y	N	S	A	11
Hibiscus	*Hibiscus lunariifilius*	6–11	DS	S	Su	WD	Y	Y	N	N	A	Y	F	A	5, 10, D
Hickory, bitternut	*Caryacordiformis*	5–8	DT	L	Su	D	N	N	Y	Y	Y	Y	F	A	3
Hickory, mockernut	*Carya tomentosa*	4–10	DT	L	Su	NP	N	N	Y	Y	Y	Y	A	A	3
Hickory, shagbark	*Carya ovata*	3–9	DT	L	Su/Sh	WD	Y	N	Y	YE	Y	A	Y	S	L	3

Hoheria	*Hoheria populnea and foliis purpureis*	9–10	DS	L	Su	D	Y	Y	Y	N	Y	Y	A	A	11
Holly, American	*Ilex opaca, aquifolium, and crenata*	5–9	ES/DS	M/L	Su/Sh	WE/M	Y	A	Y	Y	N	N	S	L	1, 3, 11, D
Holly, false	*Osmanthus*	6–10	ES	L	Su/Sh	NP	Y	Y	Y	Y	Y	Y	A	A	11
Honey locust	*Gleditsia triacanthos*	3–9	DT	L	SU	NP	Y	N	Y	Y	Y	Y	A	A	7, 11, 13
Honeysuckle	*Lonicera*	5–9	S	M	NP	NP	Y	Y	N	Y	Y	N	F	L	7, 10–11, 17, 23
Hop hornbeam, eastern	*Ostrya virginiana*	2–9	DT	S/M	Su/Sh	NP	Y	N	Y	Y	Y	A	S	L	7
Horsechestnut	*Aesulus hippocastarum*	5–9	DT	M	Su	WD	Y	Y	N	N	Y	N	A	L	4, D
Huckleberry	*Gaylusscia, baccata*	6–8	DT	S	Su/Sh	M	Y	Y	Y	Y	Y	N	F	A	2
Hydrangea	*Hydrangea paniculata*	4–8	DS	L	Su	WD	Y	Y	N	N	Y	N	A	A	10, 17, 23
Incense cedar	*Calocedrus decurrens*	9	ET	L	NP	W	Y	N	Y	N	Y	N	S	L	7
Japanese angelica tree	*Aralia elata*	4–9	DS	L	Su	NP	Y	Y	Y	Y	Y	N	S	A	D
Japanese pieris	*Pieris japonica*	5–8	ES	M/L	Su/Sh	NP	Y	Y	Y	N	Y	N	S	A	n/a
Joshua tree	*Yucca bievifolia*	6–10	ET	S	Su	D	Y	N	Y	N	Y	N	S	L	6
Juneberry	*Amelanchier arborea*	4–9	DT	S	NP	WD	Y	Y	Y	Y	N	Y	A	A/L	10
Juniper, Utah	*Juniperus osteosperma*	3–7	ET	S	Su	E	Y	N	Y	YE	Y	N	S	L	6
Kentucky coffeetree	*Gymnocladus dioicus*	3–7	DT	L	Su	NP	Y	Y	Y	Y	Y	Y	S	L	7
Kerria	*Kerria japonica*	5–9	DS	M	Su/Sh	NP	Y	Y	Y	N	Y	Y	A	A	23
Kew broom	*Cytisus kewensis*	6–8	DS	S	Su	WD	N	Y	N	N	Y	N	A	A	D

Name	Latin Name	Zone(s)	Type	Size	Light	Soil, Moisture	Wind	Flowers	Foliage	Fruits	Predator Hardy	Street Tolerant	Growth	Length of Life	Where in Book
Lace bark	Hoheria populneaDS	DS	L	Su		D	Y	Y	Y	N	Y	Y	A	A	11
Laurel, bay	Laurel nobilis	8–10	ES/ET	M/L	Su/Sh	WD	N	N	Y	N	N	N	A	A	23, D
Laurel, davids mountain	Sophora davidii	6–9	DS	L	Su	NP	Y	Y	Y	N	Y	Y	A	A	10
Lilac, Japanese tree	Syringa reticulata	3–8	DS	M	Su	WD	Y	Y	N	N	Y	Y	A	A	7
Linden	Tilia Americana	3–8	DT	L	Su/Sh	M	Y	Y	Y	Y	Y	Y	A	L	7, 9, 12, 19, 24
Loblolly-bay	Gordonia lasianthus	7–9	ET	M	Su/Sh	NP	N	Y	N	N	Y	N	S	L	n/a
Lotus, red	Manglietia insignis	7–9	ET	M	Su/Sh	WD/M	Y	Y	Y	Y	Y	Y	A	A	n/a
Magnolia	Magnolia grandiflora and tripetala	5–10	DT	M	Su	W	Y	Y	N	N		N	A	A	3, 10, 16–17, 21, 23, D
Magnolia Leonard Meisel	Magnolia × loebneri Leonard Meisel	5–10	DT	M	Su	W	Y	Y	N	N	Y	N	A	A	10
Mahonia	Mahonia	5–11	ES	S/M	Su/Sh	NP	Y	Y	Y	N	Y	Y	A	A	D
Mallow, Indian	Abutilon	9–11	S	S	Su	NP	Y	Y	Y	N	Y	N	A	A	10
Mangrove, red and black	Rhizophora Avicennia germinans	9–10	ET	M	Su	W	Y	Y	N	N	Y	N	F	A	3, 9, 22
Maple, amur	Acer ginnala	3–7	DT	M	NP	WD	Y	N	Y	N	Y	Y	F	S	7, 11
Maple, autumn blaze	Acer × freemanii	3–8	DT	L	Su	NP	Y	N	Y	N	Y	Y	F	M/L	7, 11
Maple, Norway	Acer platanoides	3–7	DT	M	Su/Sh	NP	Y	N	Y	N	Y	Y	F	L	9, 11, 13
Maple, red	Acer rubrum	3–9	DT	L	NP	WD/NP	Y	N	Y	N	N	Y	F	A	4, 6, 11
Maple, silver	Acer saccharinum	3–9	DT	L	NP	NP/W	Y	N	Y	Y	Y	Y	F	L	7–8, 10, 13, 19

Common name	Scientific name																
Maple, sugar	Acer saccharum	3–9	DT	L	NP	WD	Y	N	Y	N	Y	Y	N	Y	S	L	2–3, 6, 9, 11, 24
Mesquite, velvet	Prosopis velutina	7–9	DT	S	Su	NP	Y	Y	N	Y	N	Y	N	N	S	A	5–6
Mexican orange blossom	Choisya ternata	8–10	ES	M	Su	NP	Y	Y	Y	N	Y	Y	Y	Y	A	A	23, D
Mexican pinyon	Pinus cembroides	9	ET	S	Su/Sh	D	Y	N	Y	N	Y	Y	Y	Y	S	L	6
Mockorange	Philadelphus	4–9	DS	S	Su	WD	Y	Y	Y	Y	A	Y	Y	Y	A	A	7, 10–11, 23, D
Mockorange, Japanese	Pittosporum tobira	8–10	ET/ES	L	Su	WD	Y	Y	Y	N	Y	Y	N	N	A	A	11
Monkey puzzle	Araucaria araucana	7–10	ET	M	Su	W/D	Y	Y	Y	N	Y	Y	N	N	A	A	9
Mulberry, red	Morus rubra	4–11	DT	M	Sh	WD	Y	N	Y	Y	Y	Y	Y	Y	F	A	11
Nannyberry	Viburnum lentago	2–8	DS	L	NP	NP	Y	Y	Y	Y	Y	Y	N	N	S	L	5, 7
Ninebark	Physocarpus	2–8	DS	M	NP	NP/WD	Y	Y	Y	N	Y	Y	N	N	F	A	7, D
Oak, black	Quercus velutina	4–7	DT	L	Su	NP	Y	Y	Y	Y	Y	N	Y	N	A	A	24
Oak, blackjack	Quercus marilandica	5–9	DT	M	Su	D	Y	N	Y	Y	Y	Y	N	N	S	L	24
Oak, bur	Quercus macrocarpa	4–7	DT	L	Su	NP	Y	N	Y	Y	Y	Y	Y	Y	S	L	3, 6, 9, 13
Oak, chestnut	Quercus prinus	4–7	DT	L	Su	NP	Y	N	Y	Y	Y	Y	N	N	S	L	6
Oak, chinkapin	Quercus muehlenbegii	4–10	DT	L	Su	NP	Y	N	Y	Y	Y	Y	N	N	S	L	6
Oak, live	Quercus virginiana	8–11	DT	L	NP	D/NP	Y	N	N	Y	N	N	N	N	S	L	3, 9
Oak, overcup	Quercus lyrata	5–8	DT	L	Su	NP	Y	N	Y	Y	Y	Y	Y	Y	S	L	6
Oak, pin	Quercus palustris	4–8	DT	L	Su	W/WD	Y	N	Y	Y	Y	Y	Y	Y	F	L	6, 9, 11, 21

Name	Latin Name	Zone(s)	Type	Size	Light	Soil, Moisture	Wind	Flowers	Foliage	Fruits	Predator Hardy	Street Tolerant	Growth	Length of Life	Where in Book
Oak, post	*Quercus stellata*	5–9	DT	L	Su	NP	Y	N	Y	YE	Y	N	S	L	6, 9
Oak, red	*Quercus rubra*	3–8	DT	L	NP	WD	Y	N	Y	Y	N	Y	F	L	2, 5–6, 9, 11, 13, 19
Oak, scarlet	*Quercus coccinea*	5–9	DT	L	Su	D	Y	N	Y	Y	Y	N	F	L	9
Oak, scrub	*Quercus berberidifolia*	6–10	ET/ES	S	Su	D	Y	N	Y	Y	Y	N	S	A	6
Oak, silk	*Grevillea robusta*	10/11	ET	M	Su	WD	N	N	N	N	Y	Y	F	A	4, 7, 19
Oak, swamp white	*Quercus bicolor*	4–7	DT	L	Su	NP	Y	N	Y	Y	Y	Y	S	L	6
Oak, white	*Quercus alba*	3–8	DT	L	Su	WD	Y	Y	N	Y	Y	N	S	L	2, 6, 11, 19
Oak, willow	*Quercus phellos*	6–9	DT	L	Su	W	Y	N	Y	Y	N	Y	F	L	6
One seed juniper	*Juniperus monosperma*	7	ES/ET	S/M	Su	D	Y	N	Y	Y	N	N	S	L	6
Orange, sour (or Seville orange)	*Citrus × aurantium*	9–11	ET	S	Su	M	Y	Y	Y	Y	Y	Y	A	A	6
Pacific yew	*Taxus brevifolia*	6–9	ET	M	Su/Sh	M	Y	N	Y	Y	Y	N	S	L	6
Palm, California fan	*Washingtonia*	9–10	P	L	A	A	Y	N	Y	Y	Y	Y	F	A	7
Palm, Canary Island date	*Phoenix canariensis*	8–11	P	L	Su	WD/D	Y	N	Y	Y	N	Y	S	A	10–11
Palmetto, dwarf	*Sabal minor*	7–11	P	S	Su/Sh	D	Y	N	Y	YE	Y	Y	S	A	4
Palmetto, saw	*Serena repens*	7–11	P	S	Su/Sh	D/W	Y	N	Y	Y	N	Y	A	A	4
Paperplant Fatsia	*Fatsia japonica*	8–11	ES	S	Su/Sh	NP	Y	Y	Y	Y	N	N	F	A	11
Pawpaw	*Asimina triloba*	5–10	DT	S	NP	NP	Y	Y	Y	YE	A	Y	S	S	2, 4, 9

Common name	Botanical name																	
Pea shrub, Siberian	*Caragana arborescens*	2–7	DS	L	Su	D	Y	Y	N	Y	Y	Y	Y	Y	A	F	A	D
Peach	*Prunus persica*	5–9	DT	S	Su	WD/NF	Y	Y	N	Y	YE	Y	N	N	A	A	A	4, 6, 11
Peacock flower	*Caesalpinia*	8–11	DS	L	Su/Sh	WD	Y	N	Y	N	N	Y	N	F	N	F	S	10
Pecan	*Carya illinoinensis*	5–9	DT	L	Su	WD/NP	Y	N	Y	N	YE	A	Y	N	L	S	L	3, 6, 9
Pepper tree	*Schinus molle*	8–11	ET	M	Su	D	Y	N	N	Y	Y	A	Y	N	A	A	A	7
Persimmon	*Diospyros virginiana*	5–9	DT	L	NP	NP/D	Y	Y	Y	Y	Y	Y	Y	Y	L	S	L	6, 9, 11
Photinia	*Photinia fraserii and robusta*	9–11	ES	L	Su/Sh	WD	Y	Y	N	Y	Y	Y	Y	Y	A	A	L	9, 11, 21, D
Piersis	*Piersis floribunda*	5–7	ES	M/L	Su/Sh	NF	Y	Y	Y	Y	N	Y	N	Y	A	A	A	10
Pine, Austrian	*Pinus nigra*	6	ET	L	Su	NP	Y	N	Y	N	N	Y	Y	N	A	F	L	6, 9
Pine, eastern bristlecone	*Pinus longaeva*	4–7	ET	M	Su	WD/D	Y	N	Y	N	N	Y	Y	N	S	S	L	6
Pine, jack	*Pinus banksiana*	2–7	ET	M	Su	WD/NP	Y	N	Y	N	N	Y	N	N	S	S	L	1, 3, 6
Pine, Japanese white	*Pinus parviflora*	4–7	ET	M	Su	WD	Y	N	Y	N	N	Y	N	N	A	A	A	9
Pine, loblolly	*Pinus taeda*	5–8	ET	M/L	Su	NP	Y	N	Y	N	N	Y	N	N	F	F	S	3, 9
Pine, lodgepole	*Pinus contorta*	2–7	ET	L	Su	WD/D	Y	N	Y	N	N	Y	Y	N	F	F	L	3, 4, 6
Pine, Monterey	*Pinus radiata*	8–10	ET	L	Su	D	Y	N	Y	N	N	Y	N	N	F	F	A	4, 9
Pine, Ponderosa	*Pinus ponderosa*	3–7	ET	L	Su	WD	Y	N	N	N	N	Y	N	N	S	S	L	7
Pine, red	*Pinus resinosa*	2–6	ET	L	Su	NP	Y	N	N	N	N	Y	Y	N	A	A	L	6, 9, 19
Pine, sand	*Pinus clausa*	9–11	ET	S	Su	D	Y	N	Y	N	N	Y	Y	N	S	S	S	6
Pine, Scotch	*Pinus sylvestris*	2–5	ET	L	Su	WD	Y	N	Y	N	N	Y	Y	N	S	S	L	6
Pine, shortleaf	*Pinus echinata*	5–8	ET	L	Su	D	Y	N	Y	N	N	Y	N	N	F	F	L	6
Pine, slash	*Pinus elliotii*	7–10	ET	L	Su	NP	Y	N	N	N	N	Y	N	N	F	F	S	4, 6, 9

Name	Latin Name	Zone(s)	Type	Size	Light	Soil, Moisture	Wind	Flowers	Foliage	Fruits	Predator Hardy	Street Tolerant	Growth	Length of Life	Where in Book
Pine, western bristlecone	*Pinus aristata*	8–9	ET	S/M	Su	NP	Y	N	Y	N	Y	Y	S	L	6
Pine, white	*Pinus strobus*	2–8	ET	L	Su	NP	Y	N	N	N	N	N	S	L	3–4, 6, 9, 20–21
Pistachio, Chinese	*Pistacio chinensis*	9–11	ES	L	Su	D	Y	N	Y	Y	N	N	A	A	11
Plum, American	*Prunus americana*	5–8	DT	M	Su	M	Y	Y	Y	Y	N	Y	A	A	D
Plum, beach	*Prunus maritima*	3–6	DS	M	Su	D	Y	Y	N	YE	Y	Y	A	A	11, 23, D
Plum, wild	*Prunus Americana*	3–8	DT	S	Su	WD	Y	Y	Y	YE	N	N	S	A	6, 11, D
Potentilla or cinquefoil	*Potentilla fruticosa*	3–7	DS	S	Su/Sh	NP	Y	Y	Y	N	Y	Y	F	A	7, 10–11, 17, 23, D
Prairie crabapple	*Malus ioensis*	4–10	DT	S	Su	WD	Y	Y	Y	YE	N	Y	F	S	6
Prickly pear	*Opuntica macrorbiza*	4–10	ES	S	Su	D	Y	Y	Y	Y	Y	Y	A	A	4, 6
Privet, glossy	*Ligustrum lucidum*	6–10	DS	L	NP	NP	Y	Y	Y	Y	Y	Y	F	L	17, D
Privet, swamp	*Forestiera acuminata*	6–10	DS/DT	S/M	Su/Sh	NP/W	Y	Y	N	Y	N	N	F	A	D
Quince, Japanese	*Chaenomeles japonica*	4–9	DS	S	Su/Sh	WD/D	Y	Y	Y	Y	Y	Y	A	A	10
Raspberry	*Rubus idaeus crataegifolis and lasiostylus*	2–8	DS	M	NP	NP	Y	Y	Y	YE	Y	N	F	S	10–11, D
Red Rivergum	*Eucalyptus camaldulensis*	7–11	ET	L	Su	M	Y	Y	N	Y	Y	Y	F	L	3, 19, 23–24
Redbud	*Cercis canadensis*	4–9	DT	S	NP	WD	Y	Y	Y	Y	N	A	Y	S	L	3, 7, 11, 17

Common name	Scientific name													
Redwood, dawn	*Metasequoia glyptostroboides*	8–10	DT	L	Su/Sh	W	Y	N	N	Y	N	S	L	8
Red cedar, eastern	*Juniperus virginiana*	3–9	ET	M	Su	WD	N	N	Y	N	Y	F	L	7
Rhododendron	*Rhododendron*	5–9	ES	M/L	Su/Sh	NP	Y	Y	N	Y	N	A	A	10–11, 23
Russian olive	*Elaeagnus angustifolia*	2–9	DT	M	Su	WD/D	Y	N	Y	Y	Y	A	S	7, 9, 21
Russian saltree	*Halimodendron halodendron*	3–8	DT	M	Su	NP	Y	Y	N	Y	Y	A	L	11
Saguaro	*Cereus giganteus*	9	DT	L	Su	D	Y	Y	YE	Y	Y	S	Y	3, 6–7, 9
Salmonberry	*Rubus spectabilis*	5–8	DS	M	Su/Sh	NP	Y	Y	YE	Y	Y	F	A	D
Sand cherry, western	*Prunus pumila × besseyi*	4–8	S	S	Su	WD	Y	Y	YE	Y	Y	A	A	D
Sassafras	*Sassafras albidum*	2–6	DT	M/L	Su	NP	Y	Y	Y	Y	Y	F	A	7, 23
Sea buckthorn	*Hippophae rhamnoides*	3–7	DS	M/L	Su	D	Y	N	YE	Y	Y	F	A	11
Sequoia, giant	*Sequoiadendron*	9	ET	L	Su/Sh	WD/W	Y	N	N	N	Y	S	L	2, 9, 24
Serviceberry, downy	*Amelanchier Canadensis*	3–7	DT	M	Su/Sh	WD/NP	Y	Y	Y	N	Y	A	A	10–11, 17, D
Sheep laurel	*Kalmia angustifolia*	2–7	DS	S	Su	WD/W	Y	Y	N	Y	Y	F	S	10, 23
Silverbell	*Halesia tetraptera*	5–8	DT	L	Su/Sh	M	Y	Y	Y	Y	Y	F	A	n/a
Skimmia, Japanese	*Skimmia Japonica*	7–9	ES	S	NP/Sh	NP	Y	Y	Y	Y	Y	A	A	11, 23, D
Snowball	*Ceanothus rigidus*	9–10	DS	L	Su	WD	Y	Y	N	Y	Y	A	A	10, 23
Snowbell, Japanese	*Styrax japonica*	5–9	DS	L	Su/Sh	M	N	Y	Y	Y	N	A	A	10
Snowberry	*Symphoricarpus albus*	2–4	DS	S	NP	NP	Y	Y	Y	Y	Y	A	A	7, 11, 23, D

Name	Latin Name	Zone(s)	Type	Size	Light	Soil, Moisture	Wind	Flowers	Foliage	Fruits	Predator Hardy	Street Tolerant	Growth	Length of Life	Where in Book
Soapberry	*Sapindus saponaria, drummondii*	7–10	DT	M	S	NP	A	Y	Y	Y	Y	Y	A	L	6–7
Sophora	*Sophora tetraphera*	9–10	DS	L	Su	WD	Y	Y	Y	Y	Y	N	A	A	10
Sophora (or necklace pod)	*Sophora tomentosa*	9–11	DS	M	Su	WD	Y	Y	Y	Y	Y	N	A	A	10
Sourwood	*Oxydendrum arboreum*	5–9	DT	M	NP	NP	Y	Y	Y	Y	Y	N	F	A	5, 9
Spice bush	*Lindera benzoin*	4–9	DS	M/D	Sh	W	Y	Y	Y	Y	A	N	S	A	5, 9, D
Spiraea	*Spiraea japonica*	4–9	S	S	Su	NP	Y	Y	N	N	Y	Y	F	A	4, 9–12, 17, 23, D
Spruce, blue	*Picea pungens*	6–8	ET	L	Su/Sh	Y	Y	N	Y	Y	Y	Y	S	L	19, 23
Spruce, Sitka	*Picea sitchensis*	7–8	ET	L	S	WD	Y	N	N	Y	N	S	L	6, 19
Spruce, white	*Picea glauca*	3–8	ET	L	NP	NP	Y	N	N	N	Y	N	F	A	3, 5, 24
St. John's wort (or Rose of Sharon)	*Hypericum calycinum*	6–8	DS	S	Su/Sh	NP	Y	Y	Y	N	Y	Y	A	A	23
Stephanandra	*Stephanandra*	4–8	DS	M	Su/Sh	M	Y	Y	Y	N	Y	Y	A	A	D
Stranvaesia	*Stranvaesia*	6–10	ES	L	Su/Sh	NP	Y	N	Y	Y	Y	N	A	A	D
Sumac, scarlet	*Rhus glabra*	2	DS	L	Su	NP	Y	N	Y	Y	Y	Y	F	A	D
Sumac, staghorn	*Rhus typhina*	4–8	DT	S	Su	WD/NP	Y	N	Y	N	N	N	F	S	6
Summersweet	*Clethra acuminata*	6–9	DS	L	Su	M	Y	Y	Y	Y	Y	Y	A	A	D
Sun rose (or orchid rock rose)	*Cistus × purpureus*	9–10	DS	S	Su	WD	Y	Y	Y	Y	Y	Y	A/F	A	10
Sweet pepper bush	*Clethra alnifolia*	4–9	DS	M	Su	M	Y	Y	Y	Y	Y	Y	A	A	D

Common name	Scientific name														
Sweetbox	*Sarcococca*	6–8	ES	S	NP/Sh	WD	Y	Y	Y	N	Y	Y	A	A	D
Sweetgum	*Liquidambar styraciflua*	6–9	DT	L	Su/Sh	WD	Y	Y	Y	Y	N	Y	A	L	19, 21
Sycamore	*Platanus occidentalis*	4–9	DT	S	Su	W	Y	N	N	N	Y	Y	F	L	3, 9, 12, 16, 19
Tamarack	*Larix laricina*	2–5	DE	M	Su	NP/W	Y	N	Y	N	N	Y	S	L	1, 3, 6–7
Tamarisk	*Tamarix ramosissima*	3–9	DS	M	Su	M	Y	Y	Y	N	Y	Y	F	A	10
Thornless cockspur hawthorn	*Crataegus crus-galli iner*	4	DT	S	NP	NP	Y	Y	N	YE	N	Y	F	A	n/a
Tree peony	*Paeonia suffruticosa*	4–6	DS	M	Su/Sh	NF	Y	Y	Y	N	N	N	S	A	10, 23
Tree poppy, California	*Romneya*	8–10	DS/ES	M	Su	WD/NP	Y	Y	Y	N	Y	Y	A	A	23
Tulip tree (or tulip poplar)	*Liriodendron tulipifera*	4–9	DT	L	Su	WD	Y	Y	Y	N	Y	Y	A	L	1, 6–7, 9, 11, 22, 24
Tupelo, black	*Nyssa sylvatica*	5–9	DT	S	Su	W	Y	Y	Y	N	Y	Y	A	L	3, 9
Verbena	*Verbena*	8–10	DS	D/S	Su	NF	Y	N	Y	N	N	N	A	A	n/a
Wahoo, eastern	*Euonymus atropurpureus*	3–8	DS	S	NP	NF	Y	Y	N	N	Y	Y	A	A	7
Wax myrtle California	*Morella californica*	7–10	DS/DT	S	Su/Sh	D	Y	Y	Y	Y	Y	Y	S	A	n/a
Wayfaring tree	*Viburnum lantana*	3–7	DS	L	Su/Sh	NP	Y	N	A	Y	A	Y	A	A	23
Weigela	*Weigela*	4–9	DS	M/L	Su	NP	Y	Y	A	Y	Y	Y	F	A	10–11, D
Willow	*Salix*	2–6	DT	M/L	S	M	Y	Y	Y	N	Y	Y	F	S	1–2, 5–7, 9, 13, 19, D

Name	Latin Name	Zone(s)	Type	Size	Light	Soil, Moisture	Wind	Flowers	Foliage	Fruits	Predator Hardy	Street Tolerant	Growth	Length of Life	Where in Book
Willow, arctic	*Salix arctica*	1–5	DS	S	Su	NP	Y	N	Y	N	A	Y	S	L	D
Willow, black	*Salix nigra*	3–10	DT	L	Su	W	Y	N	Y	N	Y	N	F	S	6
Wineberry	*Prunus phoenicola-sius*	6–8	DS	M	NP	NP	Y	Y	Y	YE	N	Y	A	A	10, D
Winter hazel	*Corylopsis pauciflora*	6–8	DT	S	Su/Sh	NP	Y	Y	Y	N	Y	N	S	A	11, D
Witchhazel	*Hamamelis virginiana*	3–7	DT	S	Su/Sh	NP	Y	Y	Y	Y	N	Y	A	A	n/a
Yellow paloverde	*Cercidium microphyllum*	10	DT	M	Su	D	Y	Y	N	Y	Y	Y	A	A	6
Yellowwood	*Cladrastis kentukea*	3–10	DT	M	NP	WD	Y	Y	Y	N	A	Y	S	L	n/a

Index